D1824163

Industrial tribunals

After a law degree at London School of Economics, **Roger Greenhalgh** obtained professional qualifications in personnel management. He worked in the electricity supply industry for 10 years. Since 1972, when he became an independent consultant, he has worked at the personnel management/law interface, advising and representing employers, trade unions and individual employees. He wrote the first ever practical guide to Industrial Tribunals, for the IPM in 1973, and has written or contributed to books on many aspects of employment law, particularly racial and sexual discrimination. He is a former Chairman of the Industrial Law Society.

Law and Employment series

General editor: Olga Aikin

The law relating to employment can seem labyrinthine – but with today's escalating number of legal claims, managers ignore it at their peril.

Managers must be able to construct sound yet flexible and progressive employment policies built on firm legal foundations. This important new series will enable them to meet the challenge. It forms a superbly practical and, above all, accessible source of reference on employment practice and the law.

The IPM has specially commissioned Olga Aikin – one of the country's foremost authorities on employment law, a qualified barrister and well known legal writer – to steer the project. The books have been written by leading employment law experts and human resource practitioners. Together they provide a unique combination of up-to-date legal guidance with in-depth advice on current employment issues.

Other titles in the series include:

Discipline
Philip James and David Lewis

Contracts
Olga Aikin

Redundancy
Alan Fowler

Law and Employment series

Industrial tribunals

Roger Greenhalgh

Institute of Personnel Management

To a pearl

Typesetting by The Comp-Room, Aylesbury
and printed in Great Britain by
The Cromwell Press Ltd, Wiltshire

British Library Cataloguing in Publication Data

Greenhalgh, Roger
    Industrial Tribunals. – (Law &
    Employment Series)
    I. Title   II. Series
    344.1040269

    ISBN 0-85292-496-8

The views expressed in the book are the author's own, and may not necessarily reflect those of the IPM.

Contents

General editor's foreword

This series is essentially a user's guide to employment law and good employment practice. The objective is to provide managers, trade unionists and the employees themselves with a basic understanding of the legal rules and basic principles which affect the employment relationship. There is no intention of turning everyone into a lawyer, but today a little knowledge of employment law is far from dangerous and a fair amount can be a positive advantage.

In the past thirty years we have moved away from a situation in which the law relating to employment could be ignored, in which legal actions were few and far between, into one in which the number of legal claims is increasing and in which the law is becoming far more complex. But this does not mean that it is a matter for lawyers, or, even when lawyers are essential, that the decisions have to be left to them alone. Lawyers and consultants can only advise. Business decisions have to be made by managers; employees have to decide whether there is an advantage in suing. The law is rarely 100 per cent certain and the ultimate decision has to be made by the client.

The law is not enough. The purpose of the law is to set minima and devise means of dealing with the fall-back situation when the parties cannot reach a solution. Good employment relations demand far more than mere compliance with legal requirements. They require an understanding of the nature of the relationship between employer and employee and how the manager manages it.

This series is concerned not only with the practical application of the law but also with the problems and issues which arise before, during and after employment. For this reason it starts with the practical situation and explains the law relating to it, the pitfalls and advantages, and suggests approaches which may be helpful.

The authors are all experts in their fields and combine legal knowledge with practical expertise.

Olga Aikin

List of abbreviations

ACAS	Advisory, Conciliation and Arbitration Service
CRE	Commission for Racial Equality
EAT	Employment Appeal Tribunal
EC	European Community
EOC	Equal Opportunities Commission
EPCA	Employment Protection (Consolidation) Act 1978
JP	Justice of the Peace

This series has been produced for instruction and information. Whilst every care has been taken in the preparation of the books, they should not be used to provide precedents for drawing up contracts or policies. All terms should be carefully considered in the light of the prevailing law and the needs of the organization. When in doubt, it is recommended that professional legal advice is sought.

Chapter 1
Introduction

Some employers view industrial tribunals as bodies from a different world, largely irrelevant to the industrial and commercial world in which they themselves operate. They feel that having to deal with a tribunal case is no part of what management is, or should be, about.

A central thesis of this book is that industrial tribunals and dealing with cases before them have become, for better or worse, as much a part of real management as dealing with trade unions, customers or bankers. Industrial tribunals and how they may be expected to react to what a business does should be taken into account in management decision-making in the same way as the existence of trade unions and how they may react, of the business's customers and how they may react, and of the company's bankers and how they may react. Industrial tribunal cases that do occur should be approached in the same way and using the same skills and disciplines as other problems with which management has to deal.

Within any business there will be one or more people who develop the necessary skill, knowledge and experience to deal with particular aspects of management. The larger the business the more limited each area of specialisation may be. A sole proprietor has to be able to handle the customers, the suppliers, the VAT office, the bank, the staff, and so on. A major company may have whole departments coping with design, with marketing, with finance, with personnel, with operations, etc. Within one department it may have different sections dealing with different aspects of the department's overall responsibilities. But, although they may affect how it is handled in practice in a particular business, size and organisation do not determine whether an issue is one which should be regarded as a normal aspect of management.

The sole proprietor can only personally do so much and may seek outside help with, say, invoicing and debt collection. That does not mean that looking after cash-flow ceases to be an integral and important aspect of management or that the sole proprietor ceases to be interested in and ultimately responsible for it. Rather, given the overall range of functions which have to be performed and the resources available to perform them in the business concerned, a management decision is made that cash flow will be handled externally whilst other aspects of management are dealt with internally. A different person in the same position may decide that,

1

while there was still too much for one person to do, expertise in a different aspect of management should be bought in: 'I will continue to do the invoices and debt-collection, but I will get in someone to do the deliveries.' Different people have different skills and interests and priorities and will rightly decide that 'I will do this, but I had better get someone else to do that.' On a grander scale the large business will be making similar decisions, but in terms of creation, organisation and staffing of departments, establishment of procedures, provision of training and so on.

In making these decisions a business, whether large or small, should not treat industrial tribunals and the handling of industrial tribunal cases as any more of 'a special case' than any other function. The necessary skills are likely to be available: problem-solving, decision-making, communicating. If such skills were not available the business would not be functioning.

One reason why tribunal cases are often regarded in a special way is that they are seen as involving a moral judgement on the participants. A dismissal is 'fair' or 'unfair'. It has to be decided whether an employer acted 'reasonably' or 'unreasonably'. One person 'discriminates against' another, perhaps 'by way of victimisation'. The moral element should not be underplayed. The law which industrial tribunals apply has derived much of its impact from the general feeling which has grown up from the reporting of decisions that to do things one way is 'right' and to do them in a different way 'wrong'. Businesses should not be encouraged to do 'wrong' things just because there may be more profit in it. Indeed, industrial tribunals have an exceptional power to award exemplary damages against employers who deliberately discriminate on racial or sexual grounds, reasoning that the compensation they may have to pay for doing so will be 'worth it'.

But nor should morality play too large a part in an employer's thinking. What is 'fair' or 'unfair' is a legal question, not essentially a moral one. It can turn on issues which have no moral connotations at all, such as the length of an employee's period of employment. If an employer is found to have acted 'unreasonably', what it often really means is that one individual in an organisation has made a wrong decision, or even made the right decision but in the wrong way. Legally the company is responsible. Morally, although the company should perhaps take steps to ensure that the same mistake is not made again, its responsibility is very oblique. How far, anyway, should the company, in this area or in others, base its business decisions on moral criteria? If the company is perceived to be immoral, that may affect its public relations, human relations or customer relations. Morality may properly be a factor in business decision-making. But there is no intrinsic reason why decisions relating to industrial tribunal cases should be any more or less conditioned by morality than any other business decisions.

A business has objectives. In well managed companies they are probably set out in a business plan. Within overall objectives, subsidiary objectives are set in particular business areas, for particular departments and/or for particular individuals. Even where it is not expressly stated, there must be some reason for the business to exist: some goal or goals for it to achieve. A good business decision is one which promotes the achievement of those objectives. A bad decision is one which hinders their achievement. This is as true of decisions about whether and how to deal with tribunal cases as it is about other business decisions.

So the purpose of this book is to look at dealing with industrial tribunals specifically as a part of business management. It is directed at managers in general, and in particular at personnel or industrial relations or human resource managers and practitioners: at those who as part of their job may have to make or advise on decisions that bear upon matters within the jurisdiction of industrial tribunals. It is not a book about substantive law: unfair dismissal, sex and race discrimination, the Wages Act, etc. As those are the issues with which tribunals deal, examples are taken from those areas, but the emphasis is on what industrial tribunals are, how they work and the ways in which a business may react to them and the cases they raise.

Chapter 2 briefly outlines the history, jurisdiction and composition of industrial tribunals. The next four chapters look at how tribunals work. Three of these chapters look at the outward manifestations. Chapter 3 covers practices and procedures prior to a hearing and Chapter 4 those of the hearing itself. Chapter 5 is concerned with what can happen after, or instead of, a hearing: with how a case is ultimately disposed of. The last of the four chapters, Chapter 6, is more concerned with the internal workings of tribunals: the mental rather than the physical processes, the concepts that lie behind and the factors that influence those processes.

The emphasis then turns from the tribunal to the business. An industrial tribunal's legal problem is a manager's business problem. The manager needs to handle it in business terms. Information needs to be gathered. Options for action have to be identified and assessed. A plan of action needs to be decided. At all these stages it has to be remembered that if no other solution is found the tribunal will impose its legal one. It is with this in mind that Chapter 7 considers investigation – what a manager needs to know about the facts of a case. Chapter 8 looks at analysis and assessment – what a manager needs to know about the law which may be involved. Chapter 9 discusses business factors which may influence the decision about how to proceed and the shape which an action plan may take.

Implementing the action plan is next. Looking at in business terms, management's preferred solution has to be 'sold'. The 'buyer' may be the employee who started the case. If the action plan does not involve the possibility of settlement, or if the employee's withdrawal of the case cannot be bought at the right price, then a different solution has to be sold to a tribunal. That involves argument, which has to be based on evidence. Chapter 10 is concerned with the structure, preparation and presentation of such argument; Chapters 11 and 12 with the identification and effective presentation of evidence, in person and on paper. Whatever the result of a tribunal case, whether management succeeds in selling its preferred solution or not, something of business value can come from it, provided any lessons that the experience offers are learned. Chapter 13 suggests the need for a post-case management review.

This is not a legal textbook. The law is frequently mentioned but that is because it provides the subject matter of the problems which have to be solved and the framework within which solutions have to be found. Where cases are referred to, it is to provide examples and to explain why one approach or technique may be preferred to another and not as citation of legal authority. For this reason no case names or law report references are given. Some legislative provisions are quoted, but only to exemplify or explain points of procedure or technique.

The rules which govern industrial tribunals' procedures are slightly different. They specifically and expressly set the limits of the area with which this book is concerned. Extracts from them are quoted where appropriate in the body of the text, but the rules as a whole appear in the Appendix. For the sake of completeness the Appendix includes the special rules relating to some equal pay cases – but those are worth a book on their own and, in so far as they differ from 'normal' cases, this one does not deal with them.

Chapter 2
What industrial tribunals are

Industrial tribunals have developed, from small beginnings under the Industrial Training Act 1964, into a significant part of the legal system. The years since 1960 have seen a continual process of statutory intervention in and regulation of the employment relationship. From the Contracts of Employment Act 1963 to the Employment Act 1990, new legislation has created new employment rights and added adjudication on those rights to industrial tribunals' functions. The process is not over. Further extension of employment statutes is inevitable. Power already exists for tribunals' jurisdiction to be extended to hear claims for breach of employment contracts. It is increasingly clear that tribunals have the power, and duty, to apply European Community law directly in appropriate cases, although the limits of what are 'appropriate cases' are still in the process of judicial definition and development.

The range of jurisdiction

Whilst all industrial tribunal jurisdictions have some connection with 'employment', they form a very mixed bag. In some – under the Health and Safety at Work, etc., Act 1974 or the Industrial Training Act 1982, for instance – the tribunal is an appellate body, hearing appeals against orders made by a public authority. Much more often it is the court of first instance in a dispute between two individuals, although one of the 'individuals' will often be a company.

In such cases the applicant will normally be an employee, ex-employee or an applicant for employment and the respondent an employer, but not always. The Sex Discrimination Act 1975 and the Race Relations Act 1976 both provide for the agencies they created, the Equal Opportunities Commission (EOC) and the Commission for Racial Equality (CRE) respectively, to complain to industrial tribunals about discriminatory employment advertisements and instructions and pressure to discriminate. These Acts include further examples of an appellate jurisdiction: against non-discrimination notices. Both also provide that complaints about illegal discrimination may be brought not only against an employer but also against the individual manager, supervisor or other agent who took the illegal action or decision on the employer's behalf.

Thus a respondent need not be the 'employer'.

The Employment Protection Act 1975 requires consultation with trade unions in respect of impending redundancies and, if the requirements are not met, provides for a protective award to be made. Although once such an award has been made it is the individual employee who asks a tribunal to enforce it, it is the trade union which must make the initial application for the protective award to be made. A trade union may also complain, under the Employment Act 1980, that an employer has unjustifiably failed to comply with a request for facilities for a workplace ballot. In either of these cases the trade union, rather than an individual employee, initiates the tribunal case. Also under the 1980 Act

> a complaint may be presented to an industrial tribunal against a trade union by a person that an application by him for membership of the union has been unreasonably refused, or that he has been unreasonably expelled from the union . . .

There the trade union would be the respondent.

The above description, though not exhaustive, illustrates that industrial tribunals are not concerned only with employee/employer disputes. It also begins to show the range of employment areas into which their jurisdiction extends: from pre-employment practices under the Sex Discrimination Act and Race Relations Act at one end to termination of employment in redundancy provisions at the other. Other statutory provisions fill out that range.

Employment legislation was consolidated in 1978, and it is in the Employment Protection (Consolidation) Act 1978 (EPCA) that many of the employment rights on which industrial tribunals adjudicate are to be found. They cover:

- The provision of written particulars of terms of employment and itemised pay statements.
- The granting of time off – sometimes with pay, sometimes without – for purposes as diverse as trade union duties and activities, fulfilling duties as a JP, through antenatal care to job-seeking when under notice of redundancy.
- Payments during lay-off and short time or when prohibited from working by some statutory medical requirement.
- Returning to work after confinement.
- Periods of notice required to terminate employment.
- The provision of written statements of reasons for dismissal.
- Unfair dismissal.
- Redundancy payments.

The Sex Discrimination Act, the Equal Pay Act 1970 and article 119 of the Treaty of Rome together with EC directives, particularly those on equal pay and on equal treatment, outlaw sexual discrimination not only in relation to advertising and other pre-employment matters but at all stages of the employment relationship – recruitment, training, promotion, termination – and with respect to all aspects of terms and conditions of employment – pay, hours, allocation of work, discretionary benefits – up to and including pensions. The Race Relations Act has similar, but not identical, coverage.

Payment of wages is covered by the Wages Act 1986, although only in the sense that unauthorised deductions are outlawed. Disputes about amounts due, or claims in relation to complete non-payment, cannot be dealt with by industrial tribunals until an order under section 131 of the EPCA has been made. This is the provision by which industrial tribunals' jurisdiction can be extended to cover breach of employment contracts where the claim:

- Arises out of or is outstanding on the termination of the employee's employment; or
- Arises in circumstances which also give rise to proceedings already or simultaneously brought before an industrial tribunal otherwise than by virtue of section 131; or
- If the order so provides, it satisfies both these conditions.

A similar provision has existed since 1971. Increasingly strong and frequent suggestions from judges and commentators that the jurisdiction should be extended in this way have increasingly been met by official statements that it will be done. At the time of writing no such order, even in draft, has been published; nor has any Bill which would have that effect.

One argument against such extension is that it would move tribunals out of the area for which they were created and designed to deal – the enforcement of specific statutorily defined rights – into a more general common law area: the law of contract. Whatever validity that argument may initially have had, which is probably very little, it now has none. As soon as entitlement to a statutory right was stated by the statute concerned to be dependent on the existence of a 'contract of service or of apprenticeship' the industrial tribunals had to look at the common law concerned with contracts to determine whether an applicant was entitled to claim that right. Once qualification to claim a right was made dependent on the hours worked under a contract, or the amount of any payment was fixed with reference to remuneration provided for under a contract, industrial tribunals had to interpret contracts in accordance with common law rules. 'Dismissal' is a statutory concept but is statutorily defined with reference to common law concepts –

contract, termination, fundamental breach, repudiation, acceptance.

Industrial tribunals are, then, already 'common law' courts, in the sense that they are bound by, and apply, the general body of law as well as the specific statutory provisions on which applications are based. But common law principles are used as steps in reaching decisions in relation to specific statutory jurisdictions. Industrial tribunals have no power to deal with an issue, even if patently justiciable at common law, just because it arises out of employment. Many such cases, even after any order that may be made under section 131 of the EPCA, will go to the 'ordinary courts of law'.

Tribunals or courts?

The Franks Committee was appointed to 'consider and make recommendations on the constitution and working of tribunals other than the ordinary courts of law'. In its 1957 report it agreed that:

> tribunals have certain characteristics which often give them advantages over the courts. . . . But as a matter of general principle we are firmly of the opinion that a decision should be entrusted to a court rather than a tribunal in the absence of special considerations which make a tribunal more suitable.

Industrial tribunals did not exist in 1957 and the Franks Committee did not cover them in its study. It is, though, worth considering briefly what 'special considerations' lead to such extensive delegation of employment law matters to tribunals rather than courts.

Characteristics which Franks felt often gave tribunals advantages were 'cheapness, accessibility, freedom from technicality, expedition and expert knowledge of their particular subject'. Industrial tribunals *are* cheaper, more accessible, less technical and quicker than the ordinary courts. They have detailed knowledge of industrial and commercial employment which the ordinary courts lack. The characteristics overlap.

One reason why tribunals are cheaper is that there are fewer procedural technicalities. They are not bound by complicated rules about how cases should, before hearing, be defined on paper. Their proceedings are less formal. Any applicant or respondent may appear in person or be represented by any other person, legally qualified or not. Strict rules of evidence do not apply. Tribunal members will question unrepresented or poorly represented litigants and their witnesses to discover what, in legal terms, their cases are all about. The need for legal representation and for the expense of it is thus reduced. But tribunals are cheaper than ordinary courts in other ways too. There are no court fees. Travelling and meal allowances and a contribution towards lost earnings are payable to parties and witnesses. Only in an exceptional case will the loser be required to pay the winner's costs.

Lack of technicality and reduction in actual or potential expense in turn increase tribunals' accessibility. Potential litigants are less likely to be frightened off by legal mumbo-jumbo and the prospect of huge lawyers' fees. Industrial tribunals provide simple standard forms on which applicants can make and respondents can reply to complaints. There are leaflets outlining procedures and describing in lay terms the legal provisions which tribunals apply. They sit in numerous locations, making them physically as well as psychologically more accessible.

The speed with which tribunals can deal with cases is also influenced by their lack of technicality. Where there are no pre-trial procedures a case can, from the tribunal administrator's point of view, be heard as soon as an application and a response to it have been received and a tribunal is available to hear it. The lack of pre-trial procedures can sometimes mean that cases take longer to hear than where the issues have been more sharply defined before a hearing begins, which in turn means that other cases must wait longer to be heard. But that effect can be diminished by the tribunal, where it seems necessary, itself requiring further particulars to be given or modifying the procedure at the hearing. The case load on tribunals is decreased, and so the speed with which they can deal with individual cases is increased, by vetting applications, by pre-hearing assessments and by the involvement of conciliation officers to try to dispose of cases without any need for them to be heard.

Tribunal members

Some of industrial tribunals' expert knowledge of their particular subject derives from their members' specific training for their roles and their continued exposure to cases. More, in the case of 'lay members', comes from their background. Each industrial tribunal hearing a case has three members. One, in the chair, is a lawyer: a barrister or solicitor of at least seven years' standing. The other two are not legally qualified but have experience of employment either from the employees' or from the employers' point of view. There are two panels of such members: one consisting of people recommended by trade unions, the other of people recommended by employers' organisations. One person from each panel will join the legally qualified chairperson to form one tribunal.

The mix of individuals will vary from case to case. The same legally qualified chair may sit with different lay members on different days, and the same two lay members will not always sit together. Obviously, the same three members will sit together throughout the hearing of one case, even if the hearing takes place over many days. The precise composition of any tribunal, in terms of individuals, is a function more of administrative convenience and the availability of members than of picking horses for courses. It has been judicially stated that the more random the selection of the lay membership of a tribunal can be the better. That said, an attempt will usually be made in a case involving an allegation of racial or sexual discrimination to ensure that at least one of the lay members has some personal understanding of the problems of discrimination, perhaps as a member of an ethnic minority. Efforts have been made to increase the representation of minority groups and of women among lay members.

The value of lay members' employment experience is in enabling them to weigh and assess the evidence and if necessary interpret it. What a tribunal may not do is treat a member's experience or specialist knowledge as evidence which can be preferred to that which has actually been given. If, from personal experience or specialist knowledge, a tribunal member believes that evidence which is being given is wrong, or provides an incomplete picture, the member must openly raise the issue with the parties at the hearing and seek their reactions. If necessary an adjournment should be granted to allow the party to study the point and seek further evidence.

Although lay members are expressly drawn from two panels, one employee-based and the other employer-based, they are not expected to represent any sectional interest. They are expected to decide the case before them objectively, having regard to the strength of the evidence and legal argument advanced by both sides. In practice the vast majority of industrial tribunal decisions are unanimous. Where a unanimous decision is not possible it is reached by majority vote. In the few cases where that does happen, the two lay members can, and sometimes do, combine to outvote the legally qualified chair. That can happen even if the difference of opinion concerns a point of law rather than a question of fact. There are instances where a majority, lay, decision on a point of law has been upheld on appeal.

So it is possible to find in industrial tribunals the characteristics which Franks felt gave tribunals advantages over courts. What is less clear is that those characteristics always exist to the most advantageous extent or whether there are what Franks felt were the necessary 'special considerations' which make tribunals 'more suitable' than courts.

Some constraints

The speed with which tribunals can deal with cases and how much a case costs parties to pursue are significantly influenced by other factors not mentioned by Franks: the resources the State devotes to the provision and funding of the industrial tribunal service and the extent and type of jurisdictions with which the State expects it to deal. It is not intended by making this point to suggest that the service is under-funded; nor by adding this clarification to suggest that it is over-funded. The point is simply that it is a State-provided service which costs money to run.

It could be made cheaper, for the parties, by extending legal aid to tribunal representation. Cases could be heard more speedily by funding more appointments as tribunal members and staff. Either course would require more public money to be devoted to the service. Unless and until such extra money is allocated for the purpose, industrial tribunals have to cut their coat according to the available cloth. There are limits to what can be achieved by streamlining and simplifying procedures.

However non-technical most industrial tribunal procedures may be, some of the substantive law provisions which they have to interpret and apply are highly complex. Claims for equal pay for work of equal value rest on regulations: the Equal Pay (Amendment) Regulations 1983 and the Industrial Tribunal (Rules of Procedure) (Equal Value Amendment) Regulations 1983, now incorporated in the Equal Pay Act 1970 and the Industrial Tribunal (Rules of Procedure) Regulations 1985. These regulations contain syntactical and procedural mazes which have been judicially criticised as 'incomprehensible' and 'giving rise to delays which are properly described as scandalous'. Many commentators have used less judicially restrained language. Other, far less complex, employment law provisions have been compared unfavourably with the worst excesses of Finance Acts. Just as lack of technicality was seen, above, to contribute to the cheapness, accessibility and expedition of industrial tribunals, so increases in technicality tend to increase costs, reduce accessibility and increase the time taken to deal with cases.

Whether experience in employment equips tribunal members with 'expert knowledge of [the] particular subject' of racial and sexual discrimination is open to question. If it does, and if the need for such specialist knowledge amounts to a special consideration which makes a tribunal more suitable than a court to determine discrimination issues, it has to be asked why such issues are heard by ordinary courts when they arise in non-employment contexts.

The broader picture

Whatever imperfections it may have, the industrial tribunal system as it exists is what employers have to deal with. And, in practical terms, dealing with it depends not upon whether the bodies involved are called 'tribunals' or 'courts' but on how they operate. Had there been a conscious decision in the early 1960s to add, say, a Labour Law Division to the traditional court structure, the end result might have differed in its

details and in the names used for the bodies concerned. But it would still
have had many similarities to what exists today. No such decision was
taken. Industrial tribunals and the system of which they form part, like
Topsy, just growed.

The link between industrial tribunals and the rest of the legal system
was initially through the Queen's Bench Division of the High Court.
Appeals in some tribunals' jurisdictions still go there. But in 1971 the
Industrial Relations Act created a National Industrial Relations Court the
functions of which included appellate supervision of industrial tribunals.
That court was abolished in 1974 by the Trade Unions and Labour
Relations Act, and for a short time the Queen's Bench regained appellate
jurisdiction over all the work of industrial tribunals. But the Employment
Protection Act 1975 established the Employment Appeal Tribunal
(EAT). This has, since then, heard appeals against industrial tribunal
decisions in most areas in which the tribunals adjudicate. Examples of
exceptions are levy orders and improvement and prohibition notices. In
most cases where an appeal lies from an industrial tribunal decision to
the EAT it can be made only on a point of law. Exceptionally the EAT
can hear appeals against tribunals' finding of facts in cases of unreasonable expulsion or exclusion from a trade union.

Its composition is similar, at a higher level, to that of industrial tribunals. A judge presides and there are two lay members, each of whom
has an equal vote if unanimity is not possible. Although the lay members
can outvote the judge, the EAT is a 'superior court of record'. Its decisions bind industrial tribunals and other lower courts in accordance with
the doctrine of precedent on which the legal system is based. Appeals
from its decisions on points of law can be made, by leave, to the Court of
Appeal and thence, by leave, to the House of Lords.

Alongside the specialised judicial structure which was created in the
early 1970s and revised in the mid-1970s there was, and is, a conciliation
function. Since 1974 it has been part of the Advisory Conciliation and
Arbitration Service (ACAS). That body appoints a number of conciliation officers who are required, by the relevant statutes, to seek to achieve
settlements of cases without the need for a tribunal hearing. They do so
where a party requests it or where, even without such a request, they feel
a settlement seems reasonably likely to be achievable. Industrial tribunal
staff inform ACAS of applications which are made, and of the progress
of cases. The industrial tribunal rules of procedure expressly provide for
adjournments to be granted in appropriate cases to allow the possibility
of ACAS-assisted conciliation to be explored.

The legal systems of England and Wales, of Scotland and of Northern
Ireland are separate. Although much of the substantive law which industrial tribunals apply is identical across these countries' boundaries, the
industrial tribunal systems are distinct. Each has its own President of

Industrial Tribunals and its own Central Office. In strict terms, this book is concerned only with industrial tribunals in England and Wales, although much of what it says is just as applicable in Scotland and Northern Ireland. Nevertheless, there are differences in procedure and practice in different parts of the United Kingdom. Where relevant, they should be taken account of in considering how to deal with an industrial tribunal case.

In England and Wales the Central Office of Industrial Tribunals is located in Bury St Edmunds and there are Regional Offices in most of the major cities. There is a President of the Industrial Tribunals and, in each region, a Regional Chairman. There is a Secretary of Industrial Tribunals and, in each region, an Assistant Secretary. Besides legally qualified and lay tribunal members there are administrative staff who process applications, arrange dates for hearings, act as clerks at hearings, and so on. Where a judicial decision is required – for instance, postponing a hearing for which the date has already been fixed – the administrative staff must refer matters to a legally qualified chair. But, even in these cases, they will be a party's first point of contact. They should not be expected to give legal advice with regard to procedural or substantive matters but can advise on administrative arrangements and practices which are followed in their regions. This can be helpful, as there are differences, albeit small, in how different regions do things.

Chapter 3
Practice and procedure (I) Pre-hearing

A case is commenced by an originating application, and the person making it, or on whose behalf it is made, is referred to as the applicant. For the purposes of all that follows it will be assumed that the applicant is an employee, an ex-employee or a person who has been refused employment. Actually, as has been noted, others can be applicants in industrial tribunal cases.

The originating application

Under rule 1(1) the originating application has to be in writing and must set out:

- The name and address of the applicant.
- The names and addresses of the person or persons against whom relief is sought.
- The grounds, with particulars thereof, on which relief is sought.

Industrial tribunals provide a form, IT1, on which this can be done, and the form asks a number of other questions. Most originating applications are, in practice, made on form IT1 and the other questions on that form are answered. But any written application which meets the rule's requirements is sufficient to start a case. Whether the rule's requirements have been met is determined with reference to substance, not form. So, for instance, a technically incorrect naming of the 'person against whom relief is sought' will not invalidate an originating application if sufficient information is provided for the person to be identified. Similarly, the rules do not expressly require the applicant to name, with technical precision, the statutory provision under which the application is being made. If it is generally clear what it is about, that will be enough to start the ball rolling. Nor do the rules require, as form IT1 asks an applicant to provide, information about the applicant's age, starting and finishing dates of employment, job title and rate of pay. The absence of these details, on the form or in any other written application, will not make it invalid. Although the rule states that proceedings shall be instituted by the applicant, an application by an authorised representative of the applicant, such as a solicitor or a trade union, will be accepted.

Rule 1(1) requires the originating application to be presented to the Secretary of the Tribunals. In the light of the case law, 'presented' means received by the tribunal offices, even if that is on a non-working day. It has not been specifically decided whether receipt by a Regional Office, rather than the Central Office, amounts to 'presentation' for the purpose but it seems likely that it does. These points of pernickety detail are important. Each statutory employment right carries a time limit within which a claim must be made. Failure to present an originating application within the time limit, unless it was not reasonably practicable so to do, will mean that it is time-barred.

Posting an application before the time limit expires is not enough. It must be *received* before the deadline. As a judicial rule of thumb, items sent by first-class post are expected to be received by the addressee – that is, presented – on the second working day after posting; those sent by second-class mail on the fourth working day after posting. So, if an applicant posted an application with a first-class stamp a full two days before the expiry of the deadline, but it was not actually received until the day after, a tribunal would probably accept that, given the circumstances of postal delays, it was not reasonably practicable for it to be presented in time. If, however, the same application were sent by second-class post the tribunal might hold, subject to proof to the contrary, that it was reasonably practicable to have presented it in time and that it was, therefore, out of time.

After being stamped with the date of receipt an originating application is scrutinised. If it appears to show no cause of action with which an industrial tribunal could deal, the applicant is informed, with the reason, and told that, in the absence of written instructions to the contrary, the application will not be processed any further. This may occur, for instance, if the claim is on account of unpaid wages rather than an unauthorised deduction from wages, or if a short-service employee is claiming a statutory right which depends on longer service. If the applicant does write asking for the case to proceed, nevertheless, it must do so. In practice, if no further information is provided to change the appearance that it is outside the industrial tribunal's jurisdiction, a pre-hearing assessment is likely to be held. If nothing further is heard from the applicant, or if the applicant withdraws, the application is not registered and that is the end of the matter.

If the originating application does disclose a cause of action, or if the applicant writes that it should proceed anyway, it is registered, given a case number, allocated to a Regional Office and copied to each person against whom relief is sought. Each such person is called a respondent. For the rest of this book it is assumed (unless stated otherwise) that:

- There is one respondent.
- The respondent is an employer.
- The employer is a company.

It has been explained that this may not always be the case in practice. The copy originating application is covered by a standard letter, IT2, and accompanied by an explanatory leaflet and a blank form, IT3, which the respondent can use to reply.

The notice of appearance

Rule 3(1) states that:

> A respondent shall within fourteen days of receiving the copy originating application enter an appearance to the proceedings by presenting to the Secretary of the Tribunals a written notice of appearance setting out his full name and address and stating whether or not he intends to resist the application and, if so, setting out sufficient particulars to show on what grounds.

The notice of appearance is the counterpart of the originating application, and many of the above points continue to apply. Its validity depends upon its substance, not its form. It does not need to be on form IT3. It does not have to provide all the information asked for on that form, although there is usually no good reason why, even if appearance is entered by way of a letter rather than the form, the additional information should not be given. The really important questions are whether the respondent intends to resist the application and, if so, on what grounds. The grounds do not need to be given with technical precision or in great detail. Provided that enough is said to let the applicant and the tribunal know, in general terms, the defence the respondent will be advancing, the lack of quotation of specific statutory provisions or of a blow-by-blow narrative of what happened will not make the notice of appearance invalid.

Of less importance, but still required by the rules and not just by form IT3, are the name and address of the respondent. It is not uncommon for an applicant to name the respondent incorrectly. In some organisations all staff are employed by a holding company or by a service company while being individually allocated to work in various of the group's subsidiaries. If, in such a case, the applicant has named one company as the respondent when, technically, the employer was a different company, the correct company should be specified. A natural person, Mr X. or Mrs Y., might be named when the proper respondent may really be a legal person, a company or partnership, of which that natural person was a director or partner or manager. A trading name may have been given for a sole trader who, more properly, should be 'Z., trading as the Corner

Shop'. The notice of appearance should correct such errors.

It may be that an application has identified the named respondent, however imprecisely, but that the named respondent is not the person against whom an application should be made. Rather than wrongly identifying the right respondent, it has rightly identified the wrong respondent. An applicant may have named as employer the company for which s/he was doing agency work rather than the employing agency. In such a case the notice of appearance should give the correct legal name of the named respondent but say that the respondent's grounds for resisting the application are that, as the respondent is/was not the applicant's employer, it is not the proper respondent to the applicant's complaint in respect of employment rights.

Nothing of substance is likely to turn on the address given in the notice of appearance, but it will be treated as the respondent's 'address for service': the address to which, unless a representative is nominated, all communications to the respondent about the case will be addressed. Administratively it will probably be more convenient if communications about the case go direct to whoever in the respondent's organisation is actually dealing with it rather than being addressed to the organisation 'at large'. This can be achieved either by giving that person's location and 'for the attention of' that person as the address of the respondent or by nominating that person, and giving the appropriate address, as the respondent's representative. The second is the better approach, as it avoids any possibility of confusing that person's identity with the legal identity of the respondent. The respondent's address will normally be given as the registered or principal office of the employer, or perhaps of the unit or site where the applicant was employed.

Applying to extend the time limit

The notice of appearance should be submitted within fourteen days of the employer's receipt of the originating application, but the fourteen-day limit is not absolute. A respondent may apply at any time for an extension of time in which to enter a notice of appearance. Any appearance entered after the deadline is automatically deemed to include an application for an extension. Such a deemed application can be granted even though the grounds for it are not stated. It cannot be turned down without the respondent being invited to explain why it is sought. In practice a respondent's late entry of a notice of appearance will be accepted without question for some time after the deadline has passed. Whether made formally or deemed to be included in a late notice of appearance, an application will be refused only if there are no real grounds for the delay or if it is so late that injustice would result from an extension.

Again as a matter of practice, the tribunal will normally write to a respondent who has not entered a notice of appearance within a reasonable period after the expiry of the time limit for doing so, to confirm that the originating application was received and to repeat the invitation to enter a notice of appearance. Such a second letter will be sent by recorded delivery.

Despite the possibilities of extension, a respondent gains nothing by delaying a notice of appearance for any purpose other than ensuring that it can be fully and properly prepared. If it is genuinely impossible for the respondent to answer the originating application because it is so unclear what is being alleged, then an application should be made for further particulars. At the same time, an extension of time for entry of the appearance should be requested until the particulars have been provided. Where a vital participant in the events covered by the originating application – a person without whom an investigation could not be completed – is temporarily unavailable, an application for extension of time until after that person's return, explaining why it is needed, may be made.

If an appearance can be entered within a few days of the fourteen-day time limit – say, no more than a week after it expires – no explanation of the delay need be given, although an apology will do no harm. If submission will be delayed beyond that, the respondent should apply for an extension of time as soon as possible. This can be done by letter, addressed to the Secretary of the Tribunals at the address given on form IT2. The letter should quote the case number on IT2 and explain why an extension is being sought and when it is anticipated the notice of appearance will be submitted. The detail of the explanation and the strength of the grounds quoted should depend on when the application is made and how long an extension is being requested. An application made within the time limit for a short extension will be sufficiently supported by a general reference to 'insufficient time properly to prepare the notice of appearance'. An application made after the fourteen-day period and seeking an extension of a few weeks will need to include more detailed and substantial reasons, and not just the pressure of other work. In deciding how long an extension to ask for, the respondent should err on the side of caution. Although an application can be made for a time limit already extended to be further extended, doing so involves more effort and expense, and may create an unfavourable impression.

An application for more time in which to enter an appearance replaces or accompanies the notice of appearance as the first stage in the presentation of the respondent's case to the tribunal. It should be drafted with this in mind. In terms of legal analysis a tribunal's decisions depend on substance, the facts and the law, not upon presentation. In practice – particularly given that the tribunal is the final arbiter on matters of fact, and that 'reasonableness' is in many cases a crucially important fact – the members can be influenced by presentational factors. An application which demands an extension of time rather than requesting it; which cites in justification ('prays in aid') factors which, however important to the respondent, are not relevant to the tribunal's decision; which makes or implies promises that the respondent does not keep – all these may weigh in the members' minds when the substantive decisions need to be made. So, like all other aspects of presentation, an application for an extension of time in which to enter a notice of appearance should be courteous and carefully worded.

'Pleadings'

When a valid notice of appearance has been submitted, or once it has become apparent that no appearance is likely to be entered, the case can proceed to a hearing. Many ordinary courts require extensive documentation, called 'pleadings', to be exchanged between the parties and submitted to the court before the hearing stage can be reached. But industrial tribunals can and often do proceed just on the basis of an originating application and a notice of appearance; or even, if no appearance is entered, with just an originating application.

The preparation of written pleadings can be time-consuming and, given particular courts' rules of procedure, technically complex. Their purpose is to identify and clarify the issues beforehand so that the time taken actually to hear the case is reduced to a minimum. The wish to avoid technical complexity and time-consuming pre-trial procedures makes these sorts of pleading inappropriate for industrial tribunal cases. But these factors must be balanced against the need of parties to know in advance what questions will be at issue in any hearing which is held, so that they can properly prepare to deal with them, and the need for tribunal hearings to be as short as can be made consistent with a full and fair consideration of any disputed questions. So procedures are available by which industrial tribunal pleadings can, if necessary, be extended beyond the originating application and any notice of appearance. Procedures which operate before, and with a view to assisting towards, the final overall substantive decision are called 'interlocutory' procedures. Applications under such procedures are 'interlocutory' applications. Any hearings to settle such procedural questions are 'interlocutory' hearings, and so on.

Further particulars

Either party can apply to the tribunal for an order requiring the other to furnish in writing to the person specified by the tribunal further particulars of the grounds on which he or it relies and of any facts and contentions relevant thereto.

The tribunal can also issue such an order 'of its own motion' – that is, without any application having been made to it by either of the parties.

The normal practice is for a party which feels it needs more detailed information about the case to approach the other party direct, or through a representative where one has been named, before seeking an order from the tribunal. Where such a direct request is made in writing it will often be valuable for it to be copied to the tribunal as well. This prepares the ground in case the request is not met voluntarily and an application for an order does have to be made. It also lets the tribunal know that, as further particulars are being sought, at least one party is not yet ready for a hearing. Where such a request is voluntarily complied with a copy of the further particulars should also be sent to the tribunal so that they can, in effect, become part of the pleadings in the case. None of these practices is expressly required by the relevant rule, 4(1)(i), but all are, at the least, courteous and may also help to deal with the case more efficiently.

Applying for further particulars is an exception to the general rule that a respondent who has not entered an appearance may take no part in a case. An originating application may be so imprecise that the named respondent cannot even decide whether to resist the application and, if so, on what grounds. That seldom happens, but when it does, the respondent can seek further particulars before entering an appearance.

A request or order for further particulars is usually specific rather than general. It will ask for or require more detail about this aspect of the case, or about that particular allegation, and not just say, 'Tell us more.' A general statement in an originating application that the procedure followed in a dismissal was 'unfair' might be met with a request for clarification of the respects in which it is alleged to have been unfair. A respondent's statement that an applicant had 'been warned on numerous occasions' might elicit a request for each occasion to be identified and for the terms of the warning to be stated.

Orders for further particulars can be made at any time up to, or even at, a hearing and will specify a time by which the order must be complied with. An order can be made *ex parte* – that is, simply on the application of one party and without the other party having been given an opportunity to argue against it. Where that is done, or where the tribunal orders further particulars of its own motion, the party against whom the order is made can apply to have it set aside. Such an application has to be made before the date by which the order requires the further particulars to be provided – although it is possible, even after that time limit has expired, to apply for an extension either to comply with the order itself or so as to apply for it to be set aside. An application for an order for further particulars to be set aside is made by writing to the tribunal with a copy to the other party. Although the rules do not expressly require it, some reasons why the order should be set aside will need to be shown.

Further particulars cover, as the quotation above shows, 'facts and contentions', not how those facts are to be proved or how those contentions are to be supported by detailed argument. The facts and contentions they cover are those which are relevant to 'the grounds on which [a party] relies'. So a party who has the burden of proving something is not entitled to seek information about whether, and if so how, the other party may attempt to disprove it unless that other party has already stated reliance on grounds which, expressly or by implication, involve its disproof. So, for instance, the structure of unfair dismissal law is that the employer has to show what was the reason for any dismissal and that it was one of the reasons permitted by section 57 of the EPCA. If an applicant simply alleges that a dismissal was unfair the respondent cannot seek further particulars about the reason for which the applicant thinks the dismissal occurred. The reason is a matter which it is for the respondent to prove, and the applicant has not relied on any ground relating to the reason. If the applicant states that the reason for dismissal was, say, that 'the foreman had it in for me', further particulars of the allegation could be sought. The reason has expressly become a ground on which the applicant relies.

Such fine distinctions are seldom drawn in practice. The question with which industrial tribunals most often have to deal, whether a dismissal for a reason permitted by section 57 was 'reasonable', is neutral in terms of the onus of proof. In deciding whether to order further particulars to be given, as in determining whether originating applications and notices of appearance are valid, industrial tribunals are more concerned with substance than with form. They are guided by whether the provision of such particulars will ease disposal of the case while maintaining fairness between the parties. But looking at the limits of the provision does illustrate that further particulars are to clarify, in outline, the limits of the case which has to be met. They are not intended to provide additional ammunition for the party seeking them.

Where an order for further particulars has been made and has not been set aside a tribunal has the power, if the terms of the order are not met, to dismiss the whole or part of the originating application, or to strike out all or part of the notice of appearance, or even to debar the respondent completely from defending the case. Before doing so it must give the offending party 'an opportunity to show cause why such should not be done'.

Amendment of pleadings

Provision of further particulars may make amendment of an originating
application or notice of appearance necessary. A party may, in giving
such particulars, effectively extend rather than just clarify the scope of
the case. What is said may make it clear to the receiving party that the
case which has to be met is not, in all its detail, that which it originally
appeared to be. As a matter of practice industrial tribunals will usually
allow amendment of the pleadings, provided it will not result in any
injustice to the other party.

Injustice may result if one party attempts, at the last moment, to introduce a completely new allegation or defence which the other party has
had no opportunity to prepare to meet. In such a case, whether to allow
the amendment of the pleadings, or to allow a party to pursue a line
which had not been pleaded (which amounts in effect to the same thing),
will be influenced by the reason for the late introduction of the issue and
the extent of the disadvantage to which the lateness of its introduction
puts the other party. At the very least, the tribunal is likely to postpone or
adjourn the hearing to allow the party which was taken by surprise to
prepare properly to meet the new point. In such a case the tribunal can
order the party which sprang the surprise to pay the costs of postponement or adjournment. If it appears that the new point could, with reasonable diligence, have been raised earlier, or if it appears that it was
deliberately concealed with a view to catching the other party out, the tribunal may not allow it to be pursued. Similarly if the party has previously expressly stated that it did not intend to rely on the point which it
is now trying to raise.

In assessing these matters a tribunal will have in mind the skill and
knowledge of the parties and their representatives. With counsel on both
sides, and after protracted interlocutory procedures, a tribunal is likely to
take the view that their skill and experience should have ensured that the
case was properly delineated on paper well before it came to trial and
that, if it is not, the parties they represent must suffer the consequences.
With unrepresented parties who have filled in forms IT1 and IT3 as best
they can to express their general sense of grievance or of righteousness, a
tribunal is much more likely to accept that a point, although not
expressly pleaded, was meant to be covered by the words used.

Amendment to pleadings, though, cannot be used to escape time limits.
A complaint of unfair dismissal has to be made within three months of
the effective date of termination; a claim for a redundancy payment
within six months. An originating application simply mentioning 'redundancy' might cover either, or both. Provided it was submitted within the
three-month time limit, it would allow both claims to be pursued. If further particulars were sought or an application to amend it were made, the

pleadings might show that both claims were being raised. When the amendment was made – before or after the three-month time limit had expired – would not matter. But the same application, if submitted after the three-month limit but before the expiry of six months, could not be amended in the same way. If it were, the unfair dismissal claim would still fail because it was time-barred.

If, rather than mentioning simply 'redundancy', it specifically claimed a 'redundancy *payment*' the position might be different. As initially submitted the originating application does not on the face of it raise any issue about the fairness of the dismissal. If it is amended to include a claim of unfair dismissal within three months of the effective date of termination that *new* claim has been made in time. But if no amendment is made until more than three months after the effective date of termination the new, unfair dismissal, complaint has not been raised within the relevant time limit. It may still be arguable that it was not reasonably practicable for it to be presented in time, but that is a different issue. The point for present purposes is that amendments to pleadings cannot confer jurisdictions on tribunals which they would otherwise, because time limits have expired, not have.

It is worth repeating yet again that industrial tribunals are concerned with substance rather than form. In practice some cases put forward at hearings are hardly recognisable, except in very general terms, as those outlined in the pleadings. No amendments to pleadings may have been sought or made, but as neither party is disadvantaged, and because to do so appears 'most suitable to the clarification of the issues before it and generally to the just handling of the proceedings', the tribunal accepts that. But this should not hide the fact that the permission of the tribunal is needed before an originating application or notice of appearance can be amended and that a tribunal does have power to limit the proceedings before it to what has been covered by the originating application, notice of appearance and further particulars.

The rules make no express provision for the amendment of pleadings but there are general powers for a tribunal to regulate its own procedure and to issue directions. A party that wishes to amend should write to the tribunal, with a copy to the other party, setting out what amendment it wishes to make and giving reasons why the amendment is being sought. The more radical the amendment and the later it is sought the more substantial the reasons will need to be. Many such applications will be granted without more ado, but the tribunal may invite the other party's written comments or even hold an interlocutory hearing to decide the matter.

Decisions on interlocutory matters like this can be, and usually are, made by a legally qualified chair rather than by a full tribunal. That is so whether they are made *ex parte*, after written observations from the parties or at an interlocutory hearing. Any interlocutory hearing would probably be held 'in chambers' – that is, in private, probably in the office of the legally qualified chair, rather than in public in open court.

Pre-hearing assessment

Interlocutory hearings differ in that respect, as well as in their purpose, from other hearings which may take place before a full hearing of the merits of a case. Rule 6 allows a tribunal to hold a pre-hearing assessment. This must be undertaken by a full tribunal, not just a legally qualified chair, and is concerned with the apparent merits of a case, not with the procedures which are to be followed in determining it. The procedure was introduced in an attempt to discourage further pursuit of applications or defences which appear, on the face of it, to be hopeless.

The decision to hold a pre-hearing assessment may be made by a tribunal of its own motion or on application from a party. The tribunal is not bound to accede to a party's request for a pre-hearing assessment. Where it does decide to hold one it will inform the parties, specify the date and invite them to submit written representations and/or attend to advance oral argument. No evidence is taken, but the tribunal will consider the contents of the pleadings and of any written representations which have been submitted, and will listen to argument from any party that attends. If, in the light of all that, the tribunal forms the opinion that an application or defence or particular contentions in an application or defence have no reasonable prospect of success, it will warn that to persist may lead to an order of costs against the party concerned. Costs are discussed in Chapter 5; here it need simply be noted that they are awarded only in exceptional circumstances. A costs warning following a pre-hearing assessment is an indication that one tribunal feels that the necessary exceptional circumstances may exist in the case in point. Any opinion formed by a tribunal at a pre-hearing assessment will be expressed in writing and sent to the parties and will be available to the tribunal which eventually hears the case if it proceeds. No member of the tribunal which undertook a pre-hearing assessment in a case may be a member of the tribunal which hears the case.

A pre-hearing assessment is most likely to be held where, even if the facts which a party alleges are fully proved, it could not legally lead to the result for which that party is arguing. Examples were given earlier in which the applicant might be told that an originating application appeared to show no cause of action: it was raising an issue which was outside an industrial tribunal's jurisdiction – seeking unpaid wages rather than claiming that deduction was unauthorised, or making a complaint which the applicant was not qualified to make, namely, a short-service employee claiming a statutory right which depended on longer service. If the applicant wrote back to the tribunal saying that the application should nevertheless proceed, a pre-hearing assessment might result in a warning that further persistence might cause costs to be awarded. Assuming that the applicant was correct, that wages were owed or that a dismissal was for a non-permitted reason and without adequate procedures being followed, it would still not give the tribunal jurisdiction. A defence in a sex discrimination case that a decision not to promote was in line with a collectively agreed policy of restricting female employment to the non-managerial grades would fail even if the existence of such a policy could be proved.

A pre-hearing assessment leads to an opinion, not a decision. It is based on assumptions, not proven facts. A party may ignore the warning and proceed. Some do. Of those that do a proportion are successful at the full hearing of the case. Even where they are not successful, costs are actually awarded against them only in a minority of cases. The number of pre-hearing assessments has declined over the years since the power to hold them was introduced. There is disagreement about how laudable the aim of weeding out hopeless cases may be, but there is little disagreement that the holding of pre-hearing assessments does not meet it very well and that, in attempting to meet it, it is probably discouraging the pursuit of some cases which would, if proceeded with, succeed.

The Employment Act 1989 introduced the possibility of a different system of attempting to weed out hopeless cases. It provides that regulations can be made allowing 'pre-hearing reviews' to be held which could result, in appropriate cases, in a party having to pay a deposit to proceed with the case. At the time of writing no such regulations have been published, even in draft, so the details of how the system would work are unclear. The regulations could provide for any person or a tribunal to undertake the review. They would probably specify that it must be a legally qualified chair. They would probably provide that an opportunity for written representations and/or oral argument must be provided. The regulations would prescribe the circumstances in which a deposit would be payable. The maximum amount of any deposit is set in the Act itself at £150, but this maximum is subject to review by the Secretary of State. How the actual deposit would be determined, within the maximum, can be specified in the regulations. The circumstances in which the whole or part of the deposit would be refunded or paid over to the other party can also be defined by the regulations.

'Interlocutory' and 'preliminary' hearings

A distinction has been drawn above between interlocutory hearings and pre-hearing assessments. A further term, 'preliminary hearings', should

be distinguished from both. Sometimes a hearing on interlocutory matters is referred to as a preliminary hearing. As the terms are used in this
book, however, a 'preliminary hearing' is one which is held to decide a
substantive point on which the case as a whole may stand or fall. Any
hearing held to determine a procedural matter – how the case should be
dealt with – is called an 'interlocutory hearing'. So, again using the
example of an applicant who had less than two years' service but was
claiming unfair dismissal, it might be decided that the question of
whether that applicant was qualified to claim that right should be dealt
with first and on its own; and that no arrangements for any hearing about
whether the dismissal was fair or unfair should be made until the point
had been decided. The hearing to determine this point would be a preliminary hearing, as, depending on its result, the case might be finally and
substantively disposed of by it.

Given the history of this example so far, with an initial reaction to the
originating application that it disclosed no cause of action, and a costs
warning following a pre-hearing assessment, the decision that this procedural course should be adopted would almost certainly be made by the
tribunal of its own motion. In another case the situation might be less
clear. The applicant might, if the date of termination shown on the
originating application were correct, have just two years' service. The
respondent might be contending that, given the circumstances of the
termination of the applicant's employment, the effective date was earlier
than that shown by the applicant. Hence the applicant was not qualified
to claim unfair dismissal. Resolution of the issue might require considerable evidence and protracted argument. The respondent might wish it to
be settled in a preliminary hearing and apply for such a hearing to be
held. The applicant may resist such an application on the grounds, perhaps, that the evidence and argument concerned with that issue were so
closely connected with those relating to the other issues – whether there
had been a dismissal and whether that dismissal was fair – that no useful
purpose would be served.

In the light of these conflicting views the tribunal, in the person of the
legally qualified chair, might decide that a hearing should be held to
determine the procedural question: whether the issue of qualification to
claim could and should be dealt with separately. That hearing would be
an interlocutory hearing. If the decision of the interlocutory hearing was
that the qualification question should be dealt with separately, the hearing on that substantive issue would be a preliminary hearing.

Nothing of substance turns on the terminology, and the terms may be
used other than in accordance with the above explanation, but to restrict
their meanings in the way described does help in understanding the different roles and functions that apparently similar procedures sometimes
serve.

A preliminary hearing is no different, except in its coverage, from any other substantive hearing and, in that sense, is the subject of the next chapter. Before any substantive hearing is held, however, there may be further interlocutory matters to be dealt with. Further particulars are concerned with grounds, facts and contentions, not with evidence. Two interlocutory procedures are concerned with evidence.

Discovery and inspection

Under rule 4(1)(b) a tribunal may, in response to a party's application, but not of its own motion

> grant to the person making the application such discovery or inspection (including the taking of copies) of documents as might be granted by a county court.

'Discovery' means being told what documents exist; 'inspection' being allowed to look at them and take copies. The rule's reference to 'a county court' indicates that this procedure has been borrowed from the ordinary courts, where the parties will normally be represented by professional lawyers.

Besides their duty to their clients, solicitors and barristers have a duty to the court. They are 'officers of the court'. They are used to the idea that, when responding to an order for discovery, they must disclose all relevant documents in the possession or control of their client, no matter how damaging to the client's case a particular document might be. A lay representative or an unrepresented litigant quite often finds the idea more difficult to accept.

A party is under no duty to disclose the existence of any document voluntarily. If a party intends itself to rely on a document as evidence at any hearing, the existence of the document and its contents will eventually be disclosed and there is little to be gained by delaying the other party's access to it. If a party does not intend to introduce a document as evidence, then that party is not required, in the absence of an order for discovery or inspection, to reveal that it exists or to say what it contains. But a party that does voluntarily disclose documents must not do so in such a way as to mislead the other party as to the true position. If a request is made to an employer for all performance appraisals made on an employee who has, for instance, been dismissed for poor performance, the respondent may refuse to meet the request or may disclose all such appraisals but may not select for disclosure only the ones showing poor performance and conceal any of those that show good performance. The respondent is under no duty, if it decides itself to put only the poor appraisals in evidence, to offer the good appraisals in evidence, too. But purporting to meet a request for discovery by disclosing only the poor ones will, if and when it becomes apparent that disclosure was misleadingly selective, provide grounds for an order for full discovery of all appraisals to be made or for any decision already made in the party's favour to be reversed.

As with further particulars, discovery and inspection are usually sought first on a voluntary basis and, if that fails, then by application to the tribunal. An application for discovery or inspection, unless made orally at the hearing itself, should be in writing, copied to the other party, and be for specific documents or specific classes of documents which are relevant and necessary to the case of the party making the application. Although the County Court rules provide both for general discovery and for discovery limited to certain classes of documents, the judicial view is that it is usually incompatible with the role of industrial tribunals for them to order general discovery or even, as a matter of course, to order particular discovery. In particular, an application for discovery will not be granted just to allow one party to undertake 'a fishing expedition' through the other's documents. The County Court touchstone is whether discovery is necessary either for disposing fairly of the proceedings or for saving costs. To that might be added, in the context of industrial tribunals, the desirability of avoiding formality and technicality.

The limits on disclosure

An order can relate only to documents which already exist. A party cannot be ordered, for instance, to prepare a schedule or summary of information which does not already exist in documentary form or which exists only in a number of other disparate documents. Although no order can compel the preparation of such a new document, a party may offer to prepare one as a means of meeting or forestalling a request or order for the discovery of documents which contain information which is not relevant but whose disclosure would be undesirable for reasons unconnected with the case. The prime example occurs in cases alleging sexual or racial discrimination, where there may be a legitimate need to compare an applicant's own experience and qualifications and experience for a job with those of other candidates but the respondent feels that to reveal the CVs of others would breach confidentiality. The problem may be met by the respondent preparing, perhaps subject to supervision and checking by the tribunal or the applicant's representative, a schedule of the relevant details in relation to each candidate but without including the name or other details which would enable the candidate to be identified. Or the documents might, by agreement, be produced in a doctored form, with names and other identifying details blanked out.

There is no general rule protecting 'confidential' documents from disclosure. In each case the tribunal must strike a balance between the importance of disclosure to the case of the party seeking it, on the one hand, and, on the other, any cost and inconvenience that its production involves and any broader public interest which may require it to be kept confidential. Where these conflicting needs cannot be met by devices such as those described above, the normal course will be for the documents at issue to be submitted to the legally qualified chair so that the ruling on what should and should not be disclosed can take account of the precise content of the documents. Where it is then judged that the need for disclosure is paramount, the documents will be made subject to an order for discovery and inspection. The application for discovery in respect of any others will be turned down.

Communications between lawyer and client are privileged. A party to an industrial tribunal case may be advised and represented not only by a lawyer but

> by a representative of a trade union or an employers' association or by any other person whom he desires to represent him.

When this occurs the protection against disclosure of communications between lawyer and client extends to any communications between the party and the representative 'with an actual view to the litigation in hand, and the mode of conduct of it'. This does not mean that a manager who undertakes the presentation of a respondent's case at a tribunal can thereby avoid disclosure of any document just because it was created by or addressed to him or her. If that manager played a role in the events which led up to the case being brought, documents engendered in or which influenced that role are likely to be discoverable. But a memo by the manager advising the rest of the management team of possible outcomes of the case, once it has been brought, or outlining strategies for dealing with it at a tribunal, would be immune. Similarly, the provision in section 133(6) of the EPCA that

> anything communicated to a conciliation officer in connection with the performance of his functions under this section shall not be admissible in evidence in any proceedings before an industrial tribunal, except with the consent of the person who communicated it to that officer

does not mean that a document which existed quite independently of the discharge of the conciliation officer's functions can be protected from disclosure simply by being shown to a conciliation officer.

Orders for discovery or inspection will, like orders for further particulars, state a time for compliance and if made *ex parte* can be set aside on application of the party against which they are made. Similarly, non-compliance can lead, subject to an opportunity to show cause why it should not be done, to the striking out of the whole or part of the originating application or notice of appearance or to a respondent being debarred from defending altogether. Additionally, an order for discovery will state that failure, without reasonable excuse, to comply with its terms will render the offender liable on summary conviction to a fine. The maximum amount of such a fine is revised from time to time and its current amount will be stated in the order.

Witness orders

The second interlocutory procedure concerned with evidence, that providing for the attendance of witnesses and the production of documents, is also enforced by a fine. In this case, as any order is likely to be made not against a party but against some other person, striking out is not an appropriate penalty for non-compliance. Even if, exceptionally, such an order is made against a party, non-compliance cannot lead to striking out.

Rule (4)(1)(b)(iii) provides that a tribunal may, on the application of a party, but not of its own motion:

> require the attendance of any person (including a party to the proceedings) as a witness, wherever such person may be within Great Britain, and may, if it does so require the attendance of a person, require him to produce any document relating to the matter to be determined.

Discovery and inspection relate to documents in a party's possession and control. An order for production usually covers documents in the possession or control of someone else, although there are instances of such orders being made against an individual manager or other officer in a respondent's organisation and in respect of documents belonging to the organisation rather than personally to the manager or officer concerned. An order for discovery or inspection relates to documents themselves, and allows a party to decide beforehand whether the documents should be used in evidence at the hearing. An order for production is coupled with an order for a witness's attendance and gives the party seeking it no right to inspect the document before it has been produced by the witness as part of the evidence which that witness is required to give.

An order for the production of documents can be made only in conjunction with a witness order, but the reverse does not apply. Most witness orders require only the attendance of the witness and do not add any requirement for documents to be produced. Again, the issuing of a witness order does not entitle the party at whose application it was made to question the witness prior to the hearing at which attendance is required.

Before issuing a witness order a tribunal will need to be satisfied that the evidence the witness can give, or produce in documentary form, is relevant to the case of the party seeking the order and that an order is necessary to ensure that such evidence will be given. To meet the first requirement an application for such an order will have to outline the evidence which the witness could give or produce and how it would support the case which the party intends to advance. A full and detailed statement of the witness's evidence is not necessary but sufficient will need to be said to make it clear that, without the evidence, the party's case will be incomplete in an important respect. To meet the second requirement an application will have to explain why it is believed that the witness will not attend without being ordered to do so. This may not be only because the witness has been asked to attend and has positively refused to do so. It may be that the witness has not replied to a request or has given an equivocal reply. Or it may be that, despite having been given a firm 'yes', the party has reasonable grounds for doubting that the witness's undertaking to attend will be honoured. It may even be that the witness has expressed genuine willingness to attend but, for cosmetic purposes, or to facilitate release from work or some other commitment, has asked that an order should be made.

Generally the need to meet the second requirement, as well as common courtesy, means that before applying for a witness order a party will first invite the witness to attend voluntarily. If an order then seems necessary an application should be made in writing, giving the name and address of the witness and setting out the grounds. If a witness order is made the tribunal sends it by recorded delivery to the witness it covers. Besides mentioning that non-compliance could lead on summary conviction to a fine, it will explain that the witness can seek to have it varied or set aside by making an application to that effect on or before the date and time at which attendance has been ordered.

There is no express provision that a person affected by a witness order can apply for an extension of time in which to comply, but a witness who was genuinely unable to comply with an order because of the date or time it specified could apply to have it varied. A witness who was unwilling to comply for other reasons might apply for it to be set aside on the grounds that no relevant evidence could be given or that a document which had been ordered to be produced was protected from disclosure on grounds similar to those discussed above in the context of discovery.

Other interlocutory matters

An application for further particulars, for discovery or inspection or for an order for a witness's attendance or the production of documents can, if not made in writing beforehand, be made orally at a hearing. In practice this is most likely to occur in the case of an unrepresented party where it appears to the tribunal, at the hearing, that such orders are needed for the case to be dealt with properly. Although a tribunal has no power, of its own motion, to order discovery or inspection or to issue witness orders, it is under a duty to ensure that unrepresented litigants are, where necessary, aware of the relevant procedures. Although the explanatory leaflet about industrial tribunal procedures does mention such orders, their value, impact and extent may not be immediately apparent to a person with little idea of how courts work. If this seems to be the case and, on the procedures being further explained, a party does wish to make an application, it will be decided there and then. Probably the hearing will need to be adjourned to allow time for the order to be complied with and the party to make use of the information thus obtained. To avoid the necessity for such adjournments it is obviously better if applications are made as soon as the need for them becomes apparent and as long before the hearing as possible.

It is also valuable, for the same reason, if other procedural points which may affect the conduct of the hearing are raised well before it is due to take place. Powers exist for industrial tribunals to join extra respondents to a case – particularly where it is alleged that unfair dismissal by reason of non-membership of a trade union was caused by pressure from a trade union, but more generally as well. Or, where there are a number of cases from different applicants which raise common factual and/or legal questions, the tribunal has the power to direct that some or all of the cases should be heard together. The industrial tribunal systems in England and Wales, on the one hand, and in Scotland, on the other, are separate, but there are powers for cases to be transferred between them where it seems that an application made under one system could more conveniently be heard under the other. Each of these powers may be exercised by the tribunal of its own motion or on the application of a party. Where a party wishes to make such an application it should do so earlier rather than later.

Chapter 4
Practice and procedure (II) Hearings

Listing a case for hearing

Rule 5(1) provides that:

> The President or a Regional Chairman shall fix the date, time and place of
> the hearing of the originating application . . .

The administrative reality is slightly different. Matching the ever changing group of cases with the limited judicial resources available is a complex administrative task. Many of the originating applications will never
reach a hearing, but withdrawal may occur at any time, from the day
after their arrival even to the day on which they are due to be heard.

Some cases take a couple of hours to hear; others, very exceptionally,
may take months. The tribunal office itself, in many cases, has little to
guide it as to how long any particular case will take. Unrepresented litigants, even if asked, could not be expected to offer a very realistic
estimate of how long the presentation of their evidence might take.
Experienced court lawyers, who are often asked for and provide such
estimates, sometimes get them wildly wrong. A hearing not completed
within the time allocated to it will be adjourned to another date, but the
necessity to get the same members together – remembering that many of
the legally qualified chairs and all the lay members are part-timers – may
mean that the adjourned hearing cannot take place for some considerable
time. A case which finishes well within the time allocated to it means
that the time of tribunal members who, had they not been allocated to
that case, would have been available for others becomes free but may be
unusable because of the short notice at which this has occurred. Both
these phenomena mean that the final disposal of cases takes longer: one
because of the length of the adjournment, the other because judicial
resources are wasted so that other cases have to wait longer for members
to be available to hear them.

An objective of the industrial tribunal system is that it should deal
with cases expeditiously. Meeting this objective means that cases should
be fully heard as soon as possible after they have been initiated. Another
objective is justice. Meeting it requires that sufficient time should be
given to each party to prepare its case, to any reasonable extent that it

requires. Interlocutory procedures are specifically provided to enable such preparation, but they do take time. Justice also requires that one party should not by unnecessary delays deprive the other of a speedy remedy. 'Justice delayed is justice denied', but which delays are unnecessary and whether any remedy is due are open questions. Where the aims conflict the balance between them must be struck judicially, not administratively. But often there is no immediate and apparent conflict. Even where there is, a substantial administrative system is needed to stand behind the judicial decisions.

Whilst any interlocutory processes are taking place the passage of time will be advancing a case in the queue of those waiting to be heard. If the tribunal is aware, because applications for interlocutory orders have been made to the tribunal or because inter-party correspondence has been copied to it, that the case is not yet ready for hearing but that progress is being made in getting it ready, then its progress in the queue will be deliberately delayed. If, on the other hand, it appears that the originating application and the notice of appearance constitute the full pleadings, and neither party needs extra time to seek and consider further particulars or to disclose or prepare extensive documentary evidence, the case will, when it is nearing the front of the queue, be fitted into the programme of industrial tribunal hearings. This is usually called 'listing' a case for hearing.

Different methods of listing are adopted at different times and in different regions. In some the tribunal simply nominates a date without consulting the parties. In others the tribunal office advises both parties of a period within which the case will be listed and asks them which dates within it are *not* convenient; in the light of their replies a date is fixed which neither party has eliminated. In others the tribunal asks the parties individually to nominate or mutually to agree, within a given period, which date or dates would be convenient. There may be other methods, but those mentioned illustrate the range of approaches. At one extreme the date is simply dictated by the tribunal. At the other the date is effectively fixed by the parties, but within limits set by the tribunal. Between the extremes the tribunal itself fixes the date but the parties are invited to influence the tribunal's decision.

There is, in administrative terms, flexibility. Whatever system is adopted, if a tribunal is aware that some dates are more convenient for one of the parties than others an attempt will usually be made to allow for the fact. But it will always be subject to the wish to bring the case to hearing as soon as possible and to ensure that one party is not for inadequate reasons delaying a hearing which the other party is ready and anxious to have held. Where the parties are agreed about how soon a case should be ready for hearing or about the dates the weight of their views will be increased, but may still not be decisive if the tribunal feels that too much delay is involved or if there are administrative difficulties.

However a date is administratively chosen, it is, as the rule quoted above shows, fixed judicially. This means that any alteration of a date which has been fixed requires a further judicial decision. A party may apply at any time to have a hearing postponed. In common with other interlocutory applications, such an application should be in writing and state the grounds on which it is made. The decision will take account of the factors mentioned above and of why the postponement is sought. A date which has been fixed without any consultation with the party will be more readily changed than one to which the party had expressly agreed. A first request for a postponement is more likely to be granted than the last in a series of such requests. An application made well before the date which it is sought to change has more chance of success than one made a day or so beforehand. A joint application from both parties will be seen in a more favourable light than one made unilaterally. A postponement is more likely to be granted where the request for it results from an unavoidable cause – for instance, the illness of a vital participant in the case – than where it is merely an attempt to avoid some personal inconvenience.

Absence of a party

The notice of hearing must be sent to the parties at least fourteen days before the date fixed, although there is provision for the minimum fourteen days' notice to be waived by agreement with the parties. Besides stating the date, time and place at which the hearing will commence, the notice of hearing will contain.

> information and guidance as to attendance at the hearing, witnesses and the bringing of documents (if any), representation by another person and written representations.

It will explain that, should a party not attend, the case might be decided in its absence. In practice, unless a tribunal has been told that a party does not intend to be present in person or to be represented at a hearing, considerable efforts will be made to contact an absent party before such a course is adopted. The tribunal may even, of its own motion, adjourn the hearing to allow the absent party another opportunity to be present; although it is not bound to do so. Its decision on this is likely to be influenced, in some degree, by how the party has conducted the case so far. If a positive impression has been given that the party does intend to pursue the case there is more likely to be a postponement than if, after the originating application or notice of appearance, all has been silent. A respondent who has not entered an appearance has no right to be heard.

Where a tribunal does proceed to hear a case in a party's absence it will treat that party's pleadings, the originating application or notice of appearance and any further particulars, and any other representations in writing, as the full statement of that party's case and then take evidence from the party who is present in the normal way. It will itself question witnesses to test their evidence where that appears to contradict anything which the absent party has alleged. Any oral arguments will be balanced against those advanced in writing by the absent party. The absence of a party does not, therefore, mean that the decision will automatically go against that party. Its case may be sufficiently strong in substance, even without evidence being given or any oral argument being advanced, to succeed. Given, however, that any conflict on factual points would almost certainly be decided in favour of the party who was present and who produced evidence to support their version of events, and that any points put in argument by the absent party could be countered by the party who was present but the reverse would not happen, this is in practice unlikely.

On arrival

The precise administrative arrangements, physical layout, etc., of any hearing will obviously vary from region to region and from venue to venue. The general pattern, however, will be along the following lines.

On arrival at the specified address the receptionist will ask for which case the party, witness or representative is there, mark the person's name and their role in the case – 'witness', 'solicitor', etc. – on the relevant sheet and direct the person to the appropriate waiting room. There will be two waiting rooms, one for applicants and those accompanying them and one for respondents and those accompanying them. There may be some common facilities – tea/coffee machines, telephones, toilets, copying machines – at which the opposing parties may bump into each other, but they are not forced to meet face-to-face until they go into the hearing room itself.

Sometimes, particularly when both parties are represented, their representatives do wish to meet before the hearing begins or during any adjournments. They may wish to discuss procedural points, or exchange documents, or even attempt to negotiate a settlement. At some locations any such discussions have to take place in corridors, etc., but in others there are one or two rooms available for the purpose. The receptionist or one of the tribunal clerks will be able to say whether there is any such room and, if so, whether it is available.

At some point before the parties are actually called into the hearing the clerk to the tribunal which will be hearing the case may come into the waiting room to check that all the essential people are present and, generally, to ensure that everything is prepared for the case to start. For instance, the clerk may check that the relevant documents are available and have been exchanged or that sufficient copies have been made, or ask whether reference is likely to be made to a case which is not in the law reports which are to hand. The clerk will also be able to answer any questions about other administrative arrangements.

The precise time at which a case is called will depend on a number of factors, not all of which are under the tribunal's control. Have all the necessary people – parties, witnesses, representatives, tribunal members – arrived? Are they ready? If the case is listed as the first of the day it will not have to wait for an earlier case to be decided. But it may be listed as the second case for a particular tribunal which is first going to hold what is expected to be a short hearing, maybe on a preliminary point, in another case. Estimating the length of a hearing is a very imprecise science, and the thirty minutes or hour allocated to the first hearing may turn out to be far too little, so that the second case will be delayed. Another case may be a 'floater': that is, it will be listed for hearing at a location at which a number of tribunals are sitting on a given day. One or more of them will be expected to finish well before the end of the day. Its case may not, in the event, come to a hearing, or the hearing may be short. Any freed tribunal will then be able to hear the 'floater'. If, contrary to expectation, all the earlier cases do actually come to hearing, and all take longer than anticipated, the 'floater' may be kept waiting for hours. This does not often happen. Most cases are called within a short time of that for which they are listed. But people attending a tribunal hearing lose nothing by taking along something they can usefully be doing during any waiting time which does occur.

Those in the waiting rooms will be told when the tribunal is ready to begin hearing the case. The clerk may come in and tell them personally or there may be a loudspeaker announcement. In either event the participants will be directed to the room where the hearing is to take place. The clerk will tell them where to sit.

The layout of a tribunal room will be affected by its physical characteristics. It usually contains a long table at one end behind which the tribunal members sit and, some distance away, two smaller tables at which the parties and/or their representatives sit facing the tribunal members. If these two sets of tables are regarded as opposite sides of a rectangle one of the shorter sides of the same rectangle is occupied by yet another table, at which a person will sit when giving evidence: the witness's table. Somewhere else, often opposite the witness's table and forming the fourth side of the rectangle, will be a table for the clerk of the tribunal.

Looking from the back of the room towards the tribunal members, the respondent's representative will sit at the left-hand of the two smaller tables and the applicant's representative at the right-hand one. There will be two chairs at each table and – although there is no rule about this – the person actually presenting a party's case will often sit on the innermost of the two chairs: the applicant's representative in the left-hand seat at the right-hand table and the respondent's representative in the right-hand seat at the left-hand table. Who occupies the other chair at either table depends on the composition of that party's team. Where the representative is Queen's Counsel, it will be junior counsel or the instructing solicitor. It may, where the party is an individual, be the party himself or herself. It may, where the party is a company, be the individual from the company who, although not actually presenting the case, and whether giving evidence or not, knows most about the case from the company's point of view. It should be the person who, from whatever formal position, can be of most help to the party's representative in presenting the case to the tribunal: whether by taking notes, finding the way round the documents, suggesting lines of enquiry or clarifying (to the representative) terminology used by witnesses in the context of the business concerned.

Besides those already described, there will be a number of other seats. These will usually be behind the tables at which the representatives sit. They are for parties' friends, advisers, etc., who are not presenting the case or giving evidence. In England and Wales – unlike Scotland, where they are excluded until their evidence has been given – witnesses are normally allowed to be present throughout the hearing. They will occupy some of these chairs when they are not giving evidence or, if they were previously excluded, after they have given evidence. These chairs are also where any members of the public will sit.

Hearings in private

Rule 7(1) provides that:

> Any hearing of or in connection with an originating application shall take place in public unless in the opinion of the tribunal a private hearing is appropriate for the purpose of hearing evidence which relates to matters of such a nature that it would be against the interests of national security to allow the evidence to be given in public or hearing evidence from any person which in the opinion of the tribunal is likely to consist of:
>
> (a) information which he could not disclose without contravening a prohibition imposed by or under any enactment; or
> (b) any information which has been communicated to him in confidence, or which he has otherwise obtained in consequence of the confidence reposed in him by another person; or
> (c) information the disclosure of which would cause substantial injury to

any undertaking of his or any undertaking in which he works for reasons other than its effect on negotiations with respect to any of the matters mentioned in section 29(1) of the Trade Union and Labour Relations Act 1974 [that is, the section which defines the matters which may be the subject of a 'trade dispute'].

In practice hearings are seldom held in private. Where an interlocutory decision has been made – for instance, in a race or sex discrimination case – that the interests of justice require candidates' application forms to be disclosed as they stand, rather than with any individually identifying features being removed, it may be held that, although the interests of confidentiality do not lead to their protection from disclosure they nevertheless justify evidence about them being given in private under (b) above. Or where an employee had been dismissed for disclosure of trade secrets or other commercially sensitive information which would be of value to the employer's competitors, a tribunal might sit in private, under (c) above, to hear any necessary evidence about the substance of the secrets or information. But the simple fact that information may embarrass a party or individual, or give a trade union ammunition to use in collective bargaining, will not justify its being given as evidence in private.

A party who wishes evidence to be heard in private may submit an interlocutory application. This would be done either in writing before the hearing or orally at the hearing itself. The grounds would have to be stated. If, exceptionally, such an application were granted it might relate only to the giving of the evidence concerned, rather than to the hearing as a whole, although where the nature of the evidence heard in private is such as to colour the whole conduct of the proceedings, the whole hearing may be private. Tribunal decisions are normally 'entered in the register', and so available for public inspection; those in cases where a private hearing has been held may, if the tribunal so directs, be omitted from the register.

The procedure outlined

In some tribunals the tribunal members will already be in place when the participants enter the room. In others the clerk will wait until everyone is in place and then ask them to rise while the tribunal members enter. Despite their lack of formality, not all the trappings which traditionally indicate the dignity, authority and independence of the judiciary have yet been removed from industrial tribunals. Their table will often be on a dais raised, albeit only a few inches, from the floor on which the other tables stand; but that may be so that the tribunal members can see the proceedings more clearly than for any traditional, authority-enhancing reason.

Just as the physical layout of the room will vary in minor details, so the procedure by which the hearing is conducted will vary from case to case and from tribunal to tribunal. The rules, and the case law pertaining to them, provide some fixed points but the rules themselves state that tribunals are free to determine their own procedures:

> 8. (1) The tribunal shall conduct the hearing in such manner as it considers most suitable to the clarification of the issues before it and generally to the just handling of the proceedings; it shall so far as appears to it appropriate seek to avoid formality in its proceedings . . .

The general course of a tribunal hearing will be as follows.

Once all the participants and the tribunal members are settled, the legally qualified chair will probably make some opening remarks. They may cover:

- What the case appears, from the papers already before the tribunal, to be about.
- What issues need to be decided.
- Whether all the issues will be decided at this hearing or whether, for example, the hearing will be concerned only with liability, with any question of remedies to be settled at a later hearing.
- What procedure will be followed. For example, if it is a case of unfair dismissal and dismissal is admitted by the respondent, the respondent will be asked to present its case first.

The legally qualified chair may ask for confirmation on certain points and/or for specific information and invite any questions about procedure. The party which is going to present its case first will then be invited to begin.

Each party's presentation will follow similar lines. The party will call a witness and, by asking questions, get the witness to give evidence to the tribunal. The other party will then have a chance to ask questions of that witness, and so will the tribunal. The party that called the witness will be able to ask any more questions. Then the witness will leave the witness's table, the next witness will be called, and the same procedure will be followed again.

When all one party's evidence has all been called the other party, before calling its own witnesses, will sometimes seek a ruling that there is 'no case to answer'. This invites the tribunal to say that the party which went first has not, even on its own evidence, proved what it had to prove, so there is no need for the other party to prove or disprove anything. Although a tribunal has the power to rule in this way, and occasionally will, the superior courts have advised that it is a power that should be exercised rarely and with caution. In a race or sex discrimination case, for instance, it is for the applicant to prove discrimination and the applicant's evidence is therefore likely to be given first, but whether there was or was not discrimination is unlikely to become clear until the respondent's witnesses, who are likely to include the individuals who made the decisions or took the actions in issue, have been exposed to questioning. The fact that the applicant's evidence has not demonstrated less favourable treatment on racial or sexual grounds should not preclude the testing of the respondent's evidence as to what the grounds actually were.

If a submission that there is no case to answer is accepted, that will be the end of the hearing. If it is not accepted the other party will call its evidence. More often than not, no such submission will be made and the second party will simply proceed to call its evidence. Each witness will be examined, cross-examined, questioned by the tribunal and re-examined in the same way. When all the witnesses on both sides have been called, both parties will be invited to address the tribunal to explain why, in the light of the evidence which has been presented and of any submissions they wish to make about the law, the tribunal should decide in their favour.

The tribunal will then reach its decision. It may believe it can do so within a short time, and ask the parties to wait. After a short adjournment the legally qualified chair will deliver an oral decision which will subsequently be confirmed in writing. Or the tribunal may feel that it needs longer for consideration and discussion, in which case the parties will be told that a written decision will be sent to them in due course.

A tribunal regulates its own procedure

Within the above general outline there is scope for a myriad variations. The right of a party to make an opening statement to a tribunal was removed from the rules many years ago, but a tribunal may accept in a particular case that such an opening statement or statements would be 'most suitable to the clarification of the issues before it and generally to the just handling of the proceedings'. There may, before either side's witnesses can usefully be called, be a need for preliminary rulings on procedural or even substantive points about which the parties' representatives may seek, or be invited, to make submissions. Where there is a mass of documentary evidence the tribunal may wish, or agree in the light of a party's or a joint submission, to be taken through it before any oral evidence is given. The order in which a witness is variously questioned by the two parties and by the members may differ from tribunal to tribunal. Questions from the party calling a witness always come first, followed by questions from the other party. But some tribunals prefer to ask their own questions before re-examination by the party that called the witness. Others prefer to leave their own questions until after the re-examination. Whichever of these formal courses is preferred by a particular tribunal, there is always the possibility of the tribunal interjecting its own questions, to clarify a witness's answer, during the course of either party's questioning of a witness. At some hearings the evidence and argument on the various elements of the case – jurisdictional issues, liability and remedies – are so entwined that no time or expense would be saved by trying to deal with them separately. In others a tribunal will direct that at this stage it wishes only to consider evidence and argument relating to a particular issue: other issues will be considered only if its decision on this issue makes the further issues relevant. If a dismissal is not unfair, to quantify the applicant's loss and decide whether there was a failure to mitigate it would be a waste of time. If unequal pay is justified by a genuine material factor other than sex, the complex question of whether work is of equal value is irrelevant.

The procedure actually followed in any case will reflect not only the substance of the case or the legal framework within which the tribunal has to decide it but also the tribunal's perception of the forensic skill and experience of the parties' representatives. A tribunal which has before it two barristers used to court work may closely follow traditional court procedures. Faced with two lay representatives, the same tribunal might adopt a completely different procedure. Even where there are specific rules, or specific rulings from higher courts, they are more concerned with what should be achieved than with precisely how it should be achieved:

> 8. (2) . . . at the hearing . . . a party . . . shall be entitled to give evidence, to call witnesses, to question any witnesses and to address the tribunal.

The procedures adopted in the normal courts about how evidence is given and witnesses are questioned, the order in which parties present their cases, when and whether the judge should interfere, and so on, have by and large been developed for the good reason that those procedures, in that setting, provide the best means of balancing the interests of the parties, and balancing those of both against the need for efficient use of the court's time. Similar procedures, for similar reasons, will often be appropriate in industrial tribunals, but the touchstone will always be what is 'most suitable to the clarification of the issues before it and generally to the just handling of proceedings', bearing in mind that tribunals should 'seek to avoid formality'.

A party knows that an address to the tribunal will be allowed: the rules expressly provide that it must be. Normally, the party that is asked to present its case first is the party that is asked to deliver the final address to the tribunal. But there is no rule on the matter, and should a tribunal direct that the party which called its evidence first should also address the tribunal first, that party would be hard put to it to sustain a procedural objection merely on the grounds that it was not what had been expected. If such a change in order led to some sort of injustice there would be grounds for objection because the procedure proposed was not 'most suitable . . . to the just handling of proceedings' – not merely because a non-normal procedure was used. And to sustain an appeal, either against the procedural ruling or against the substantive decision made by the tribunal after the use of the questioned procedure, the aggrieved party would have to show that the ruling of the tribunal involved an improper exercise of its discretion, by taking account of irrelevant factors or failing to take account of relevant ones or being perverse, and not simply that a different tribunal, or even the court to which the appeal was being directed, would have exercised the discretion in a different way.

It is against that background that the more detailed rules of procedure must be seen.

Who goes first?

The general rule and tradition is that the party on whom the first onus of proof lies presents its case first. So, in an unfair dismissal case, if the respondent denies that the applicant was dismissed the first onus of proof – to show that there was a dismissal as statutorily defined – falls on the applicant, and the applicant's evidence would normally be called first. If, on the other hand, the respondent admitted that the applicant had been dismissed but contended that the dismissal was fair, the onus of proving the reason for the dismissal and that it was one of the statutorily permitted ones – the first questions the tribunal must decide in such a case – would fall on the respondent, and it would be the respondent's evidence which would normally be called first.

One case before an industrial tribunal is likely to involve a whole series of questions which need to be settled, and the onus may shift from party to party as one question is answered in a particular way so that the next in the series becomes relevant. Where the different questions can conveniently be answered separately a series of separate hearings may be held, and in each hearing the tribunal will probably ask the party which bears the onus of proof in relation to the question at issue to present its case first. More often than not, however, all or the majority of the questions will be tackled at the same hearing, as the same evidence and argument will be relevant to many of them. When this is the case the party which presents its evidence first, because it bears the onus of proof in relation to the first of the series of questions which has to be decided, will have to present all its evidence first. The applicant whose dismissal has been denied will, besides presenting the evidence relating to whether there was, at law, a dismissal (which it is for the applicant to prove), will also have to present any evidence relating to the reason for the dismissal and whether it was a permitted reason, even though the onus of proof on those questions lies on the respondent, whose evidence about them has not yet been given. Unless the question of remedies is separated from that of liability, the respondent who admits dismissal will at the same time as presenting evidence about the reason for the dismissal (which it is for the respondent to prove) also have to give evidence about the applicant's loss, about which the onus lies on the applicant but about which the applicant's evidence has not yet been given.

Evidence and admissibility

The order in which a party produces its evidence is for the party to decide. A tribunal has no express power to insist on one witness being called before another, and although it has a duty to assist unrepresented litigants it will be liable to appellate criticism if it attempts even to persuade a party too strongly that evidence should be given out of the order which the party prefers. This is so even if the reason for its persuasion is to make for the greater convenience of the witnesses concerned – for instance, by suggesting that their evidence should be brought forward so that they do not have to wait so long, or return another day, to give it. Witnesses can be, and usually are, required to give evidence on an oath or affirmation which will be administered by the tribunal asking the witness to read, or repeat, the prescribed words. One of the administrative points which can usefully be mentioned to a tribunal clerk before a hearing begins is whether any witness a party intends to call will wish a particular testament to be available for administration of the oath. A party who lies whilst under oath or affirmation is guilty of perjury.

Rule 8(1) expressly states that an industrial tribunal:

> shall not be bound by any enactment or rule of law relating to the admissibility of evidence in proceedings before the courts of law.

It nevertheless retains under its general powers 'to regulate its own procedure' discretion to refuse to allow evidence which is irrelevant or of so little probative value that it can have no real bearing on the outcome of the case. A statement from a witness who is not there to answer questions about it, which would automatically be excluded by an ordinary court unless specified prior procedures had been followed, might be admitted by an industrial tribunal, which is not *bound* by the rule that would cause its exclusion in the ordinary court. But the tribunal *may* refuse to admit it, of its own motion or in response to an objection from the other party, depending on its relevance and weight.

'Hearsay' evidence, in which a witness says not what 'I heard or saw' but what a third party 'told me he heard or saw', is not admissible in many courts. A tribunal may allow such evidence to be given. If it decides to exclude it, it will be not because of 'any enactment or rule of law relating to the admissibility of evidence' but because of its irrelevance or worthlessness in the context of what needs to be proved. Similarly with 'leading questions' – those that suggest, by the form in which they are asked, that they should be answered in one way rather than another. In some circumstances, in some courts, such questions are prohibited, and answers obtained by asking them are not admitted in evidence. An industrial tribunal is not bound to prohibit their use, or to exclude answers to them, but the evidential value of such answers may be so small as to be virtually worthless, and the tribunal may point this out to the questioner.

With the exception of expert witnesses, who are most often found in equal value cases, witnesses are there to give evidence as to facts and not to express opinions. The distinction is not always as easy to recognise as it is to express. What a manager thought at a particular point in time is a fact. Where, as in discrimination cases, motivation is important, it may be a crucial fact and so, as a witness, the manager may well have to be questioned about the opinion that s/he held when the action in question was taken. The witness is unlikely to admit openly to direct motivation by simple racial or sexual prejudice, and to test for it the questioner may legitimately want to ask questions about the witness's more general views to see whether they are consistent or inconsistent with a denial of prejudice. In the context of a disciplinary dismissal one of the standard tests for fairness says that 'there must be established by the employer the fact of [the] belief [that the employee was guilty of the misconduct concerned]'. Such 'belief' can be only a matter of opinion, a subjective view held by the manager making the decision, but it is a 'fact' which has to be proved and about which evidence has to be given.

In other instances an expression of opinion by a non-expert witness, where that opinion was not a relevant fact in the sense just described, would be ruled inadmissible by many courts. Industrial tribunals are not bound by the same rules of evidence and so may, at their discretion, allow such opinions to be sought and given – which is not to say that they would necessarily give them much weight.

Adjournments

An industrial tribunal has a general power to adjourn hearings and is encouraged by the rules to do so where it seems that conciliation may produce a settlement. A hearing will be adjourned, as a matter of course, for a lunch break and at the end of the day, although the exact times are up to the tribunal. If an extra half-hour's sitting would avoid the necessity for the tribunal and parties to reconvene another day the normal hearing length may be extended.

A party may request an adjournment at any point during a hearing. The tribunal has discretion to grant or refuse such a request and will take account of the reason for which it has been made and the effect that granting it will have on the progress of the hearing. A short adjournment for 'personal reasons' – for example, to meet a pressing need to visit the toilet – will usually be granted without demur. An adjournment at a particular time – for instance, to allow a participant to meet a prior commitment – might or might not be granted, depending on the commitment, how much notice had been given, how disruptive it would be, and so on.

Circumstances in which an adjournment will almost certainly be granted and in which, if not requested by a party, it may be offered by the tribunal itself are those in which a party is taken by surprise by a development in the case. The rudimentary pleadings on which cases can come to hearing and the absence of representation can often mean that the parties are genuinely at cross-purposes. It is by no means unknown for an applicant alleging race discrimination to face a respondent prepared to defend a case of unfair dismissal or refusal of time off.

Such extreme examples will not often occur, but lesser surprises are less infrequent. A respondent may have stated that the reason for an applicant's dismissal was absence from work but may make it clear only at the hearing that the absence was believed not to have been for genuine medical reasons. The respondent may perhaps produce evidence that the applicant was seen taking part, say, in some sporting activity inconsistent with the claimed disability. An applicant whose case was based on a lack of the sort of prior consultation that the authorities require in cases of dismissal on grounds of ill health would probably ask for and be granted an adjournment to produce evidence that such allegations had never previously been raised and/or to rebut or explain the alleged sporting activity.

One party may be taken by surprise through no fault of the other. There may be genuine and reasonable misunderstanding. If, however, the tribunal believes that an adjournment has been made necessary because one party or the other is at fault, it can order the culpable party to pay costs arising out of the adjournment. This might be the party for whose benefit the adjournment has been granted if it was made necessary by that party failing adequately to prepare for a development it should have foreseen. If one party needs an adjournment in order to consider or counter an unforeseeable development introduced by the other, any costs order will be made against the other party.

Chapter 5
Disposal of cases

Once a case has been formally introduced into the industrial tribunal system by the registration of an originating application, it can ultimately and formally leave that system only by virtue of a judicial decision.

This does not mean that all cases have to be decided by a full tribunal after a substantive hearing. In practice the majority of cases never reach a hearing. The decision which removes most cases from the industrial tribunal system is a formal one, made by a legally qualified chair, along lines that 'the application should be dismissed on withdrawal by the applicant'. Such withdrawals may reflect a unilateral decision by the applicant not to proceed or a settlement of the claim either by the parties themselves or with the assistance of ACAS. Exceptionally, a case is disposed of by a decision striking out the originating application.

Nor does it mean that a decision by a full tribunal after a hearing necessarily results in the case being disposed of and so leaving the system. Procedures exist for an industrial tribunal decision to be reviewed, and decisions are subject to appeal, usually only on points of law, to the EAT and thence to higher courts.

The concern of this chapter is the ultimate disposal of cases so far as the legal system is concerned, whichever of these routes is followed.

The role of ACAS

In all jurisdictions in which ACAS has power to operate, an originating application is copied by the industrial tribunal to ACAS. So is any notice of appearance. The rules require it. As a matter of practice other documents in the case may also be copied to ACAS. Even before it has been notified in this way ACAS may have become involved by the direct invitation of one or both parties. The duty of ACAS to seek a settlement of a dispute without it being determined by an industrial tribunal arises, in each of the statutes concerned:

- Where a case has been initiated in an industrial tribunal and both parties request its assistance; or
- Where a case has been initiated in an industrial tribunal and, although neither party has requested assistance, a conciliation officer considers

there is a reasonable prospect of reaching a settlement; or
- Although no case has been initiated in an industrial tribunal, it is alleged that circumstances exist in which such a claim could be made, and either party requests the assistance of ACAS.

The relevant statutes also provide that contractual terms which purport to limit or exclude each statute's operation are void, except where such contractual terms are reached with the assistance of a conciliation officer under the above provisions. So an employer which attempts to use its greater bargaining power to get employees contractually to sign away their statutory employment rights is doomed to failure unless, first, the contractual terms are agreed in order to settle an actual or potential industrial tribunal case and, second, the case is one in which ACAS has become involved.

This led to reluctance on the part of some employers to agree out-of-court settlements without ACAS's involvement, because the employee would not be bound by the agreement not to make or pursue a tribunal claim. This ground and the reluctance based on it remained when all substantive terms of such a settlement were acceptable to both parties. The employer would be concerned that, even after it had honoured its part of the bargain, the employee was legally entitled to renege on any undertaking that the matter would not be pursued further. So the practice grew up of asking ACAS to become involved in cases when agreement as to settlement terms had already been reached, not so that ACAS could conciliate in any meaningful sense but so that the agreement would be enforceable on both sides. ACAS has an extensive case load, in much of which there is scope for meaningful conciliation, and limited resources. Wishing to avoid being used as a 'rubber stamp' in this way, it now declines invitations to become involved in such cases.

The administrative justification for its change of approach is understandable. Whether, in the light of its statutory duties, ACAS is entitled to refuse to participate in such cases seems uncertain. The issue does not appear to have been litigated. Unless and until it is, ACAS will participate only in cases where the parties are, or appear to ACAS to be, in genuine disagreement. This means that an employer who is willing to agree terms but who is unsure whether the employee will indeed refrain from bringing or pursuing an industrial tribunal case must take the chance that both parts of the bargain will stick; or find some means, other than legal enforceability, of making them stick; or refuse to agree terms because there is no legal guarantee that they will stick.

Settlement and withdrawal

The problem is often not as great as it may appear to be. Industrial tribunals' financial awards are almost invariably calculated largely with reference to an applicant's net loss. Any payment which the respondent has made to an employee under the terms of a settlement will, even if that settlement is unenforceable as against the employee, be set off against what the tribunal would otherwise have awarded. Where the loss is high and the amount paid out by way of settlement is low, that can still leave a considerable sum for the employee to aim for by going back on an agreement not to make or pursue a claim. In many cases, though, the gap will be small enough to make doing so financially unattractive. The size of the gap would, anyway, be uncertain before a tribunal's finding of the necessary facts. So what an employee would be aiming for would be not £x but only a possibility of about, or up to, £x.

Thus many settlements which are not legally binding on both parties will in practice be honoured by both parties. Neither side has enough to gain by breaking its part of the bargain. The employer knows the employee and should have some idea of whether this is likely to be so. If it is felt that the employee may be motivated not just by prospective financial gain but by a desire to be 'vindicated', the employer may be less prepared to rely on the employee's unenforceable word not to make or pursue a claim.

In such a case one approach is, whilst indicating a willingness to consider settlement, deliberately to refuse to discuss detailed terms without the participation of ACAS. Another is to agree terms under which payment by the employer does not occur until the time limit for lodging a complaint has passed. A third is to delay settlement until an originating application has been made and then either to agree terms which do not involve any payment until it has been withdrawn or to ask the tribunal to dismiss the case specifically in the light of a settlement being reached.

Where ACAS does become involved, and a settlement is reached with a conciliation officer's help, its terms will be recorded on form COT3. The standard practice is for settlements reached in this way to exclude further action only in industrial tribunals and only under the statutory provisions under which any case was, or could have been, brought in respect of the events concerned. They do not stop more general claims arising out of employment. In particular, potential claims for industrial injuries or diseases or relating to pension rights are often expressly excluded from the terms of the settlement.

If an employer wishes to cover any such other matters the settlement will have to say so expressly. Saying so may make the employee's agreement less likely. It is asking a lot of a person to sign away unquantified potential rights – for instance, the right to claim compensation for an industrial disease which may be latent and will not become apparent for some time – in return for a current payment. If a settlement is intended to have such a broad extent it will have to be carefully and clearly drafted.

If it ever does have to be enforced, it will probably be interpreted very restrictively. It has, for instance, been held that a settlement made in the context of an unfair dismissal complaint, containing much less 'oppressive' terms that purported to cover only statutory rights, could not be held to exclude the pursuit of rights which had not been expressly mentioned. But if an employer wants, and an employee genuinely agrees to, such terms they can be part of a settlement. ACAS's role is to ensure that both parties understand what is being agreed and its implications, not to say what can or cannot be agreed. Settlements do not have to be in writing, but there may be evidential problems about proving their terms, if it ever becomes necessary, when they are not.

The terms of a written settlement, whether they are on a COT3 or agreed between the parties without ACAS's involvement, will usually be lodged with the tribunal. This does not have to be done. All that is necessary for the case to be disposed of so far as the industrial tribunal system is concerned is that the applicant should withdraw. The applicant may do so without any settlement being agreed. The case may simply be abandoned. So if the applicant tells the tribunal that the case is being withdrawn but does not say that a settlement has been reached or what the terms of any settlement are, it makes no difference to the outcome. The case is still disposed of so far as the industrial tribunal system and the parties are concerned. But, formally, disposal of a case by the applicant's withdrawal and disposal of it by the parties' written agreement are different. The tribunal has power to do either. Where there is a settlement, and the tribunal is told, it will be reflected in the short written decision which formally disposes of the case. The terms of the settlement are unlikely to be quoted but that the decision is the result of agreement will be mentioned. Depending on the terms of the settlement, there may be something other than straightforward and immediate dismissal of the action. For instance, it may be dismissed conditionally on the respondent meeting the terms of the settlement within a specified period. Or the case may be adjourned *sine die* – that is, it will be regarded as closed but a party can reopen it if the terms are not honoured.

Tribunals' decisions

Where there is no settlement or withdrawal the tribunal will have to dispose of the case by a substantive decision. Under rule 9

> (1) A decision of a tribunal may be taken by a majority thereof and, if the tribunal shall be constituted of two members only, the chairman shall have a second or casting vote.
> (2) The decision of a tribunal, which may be given orally at the end of a hearing or reserved, shall be recorded in a document signed by the chairman.

(3) A tribunal shall give reasons, which may be in full or in summary form, for its decision.

(4) The reasons for the decision of the tribunal shall be recorded in a document signed by the chairman, which shall also contain a statement as to whether the reasons are in full or in summary form.

The provision allowing a majority decision to be reached by the casting vote of the legally qualified chair is to take account of circumstances where, in the light of the unavoidable absence of one of the lay members, and with the agreement of the parties, a hearing is held by the legally qualified chair and only one lay member.

In some cases decisions have to be given in full as a matter of course. These include race and sex discrimination and equal pay cases, and some of those concerning trade union membership and activities. In other cases, the majority, the tribunal can choose whether full or summary reasons are given and will usually give them in summary form. Either party can ask, at the hearing or within twenty-one days of the written summary decision being sent out, for full reasons to be supplied. Where any appeal against the tribunal's decision is contemplated, it will be essential to do so.

The rule allowing summary reasons to be given was introduced to reduce both expense and the work-load of tribunal staff and members, particularly legally qualified chairs. Previously it was necessary to draft, type, approve and copy detailed and sometimes long written decisions in every case. While that was being done members could not be hearing and deciding other cases. Provided that the right mental processes of decision making are still gone through, to remove the necessity for those mental processes to be laboriously transcribed into a physical form allows more cases to be heard with the same judicial resources. But the parties are still allowed to require, as of right, that the proper mental processes are gone through. Where a party has any doubt at all about that, it is more likely to ask for full written reasons to be produced. If there is any doubt, it is more likely to be in the mind of the party which lost the case, but either party can make the request. Although the aim of increasing the efficiency of the use of industrial tribunal resources should commend itself to respondent businesses, they should have no hesitation in asking for full reasons where they could conceivably serve a useful purpose. On the other hand, a respondent that can clearly see from a decision in summary form that there is no likelihood of a successful appeal, and that full reasons will add nothing of value to what is already known about 'where we went wrong', should not ask for full reasons just because it is entitled to.

Although decisions can be given orally, they are not final until they have been put in writing and signed by the legally qualified chair. It is unusual, but can happen, that a tribunal will have second thoughts between giving an oral decision and issuing its written one. In that case, rather than issue a written decision which contradicts what it had previously said, the tribunal should 'recall' the decision – that is, reconvene the hearing to explain the position and seek further argument from the parties on the point or points which led to the tribunal's change of view. There is no statutory requirement for this to be done, but an appellate court is likely to find that a decision which was 'wrong' one minute cannot, without more being said, become 'right' the next. For that to happen suggests that some error of law is involved somewhere. Which of the decisions was 'right' and which 'wrong' would depend not only on their substance but also on the circumstances in which each had been reached and whether the parties had already taken action on the basis of the oral decision.

Once a decision has been put in writing and signed it is copied to the parties and entered in the register. Once this has been done the decision can be altered in any substantial way only by further judicial process. An accidental error, such as a miscalculation, can be corrected by a certificate from the legally qualified chair. But any greater change would require the decision to be reviewed by the industrial tribunal or changed on appeal by the EAT or a higher court.

Review

Rule 10(1) provides that:

> A tribunal shall have power to review and to revoke or vary by certificate under the chairman's hand any decision on the grounds that:
> (a) the decision was wrongly made as a result of an error on the part of the tribunal staff; or
> (b) a party did not receive notice of the proceedings leading to the decision; or
> (c) the decision was made in the absence of a party or person entitled to be heard; or
> (d) new evidence has become available since the conclusion of the hearing to which the decision relates provided that its existence could not have been reasonably known of or foreseen; or
> (e) the interests of justice require such a review.

An application for a review can be made at a hearing or within fourteen days of the decision being issued. If not made at a hearing it has to be in writing and it has to set out 'in full' the grounds on which it is made. This means that it will have to identify under which of the provisions (a) to (e) above a review is being sought and give a convincing, detailed explanation of the circumstances that make the provision applicable. Full grounds are needed because the application for a review is first considered by a legally qualified chair. If it is thought not to have a reasonable chance of success, a review can be refused. If the application is granted, the actual review is undertaken by a full tribunal. It can result in confirmation or variation of the original decision, or the original decision can be revoked and the issue will then have to be retried. Any decision can be reviewed, not just a substantive decision of a full tribunal. So an interlocutory decision, made by a legally qualified chair alone, might be the subject of a review. Where the decision under review is one that was made by a full tribunal, the same tribunal will normally undertake the review. If that is not possible, or if the decision was originally taken by a legally qualified chair alone, another tribunal will review it. If a review revokes the original decision, any retrial could be held by the tribunal that made the original decision, by the tribunal which held the review, or by a different tribunal altogether. It seems likely, although it does not appear to have been positively decided, that any decision initially made by a legally qualified chair alone which was revoked by a review would have to be made the second time by a full tribunal.

The circumstances in which a review can occur do not often arise in practice. The grounds under which most applications are made are (d) and (e) above, and they are interpreted quite restrictively. Although 'justice' is an aim, and is specifically mentioned in (e) above, there is also a need for 'certainty': for parties to know that, once matters have been decided, they will stay decided in all but the most exceptional of situations. To be admitted, new evidence must not only have been genuinely unavailable – that a party simply failed to look hard enough or decided not to use it is insufficient – but it must also be weighty and relevant evidence which would probably have had a major impact on the outcome. An estimate of how long a dismissed employee will be out of work, on which a compensatory award is based, may turn out to be wrong. That does not necessarily mean that the 'interests of justice require a review'. If the difference is great, and it becomes apparent very soon, they might. But it will generally be held that a decision which was right at the time and in the circumstances should not be changed just because circumstances have changed in unforeseeable ways.

Appeal

If the decision was wrong at the time and in the circumstances, however, the need for 'certainty' should not stop it being put right. It might, though, mean that if no attempt was made within a specified time to get it put right the entitlement to do so would be lost. Appeals from orders and decisions of industrial tribunals to the EAT have to be made within forty-two days. In the case of an order, such as an order for discovery and inspection of documents, the forty-two days are reckoned from when the order was sent to the party concerned; in the case of a substantive decision, from the date on which the full reasons were sent to the parties. An appeal has to be accompanied by full written reasons. If a decision is first given in summary form a party that wishes to appeal will have to apply to the tribunal for full reasons to be provided. Only when they have been provided will the forty-two days start to run. Although the EAT's rules do allow for an extension, the time limits are usually applied strictly.

Appeals have to be made on the prescribed form. This requires the appellant to specify how the industrial tribunal erred *in law*. With the exception of those few jurisdictions where a factual appeal is expressly provided for by statute, the EAT will not hear appeals which do not raise a question of law. If a tribunal has made a factual decision which has no evidential basis, or which is contrary to the evidence, that does amount to an error in law. But the EAT will require very detailed particulars of any such grounds before allowing an appeal to go forward. It does, anyway, have the power to refuse to entertain appeals which do not disclose a fairly arguable point of law. These can be rejected by the Registrar, subject to appeal against the rejection to one of the judges, or by the full EAT after a preliminary hearing.

Points of law concern not only the interpretation and application of the statutes from which the industrial tribunals derive their jurisdictions but also how and in what precise ways they are bound by EAT and higher court decisions. It is in this latter context that the rules of the common law, as well as those derived from employment legislation, must be applied by industrial tribunals. Besides substantive provisions of the statute and case law, tribunals are also bound by procedural provisions. Thus appeals may also be based on the specific terms of the tribunals' own rules and the more general principles relating to the administration of justice:

- The avoidance of bias.
- 'Justice should not only be done but should manifestly be seen to be done.'
- A person should have full knowledge of and a fair chance to prepare for the case that has to be met.
- Discretion should be exercised judicially, taking account of all relevant and no irrelevant considerations.

And so on. It is under these more general provisions that, besides appeals about procedural shortcomings, perverse findings of fact might be challenged.

The EAT may dismiss an appeal completely, allow it completely, or dismiss some parts and allow others. When an appeal is allowed in whole or in part the case may have to be remitted to the industrial tribunal.

Evidence or facts may need to be reinterpreted in the light of the ruling, or further facts may need to be found so that the rule of law which the EAT has now enunciated can be applied. Where the tribunal's original decision contained enough factual findings to allow the EAT's decision to dispose of the case, remission will not be needed. Where it does not, the EAT will seldom usurp the tribunal's fact-finding function by accepting evidence to fill in any necessary gaps. A decision by the EAT may not, therefore, mark the end of the road. A further hearing at an industrial tribunal may be necessary. There is also the possibility of an appeal from the EAT's decision, only on a point of law and only by leave of the EAT or the higher court itself, to the Court of Appeal.

Whether a tribunal's decision is subject to review or appeal or is not, any sum which it awards begins to attract interest forty-two days after the written decision. The rate of interest is that prescribed by order for judgement debts, and it is changed from time to time. When the decision is sent to the parties the date from which interest will accrue and the rate at which it will do so will be specified. A tribunal's monetary award can be enforced through the County Court.

Costs

An award of costs, also enforceable through the County Court, is not subject to interest. Under rule 11, 'a tribunal shall not normally make an award of the costs or expenses incurred by a party to the proceedings', but it has the power to do so in certain circumstances. Where the postponement or adjournment of a hearing has been caused by a party's conduct the tribunal may order that party to pay the costs of the postponement or adjournment. This might happen if a party failed to turn up for a hearing but telephoned asking for it to be postponed, or where a party sprang a surprise on the other at the hearing by introducing a point which should have been covered by the pleadings. A tribunal is required to order costs against a respondent who causes a postponement or adjournment by failing to adduce reasonable evidence about the availability of suitable work at a hearing when it is known that a question at issue may be whether reinstatement or re-engagement of a dismissed employee is practicable, or at a hearing about the return to work of an employee after pregnancy or confinement.

Industrial tribunals have power to award costs where a party 'has in bringing or conducting the proceedings acted frivolously, vexatiously or otherwise unreasonably.' A case is frivolous when the party well knows that it has no chance of success or when, even if the party personally genuinely believes in it, it is so manifestly misconceived that it should have been obvious that it could not possibly succeed. Given the nature of the jurisdictions involved and that industrial tribunals are expressly available to parties without legal advice and representation, it is seldom possible to say that a party should have known, from the start, that a claim or defence must inevitably fail. Tribunals themselves, in pre-hearing assessments, sometimes take the wrong view. Unrepresented parties must be very wrong before they can be judged to have acted frivolously. The judgement can take account of the party's personal knowledge and position. An educated and intelligent person who had, or should have had, access to advice may be more readily found to have knowingly pursued a hopeless case than one who was not very bright. Similarly a party that had been warned, following a pre-hearing assessment, that costs might be awarded is more likely to be held to have acted frivolously in persisting with a hopeless claim or defence than one who had not. But, in practice, few findings of 'frivolity' are arrived at.

Vexatious conduct is that which is motivated primarily by a desire to harass or cause trouble for the other party rather than by a genuine wish to pursue one's own rights. It will probably occur in connection with a frivolous application or defence, but that is not in theory an essential ingredient. A party that persisted with a case which was not obviously hopeless but of which the chances of success were very slight, for the sole purpose of making the other party incur the costs of fighting the case to the bitter end, might be found to have done so vexatiously. But few parties would openly admit that as their aim, and a tribunal would probably be unwilling to infer such a motivation just from pursuit of the case unless it was obviously hopeless.

Frivolous or vexatious conduct can relate not only to the initial bringing or defending of proceedings and to persistence in pursuing them but also to how they are pursued. It could thus cover part of a case as well as the whole of it. To argue a hopeless case that an applicant was not qualified to claim the statutory right concerned might expose a respondent to an award of costs even if, looked at overall, there had been no infringement of the statutory right. For an applicant, in advancing a complaint about breach of a statutory right, to make completely unfounded allegations about the employer's motivation or conduct which then, although unfounded, have to be disproved may expose the applicant to an order for costs. Whether such costs would be ordered because the party had acted 'frivolously', or 'vexatiously' or 'otherwise unreasonably' would not matter in practical terms. But in analytical terms it might more easily be brought within the last of these headings. There is, besides the power to award costs, a power for the tribunal to strike out an originating application or notice of appearance, or anything within one, which is 'scandalous, frivolous or vexatious'.

Costs are very infrequently awarded. Where they are, it is usually done not of the tribunal's own motion but in response to the other party's application. A request for costs would normally be made at the end of a hearing. It could also be made in writing after a written decision had been received. Where costs are awarded they can be of a specified amount or they can be ordered to be 'taxed'. That means that the party to which costs are awarded has to submit an itemised account for approval by a County Court (not an industrial tribunal) official. Whether each item is permissible and what can be charged in respect of it is determined with reference to a list applicable to County Court actions. The result bears no more than a passing resemblance to what a party actually spends. The same is true of the allowances paid out of public funds to parties or witnesses in respect of travelling, subsistence or loss of earnings. An order for costs may be accompanied by an order that the party against whom it is made should also reimburse public funds in respect of the allowances.

Chapter 6
Decision-making in tribunals

Understanding the practical and procedural framework within which tribunal decisions are made does little to explain why tribunals decide particular points this way rather than that. Nor is it sufficient, although it is necessary, to say that a tribunal's decision will depend on the substantive law it is applying. Rules of substantive law, like procedures and practices, provide only a framework and criteria for a decision. Decision-making is a process. That the decision has law as its subject does not necessarily make the process different from making decisions on other subjects. In so far as it does, simply knowing that the subject matter is the law does not explain what the differences are. That the context is an industrial tribunal hearing does not necessarily make the process any different from that in other contexts. It may do so, but knowing only that an industrial tribunal is involved does not identify in what respects any differences occur nor what they are. The aim of this chapter is to look more closely at some of these issues.

The inquisitorial and the adversarial approaches

Information-gathering and decision-making

Decision-making is decision-making whether undertaken by a single manager, a management committee, a management-union negotiating committee or an industrial tribunal. In every case, before the decision is made it will be necessary to bring together the relevant information and to determine the criteria against which the decision should be made. Even where only one person is involved, that person will often consciously test one approach against another before reaching the decision. 'Is this information right?' 'This course will be cheaper, that course may cause less disruption among the staff. Which is more important?' Where more than one person is involved the debate will usually be articulated, although neither party may expressly state the criteria against which it believes the decision should be made when it knows that the other party feels different criteria to be appropriate.

In making some decisions a manager may first have to gather the necessary information. The manager may do it personally or ask subordinate staff to, but, in either event, must decide what information is needed or, at the least, what enquiries should be made in specified areas to see whether information from those areas is relevant. In these cases it is the manager's job, as part of the decision-making process, to decide what information is needed and to get hold of it. For some other decisions a manager will be presented, perhaps by a subordinate, with a set of facts and arguments and a request for a decision. Here the manager, although able to ask for more information, or to bring to bear considerations which the presentation has not covered, has much or all of the material on which the decision must be based already to hand. The decision-making role must still be fulfilled, but the part of it concerned with deciding what information is necessary and getting hold of it is diminished. In yet other instances a manager may be asked to choose between conflicting presentations. Subordinate A says that in the light of these facts and arguments such and such should happen, whilst subordinate B says that in the light of other facts and arguments something else should happen. Here the emphasis has shifted even further away from the information-gathering aspect.

Where the decision relates, say, to operational or commercial matters concerned with the running of the business, the manager may feel that other facts and arguments, not introduced by either A or B, are relevant and/or may want to get additional input from subordinate C. Similarly where the manager is initially investigating a grievance or disciplinary complaint. But many disciplinary procedures provide that after an alleged disciplinary offence has been investigated a hearing should be held at which a senior manager decides, in the light of the facts and arguments produced by the employee and those alleging the misconduct, whether there has in fact been misconduct and if so what the disciplinary consequences should be. Here, when 'sitting in judgement', the manager may feel it unfair or unwise to take account of points which neither side has raised.

This range of situations in which an individual manager may make a decision illustrates that, although all decision-making should be based on all the relevant information, there are different ways in which, first, it can be determined what information is relevant and, second, the relevant information might be brought before the decision-maker. At one end of the range, the inquisitorial or investigative, the decision-maker is responsible for deciding what information is needed, for getting it and for making the decision based on it. At the other end of the range, the adversarial, the decision has to be based on, and only on, information and arguments put before the decision-maker by those seeking the decision.

Tribunals' investigative role

The UK legal system works at the adversarial end of this range. The essential form of an industrial tribunal hearing, like hearings in the vast majority of UK courts, is adversarial. The two parties, applicant and respondent, present conflicting evidence and argument to a disinterested third party, which then decides, on the basis of what the parties have put before it, between them: which of them has won and which has lost. In both form and substance an industrial tribunal's function is to compare opposing cases and decide between them. It is not to investigate the issue which lies at the heart of the case before it and decide the truth and determine the rights and wrongs of the matter.

It has already been said that industrial tribunals are more prepared than many other courts to adopt an inquisitorial role. This is sometimes made necessary by the people and cases with which they deal. A dismissed employee feels that the dismissal was not fair. 'Fair', in that employee's mind, has no specific legal meaning: it is almost certainly not a convenient shorthand way of expressing the multi-faceted and sometimes complex test which the law on unfair dismissal prescribes. The employee's feeling of unfairness may rest on a belief that the employer 'got hold of the wrong end of the stick', 'went off at half-cock', 'had it in for me', or whatever. The employee's grievance is real. It may, when translated from the vernacular into the terms of the statutory tests, be justified. That the employee has not the skill or knowledge to undertake the translation should not stop the grievance being investigated. That the employee has not the forensic skill to test the employer's evidence should not stop the evidence being tested.

It is in cases like this that the tribunal is most likely to descend into the arena and, by asking questions and suggesting arguments, try to ensure that the generalised complaint is crystallised, redefined and itemised in a way which allows the essential legal tests to be applied. The party whose case needs such investigation may not be the employee. Particularly with a small employer – the owner of a corner shop or a jobbing builder, for instance – where the case is defended in person by the sole proprietor, the tribunal may similarly need to translate a non-specific and vernacular defence into the terms of the statutory tests before it can reach a decision. In so doing it may have to ask questions or suggest arguments on the respondent's behalf.

This inquisitorial or investigative role is not restricted to unravelling the cases of unrepresented parties. There is no restriction on the right of representation before industrial tribunals, and, while most of those who represent applicants and respondents do so because they have some skill and experience in doing so, such is not always the case. Whether, and if so how much, a tribunal will adopt an active investigative role will depend less on whether either or both parties are represented than on whether the tribunal thinks it is being given the information it needs to reach a decision. With skilled representation a tribunal will more readily assume that what is being put forward is all that is necessary. But even then a tribunal may raise points which, it seems from what has been said, may be relevant and important but which have not been raised by the representative/s.

The duty to do so is not open-ended. It cannot be. Unless information which makes a point relevant and important is put before the tribunal in some form, however imprecise and vernacular, the tribunal has no way of knowing that the point exists, let alone that it might be a decisive factor. The function of the tribunal remains to decide between the parties. It may adopt an inquisitorial or investigative approach to try to ensure that a party's case is adequately put, but that does not change its role into one of more generally investigating to see whether a different and better case could be put. Any inquisitorial or investigative impression given by how a tribunal may conduct a hearing should not hide the fact that the decision-making process remains firmly rooted in the adversarial tradition.

The standard of proof

Industrial tribunals are civil courts and they decide matters on the civil standard of proof. That means they require a thing to be proved 'on the balance of probabilities' and not 'beyond a reasonable doubt'. If on balance A.'s story is more likely than B.'s story, then A.'s story will be accepted. If both stories are equally likely, the issue will be determined with reference to the burden of proof: who is required to prove what? If A. bore the burden of proof and A.'s story is not *more* likely than B.'s, then A. has failed to discharge the burden and will lose the point. Had the burden of proof been on B., that A.'s story was *just as* likely as B.'s would have meant that A. would have won the point: B. had not proved what was required. In theoretical outline that is simple to express and to understand. In practice it becomes more complicated.

Misunderstanding often arises where an employee has been charged with a criminal offence related in some way to the employer's business. Whatever the employer and other employees think about the case, they all know that a person is 'innocent until proved guilty'. To be found guilty there has to be proof 'beyond a reasonable doubt'. Many go on to assume that for the employer to take any action, particularly dismissal, against the employee until the criminal court has disposed of the case must be unfair. Or, if the employer is not prepared to wait for the outcome of the criminal court proceedings, it must satisfy itself beyond all reasonable doubt that the employee is guilty as charged before any dismissal could be fair.

The assumption is wrong. Confusion arises because differing standards of proof apply for different purposes. True, unless the employee's guilt is proved beyond reasonable doubt a 'not guilty' verdict will result from the criminal charge. But an industrial tribunal hearing an unfair dismissal complaint is a different court trying a different matter by a different standard of proof. First, anything the employer has to prove at an industrial tribunal has to proved only on the balance of probability. Second, in strict terms the only thing the employer has to prove is that the reason for the dismissal related to the conduct of the employee. That the conduct has resulted in a criminal charge is coincidental and irrelevant. Third, although technically the onus of proof is now neutral, the employer will want to show that it was reasonable to treat the reason as a sufficient reason for dismissing the employee.

This may involve questions about how genuine and reasonable the employer's belief in the employee's misconduct was. But that and related questions do not concern the employee's innocence or guilt of the criminal charge, and they are answered in a different way. If the employer's belief – in misconduct, not in criminal guilt – was formed after the sort of investigation that a reasonable employer would conduct, and if a reasonable employer might decide in the light of such a belief that dismissal was an appropriate reaction, dismissal will be fair. That a different employer might have had 'a reasonable doubt' – about misconduct, let alone criminal guilt – does not alter the position. All the employer has to do is act 'within the range of reasonable responses'.

Similar confusion can arise for similar reasons in other cases where two courts or tribunals are looking at essentially the same set of facts but under different jurisdictions and for different purposes. A person who loses employment for misconduct can be disqualified from the receipt of Unemployment Benefit for a specified period. Any appeal against such disqualification must obviously cover much of the same ground as an industrial tribunal would in hearing a case about the fairness of a dismissal. It is sometimes thought that a decision in the Social Security context that loss of employment was or was not the result of misconduct is tantamount to a decision that a dismissal was not or was unfair. That again is wrong, for similar reasons.

The burden of proof

A second source of difficulty may lie in determining where the burden of proof lies in a particular issue. Occasionally, legislation will state directly that it lies on one party or the other. Section 57(1) of the EPCA expressly provides that:

In determining . . . whether the dismissal of an employee was fair or unfair, *it shall be for the employer to show:*

(a) what was the reason (or, if there was more than one, the principal reason) for the dismissal and
(b) that it was a reason falling within sub-section (2) or some other substantial reason of a kind such as to justify the dismissal of an employee holding the position which that employee held. [Emphasis added]

More often the legislative language is less direct. Where it places the burden of proof may have to be discovered by analysing the statute in the light of the general principle that it is the person asserting something who has to prove it. To do that is not always straightforward. As a path is traced through detailed provisions the burden can shift from side to side. An employee makes an unfair dismissal claim and the employer responds that the employee has insufficient service. The employee has the burden of proving that the service is sufficient, but is aided in the attempt by a presumption that service is continuous. If it is alleged that service was broken, that is for the employer to prove. It can be done by showing that the service contained a week which did not count under paragraphs 3–12 of Schedule 13 to the EPCA. To escape any such break the employee may argue, and will have the burden of proving, that the week still counts because it was one in which a strike or lock-out occurred.

In practice such complexity is of little moment. Very seldom is a case ultimately determined with reference to the burden of proof. The standard of proof is 'on the balance of probabilities', and few cases are so evenly balanced that the tribunal has to resort to saying 'It was A.'s job to prove this point, and it has not been proved, so A.'s case fails.' Where the burden of proof lies may be relevant to decide not only cases which are otherwise evenly balanced. As has been noted, tribunals will usually – and higher courts have encouraged them to – decide which party should present its case first by looking to see where the first burden of proof lies. But this is a rule of thumb, not a strict rule of law. The procedural decision about 'who goes first' is likely to be based more on a broad view of where the burden of proof lies than on a detailed statutory analysis.

A third source of confusion can arise from cases and commentators that refer to an 'evidential' burden as additional to, and distinct from, the 'formal' or 'legal' burden. The legal burden of proving direct discrimination on racial or sexual grounds rests on the person alleging it, the applicant. But the respondent is the only one who really knows whether any action was due to the race or sex of the applicant and is unlikely to admit openly that it was. So the higher courts have held that industrial tribunals are entitled, if there was less favourable treatment, and if the person treated less favourably was of a particular race or sex, to infer, if there is no other adequate explanation from a respondent, that the less favourable treatment was on the grounds of race or sex.

Once the applicant has shown that there was less favourable treatment, and there was a race or sex differential, the evidential burden shifts to the respondent. The formal burden of proof remains on the applicant but it will have been discharged unless the respondent brings forward sufficient satisfactory evidence to show that is was not race or sex which caused the less favourable treatment. The higher courts have now criticised that analysis and explanation as misleading. Some may still find it helpful. Provided it is not treated as prescribing the precise standard which a respondent's evidence must meet, it still makes the useful point that the respondent cannot simply say, 'It was not race or sex, and you have not proved that it was.' Similar analyses are possible, and may be helpful, in other areas of substantive law with which tribunals deal.

Finding the facts

The grounds on which an action was taken are a question of fact. Deciding whether evidence produced by a respondent is enough to rebut the factual inference which might otherwise be drawn is no different from deciding any other disputed question of fact. In some cases there will be little or no dispute over the facts. The parties will agree about what actually happened: any dispute will be about whether what happened was discriminatory or non-discriminatory, fair or unfair. But in other cases the parties will put forward different versions of what happened. The first thing the tribunal must do is decide which version, or what combination of the two versions, it thinks is correct. The tribunal has to find the facts.

The very phrase 'find the facts' highlights that a fact is not a fact until it has been 'found'. One individual may go along to a tribunal knowing that such and such happened. 'I said or did precisely this', 'I saw or heard precisely that.' That individual is sure, from personal experience, of a particular fact. But if a second individual goes along and says that something else happened there is conflict between the stories. The tribunal must resolve it. It may decide that it prefers the second individual's version. The first individual will then probably feel that the tribunal is wrong. It must be wrong because what it decided is contrary to what that individual experienced personally. The tribunal said that the facts were so, when the individual knows them to be different.

Emotionally that is understandable but logically it is based on a false premise: that what the individual knows and believes and has experienced is fact. What one knows and believes and has experienced (or, more properly, what one says about what one knows and believes and has experienced) is evidence of a fact. It is not, in' itself, a fact. It is only when, in the light of that evidence and of any other evidence about the same point, a tribunal makes up its own mind what happened that it can properly be said, for present purposes, that there is a fact. And, generally, once a tribunal has made up its mind about what happened, its findings of fact are immutable and irrevocable. That our disappointed individual *knows* them to be wrong is of no account. Industrial tribunals are the final arbiter on matters of fact. In the vast majority of their jurisdictions, there can be no appeal against a tribunal's findings of fact. A tribunal's findings of fact can be overturned on appeal only if they are unsupported by any evidence, or run totally contrary to the evidence.

Weighing the evidence

The grounds on which an appeal against a factual finding can be brought illustrate that findings of fact must depend on evidence. Facts are found by weighing evidence. As the phrase suggests, it is a comparative process. Where all the evidence points the same way there is no need to weigh this piece against that to decide which to accept: the fact to which all the evidence points is that which must be found. In theory this remains so even if what all the evidence points to is an obvious absurdity or a physical impossibility. In practice that situation would be met by the tribunal introducing the evidence of its own experience to demonstrate the absurdity or impossibility and giving the parties the opportunity to produce further evidence or argument to show that it was not absurd or impossible. That evidence may just, of itself, seem incredible does not entitle a tribunal to reject it. The tribunal can do so only if some more credible alternative is on offer.

This still leaves tremendous scope for tribunals. Returning to the example of direct race or sex discrimination, the factual question on which the whole of such a case would turn is 'What was the reason for this person being less favourably treated?' It is likely that the respondent will give evidence that race or sex was not the reason. As Mandy Rice Davies said when told that Lord Astor had denied her allegations, 'He would, wouldn't he?' This evidence will be the only direct evidence relating to that crucial fact and, because it is direct, will normally carry considerable weight. That the evidence could not be expected to be anything else may diminish its weight in absolute terms. But that does not entitle a tribunal to reject it and find a fact which is inconsistent with it. There has to be a greater weight of evidence pointing to a different fact before that can be found.

Evidence that a person received less favourable treatment, or that a person was of a particular racial group or sex, does not directly touch on the crucial question. But taken together the two pieces of evidence suggest the possibility of a link between the treatment and the racial group or sex. In that suggestion such evidence conflicts with the direct evidence of the respondent's denial. But the issue now is not whether the denial can of itself be rejected. It is: which of the conflicting sets of evidence should be given more weight? This is a factual matter, and so is for the industrial tribunal to decide. Where evidence is legally incapable of supporting a factual finding the tribunal can be overruled on a point of law. But the higher courts have ruled as a matter of law that – in the special circumstances of a discrimination case, at least – the inference raised by the simple juxtaposition of less favourable treatment and belonging to a particular racial group or sex can be sufficient to outweigh the respondent's direct denial.

Weighing evidence involves balancing all factors tending one way against all factors tending another way. That one piece of evidence is more direct than another does not mean that it necessarily carries more weight. It will tend to do so, but the tendency may be countered by another of its characteristics. Less direct evidence which is less tainted by the possibility of bias may, overall, be more weighty. Uncorroborated direct evidence, particulary if there seems no good reason for the lack of corroboration, may be regarded as of reduced weight relative to indirect evidence which is not contested or for which it seems less likely there could be corroboration. Indirect evidence which is internally consistent and which produces a consistent, coherent and comprehensible overall picture will be preferred to direct evidence which is internally inconsistent or which leaves points unexplained or seeming to conflict with other points.

Direct and circumstantial evidence

Directness of evidence depends on how closely it relates to the fact that has to be found. If there is a factual dispute about whether Fred was in the stores at nine o'clock the most direct evidence would come from Fred's saying, 'I was in the stores at nine o'clock', or 'I was not in the stores at nine o'clock.' Also direct would be the evidence of someone else saying, 'I saw Fred in the stores at nine o'clock', or 'I saw Fred somewhere else than the stores at nine o'clock.'

Less direct although still of considerable value would be evidence, from Fred or someone else, that he was going towards the stores immediately before nine o'clock and/or coming away from the stores immediately after nine o'clock. Although this evidence would not relate directly and immediately to the fact which has to be found, it suggests that Fred must have been in the stores at nine o'clock. The circumstances about which direct evidence has been given are consistent with him being in the stores at nine o'clock. It may be that the circumstances are not inconsistent with a different explanation. But in the absence of such an alternative explanation a tribunal is likely to find on the basis of the circumstantial evidence that Fred was in the stores at nine o'clock.

The further removed from the event in question the evidence is, the less direct it is and the less probative value it has. That Fred was seen going towards the stores at 8.30 a.m. is probably of little intrinsic value. That he was seen arriving at work at 8.00 a.m. probably of none. But if Fred was seen going towards the stores at 8.30 a.m. it might, although of little immediate apparent help on the question of whether he was in the stores at nine o'clock, still contribute to the answer to that question. If evidence were given that Fred went to the stores to do a job which usually took an hour, the fact that he was seen going there thirty minutes beforehand would be consistent with his being in the stores at the crucial time. This evidence would be unlikely of itself to cause a tribunal to find that Fred was in the stores at nine o'clock but it might, when looked at with other evidence, tilt the overall balance in favour of that finding.

Primary and secondary facts

All evidence is in one sense direct, in that it relates directly to the fact which it immediately concerns. So Mary's evidence that she saw Fred going towards the stores at 8.57 a.m. and coming away at 9.03 a.m. is direct evidence of the fact that that is what Fred was doing at those times. That can be found as a 'primary' fact on the basis of that direct evidence. A tribunal is entitled to infer 'secondary' facts from primary facts. In this case, from the primary facts, one, that he was going towards the stores at 8.57 a.m. and, two, that he was coming away from the stores at 9.03 a.m. can be inferred the secondary fact that he was in the stores at nine o'clock. Because this finding involves an inference it is not intrinsically as strong as a finding of a primary fact based on Fred's own direct evidence about where he was at nine o'clock. If it is consistent with Fred's own statement, if he says he *was* in the stores at nine o'clock, it confirms or corroborates that statement. If there is other evidence which tends to show that Fred was elsewhere at that time, it will support Fred's story as against the other.

But what if Fred's evidence is that he was *not* in the stores at nine o'clock? To hold that he was requires, first, that Mary's evidence is accepted and, second, that Fred's being in the stores at nine o'clock can be validly inferred as a secondary fact from the primary facts found from Mary's evidence. For an inference to be valid, the secondary fact does not have to follow inevitably from the primary facts. That, on balance, when taken with all other relevant evidence, it provides a more credible and probable explanation than any other may be sufficient. But if a credible and possible alternative explanation is offered – he may have been going towards the stores just before nine o'clock but have found them locked and been coming away from them just after nine to get the key – Fred's evidence is likely to be accepted.

Fred's direct evidence points unequivocally to one finding: he was not in the stores at nine o'clock. To accept Mary's evidence without reservation does not inevitably lead to a different finding. Interpreted one way, it is consistent with a different finding, but interpreted another way it can be made consistent with Fred's evidence. There is a greater weight of evidence pointing one way if Mary's evidence is interpreted consistently with Fred's than if it is interpreted inconsistently with it.

A tribunal's decision is most unlikely to set out an analysis like this of how each piece of evidence was regarded and precisely what reasoning process led to this finding rather than that. In some cases it may do so with respect to some evidence – for instance, in a race or sex discrimination case, where an inference of discrimination, drawn from less favourable treatment and the existence of a particular racial group or sex, has been held to outweigh a direct denial of discrimination by the respondent. In all cases where there was a dispute about the facts, a tribunal should say in a full decision what facts it has found and, where appropriate, outline which evidence it has accepted and which rejected in finding those facts. But each case will involve a tremendous amount and mixture of evidence. A tribunal will decide – perhaps without consciously ascribing a weight to each individual piece of evidence, and almost certainly without articulating what weight has been given to each piece of evidence, and which of its findings are of primary facts and which are secondary – what overall story it found more convincing and find the facts accordingly. But that a tribunal's decision may not expressly identify the different weight which has been ascribed to different evidence, or may not specifically indicate how secondary facts have been found by inference from findings of primary facts, should not obscure the processes concerned.

Perversity and credibility

It is when it can be shown that those processes are flawed that a tribunal's finding of fact will be reversed on appeal. That the process is flawed amounts to an error of law. The decision of the appellate body is not, as such, that the wrong finding of fact has been made, only that the process by which the fact has been found was wrong. That the process was wrong may occasionally be inferred from the finding of fact itself: if it is 'perverse'. If no reasonable tribunal could possibly have decided this fact from that evidence, then the process by which the tribunal did so must have been the wrong process. But it is only rarely that an appellate body is prepared to draw such an inference.

Weighing the evidence involves balancing many factors. One of them is credibility. Whether evidence is believable depends not only on what it is, on how consistent it is with other evidence, on how closely it relates to the fact which has to be found or on whether it is only what the person giving it might be expected to say in the light of a special interest. It can also legitimately depend on how it is given. Evidence given firmly and confidently and without prompting as to its content from the questioner is inherently more believable than evidence which appears unsure or equivocal or is given in response to leading questions. A witness who admits not knowing the answers to some questions or who readily acknowledges disadvantageous facts may be more credible than one who invents answers to fill gaps in knowledge or avoids or equivocates about unpleasant truths. Witnesses' 'body language' may give important clues as to their evidence's trustworthiness. That these clues may be unconsciously given and subconsciously interpreted does not diminish their value and validity. How evidence is given is apparent only to those present at a hearing. The tribunal members can thus form a judgement on credibility which EAT and higher judges, who do not see and hear the evidence being given, cannot. This is a major factor in higher courts' reluctance to interfere with tribunals' factual findings and highlights the need for those appearing at tribunals to concentrate on getting the tribunal to find the right facts. If a decision is wrong in law, there can be an appeal. But there is no second bite of the cherry on factual matters.

The law

Having found the facts the tribunal must apply the law to those facts. Often this is straightforward; sometimes it is not. Where the statutory language is itself clear or has already been clarified by EAT or higher courts' rulings the only issue is how closely the facts match what the law requires. In some cases what the law requires is less clear. Before it can compare the facts found with the law's requirement the tribunal has to decide what the requirement is. It will, in doing so, be bound by the provisions of the statute and by higher courts' decisions. But its own decision is necessary because, at least in one party's contention, the statute and the binding precedents do not finally and unequivocally answer the question that has now been raised.

Binding precedents and distinguishing cases

The tribunal may decide that, contrary to the party's contention, the issue has been settled finally and unequivocally by some binding precedent. It may, on the other hand, 'distinguish' the case with which it is dealing from that covered by any higher court's decision. Decisions of higher courts, like those of tribunals, cover facts as well as law. That the higher courts may not have found those facts themselves but have been relying on findings reached by tribunals does not alter this. The principles of law which higher courts' decisions enunciate are often very broadly stated but, strictly, the only binding elements are those which are needed to settle the facts of the case concerned. Where the facts in the case with which a tribunal is dealing differ from those in a case cited as a precedent only in unimportant or irrelevant respects the tribunal is bound by that precedent. But if a different fact is felt to raise an issue of principle which is not clearly decided by the quoted authority, the tribunal may explain what that difference is and what different question of principle it raises and proceed to arrive at its own decision on the new issue of principle which it has identified.

In deciding whether any new issue of principle is involved, and in deciding any such issue that is involved, it will have regard to parts of higher courts' judgements which are not strictly binding as well as to any that are. That a precedent would technically be distinguishable will not lead a tribunal to ignore it if it clearly establishes a general line of judicial thought which would inevitably lead to any different decision by the tribunal being overthrown on appeal. On the other hand tribunals will be criticised and overruled on appeal for too slavish reliance on precedent where a new issue has indeed been raised by the facts of a case.

A tribunal must also avoid over-reliance on the wording of judgements. The law which industrial tribunals are applying is that passed by the legislature. The role of courts is to clarify the legislation where its meaning is unclear and to resolve any ambiguities it contains. They do this by making decisions in particular cases and explaining the reasons for the decisions. As more and more decisions are made there is, given the need for consistency and the operation of the doctrine of binding precedent, more and more cross-reference between decisions, with this case being distinguished from that in a particular respect or drawing on the other case for a guiding analogy. Cases inevitably comment on cases. This can lead to the impression that it is the cases, particularly those which are frequently commented upon, which themselves set out the law. The better view is that all any case can actually do is comment on the legislation. In so far as it comments on other cases its real purpose is to adopt or amend those other cases' comments on the legislation.

That is the better view for the purpose of studying how tribunals decide questions of law. In terms of practical management the case law usually provides more comprehensive and comprehensible guidance as to what should and should not be done than the statute does. But the danger of regarding the cases as themselves the source of the law which has to be interpreted and applied by industrial tribunals lies in the temptation that it provides to concentrate on the precise words of judgements rather than on the principles they are intended to express: to interpret judgements as though they were statutes.

Statutory interpretation

Statutory interpretation, or 'construction', can be approached in a number of ways. At one end of the range is a 'literalist' or strict approach which relies, to the exclusion of all else, on the precise words which the statute contains. If a word, when given its ordinary and everyday meaning, leads to a certain result, then that is the result which the courts must apply. At the other end of the range is a 'purposive' or liberal approach which asks, using all the indicators it can find, what it was that the legislators were intending to achieve and then seeks to apply the law in the way that is judged most likely to achieve their intention. Between these extremes more or less of one approach is combined with less or more of the other.

Traditionally the UK legal system has operated more towards the literalist end of the range. The use of this word in this place in this statute may be compared with the use of the same word in a different place in the same statute or even in some limited conditions with how the same word has been used in a different statute, but other guides to meaning or intention are forbidden. If the end result is anomalous, that may be unfortunate, but it must be taken as what the legislators intended. The rigours of such pure and isolated semantic analysis have often been tempered in practice, but to varying degrees on different occasions and in an *ad hoc* way. The literalist constraints are still there for those who wish to argue them.

The purposive tide is, however, advancing. The European continental tradition tends more to the purposive end of the range. With the increasing and direct influence of the European Court of Justice on the UK legal system, particularly in the area of employment law, it seems inevitable that the purpose of any provision will as a matter of course assume more importance in deciding what it means and how it should be applied than the precise words in which the provision is couched. This is not to say that the precise words can be ignored. In so far as they can be given their ordinary meaning and achieve the overall purpose of the legislation, they must be applied as they are written. But the words themselves cease to be the sole guide to the purpose of the legislation. In so far as giving them their ordinary meaning appears contrary to that purpose, their meaning may be strained or even, in exceptional cases, ignored.

The movement in this direction is evolutionary. There has been, nor will be, any revolutionary overnight sea-change. The extent to which an industrial tribunal will be prepared, or be allowed by an appeal court, to take account of extraneous material – Consultative Documents, Green Papers, White Papers, parliamentary debates, ministerial speeches and so on – in deciding that the purpose of legislation is other than what its plain words mean will vary from tribunal to tribunal and from case to case. How far a tribunal will wish or be allowed to go in stretching the ordinary meaning of statutory words to meet a perceived legislative purpose is and will remain difficult to foretell. What is clear is that both are more likely now than they were a few years ago, and will become more likely still as time passes.

Chapter 7
Investigation

It is not unusual for a company's decision to appear in an industrial tribunal to be little more than a knee-jerk reaction to the arrival of an originating application. The applicant's decision to bring a case is conscious and deliberate. But the named respondent often feels that the case must, as a matter of course, be defended. That is far too simple a view.

The need for a choice

The options that exist

A case may be disposed of in two main ways. It may be determined by a substantive decision of an industrial tribunal or higher court, or it may be withdrawn by the applicant. Withdrawal may be at an applicant's own initiative or as a result of some action by the respondent. The respondent's action which results in withdrawal may be purely persuasive or there may be some element of purchase in it. That is, the applicant may withdraw having been convinced that the case is hopeless or that it will cost more to pursue than it is worth; or may withdraw in response to some *quid pro quo* from the respondent. A substantive tribunal decision may dispose of a case at an early stage – on a jurisdictional point, for instance – or at a late stage – only after awarding precise and quantified remedies – or at any stage between. Appeals move, quite slowly, from one level of court to another. Withdrawal – by persuasion or purchase – can occur at any point along the tribunal's decision-making road or whilst any appeal is pending. Without analysing the mathematics of the combinations and the permutations, it is clear that there are a vast number of ways in which a case can, in theory, be disposed of. Not all will apply in all practical situations. But there are few practical situations in which only one is realistically available.

The means by which disposal occurs are essentially different as between determination by a tribunal, on the one hand, and withdrawal by the applicant, on the other. But there is no essential financial difference between the end results. The financial implications of a solution, however it is achieved, contain two elements. First, what has to be paid out as a consequence of that solution? Second, what does it cost to achieve?

How much is paid out as a consequence of disposing of any case does not essentially depend on whether the sum is awarded by a tribunal or agreed in an out-of-court settlement. A tribunal decision may result in no award being made, if the case is dismissed or if, for example, it is held that although the respondent is liable the applicant has suffered no loss; or it can result in an award up to the appropriate statutory maximum, which can be substantial. The same, or an even larger, range of possibilities exists where a case is disposed of by withdrawal. An applicant may withdraw without any payment from the respondent, or a sum even greater than a tribunal has the power to award may be offered in return for such withdrawal. The time, effort and expense involved in achieving a tribunal decision are potentially much greater than those which achievement of withdrawal or a settlement might involve, but it need not always be so. A respondent who does not even enter an appearance may ultimately face an award of less than an applicant was seeking, in protracted negotiations, in return for the case being withdrawn.

Assessing the options

A 'cost–benefit analysis' is desirable. It is not possible to put a simple money value on all the factors which need to be considered, but that is true in many other areas of management. There it does not stop the pros and cons being weighed so as to decide what is best for the company. Many management decisions require intangibles such as 'image' and 'morale' to be weighed. What appears desirable in the short term and in one area of management may seem less attractive when account is taken of the longer term and of a company's strategic plans and objectives. It sometimes has to be recognised that individual or sectional interests, of managers or departments, are not the same as those of the company as a whole. How a respondent should react to an originating application is not essentially different from any other management decision. Why should it be approached in a different way?

The respondent has a number of options and should choose among them on a fully informed and rational basis. An objective factual investigation and some legal analysis are necessary to determine the range of options that are available and how likely they are to be achievable. The relative desirability of the options then needs to be decided against business criteria. There will seldom be only one possible outcome to a case. What is most desirable may look least achievable. Whether an attempt should nevertheless be made to achieve it will be influenced by the relative desirability and achievability of other options and of how such an attempt would impact on them. If they remain available nothing is lost by aiming first for the most desirable option and, if it is not achieved, then lowering the sights. But if pursuing that option now precludes the later pursuit of others, a choice must be made between aiming higher with less chance of success or aiming lower with more chance of success. A strategy which will, as far as possible, allow pursuit of the best option while preserving the availability of others is desirable.

A three-stage approach

This chapter is the first of three concerned with the development of such a strategy. It looks at investigation: the collection and testing of evidence on which, if a case eventually goes to a hearing, the tribunal's decision will be based. The next chapter is about analysis and assessment: identifying the legal framework and criteria against which a tribunal would decide the case and estimating how strong or weak the respondent's case is in its parts and as a whole. The investigation, analysis and assessment are intended to identify the limits within which the respondent has room for manoeuvre. A respondent cannot force an applicant to withdraw, and if there is no withdrawal the case will be decided by a tribunal. What a tribunal would decide will therefore be a yardstick against which other solutions, which do not require a tribunal decision, can be measured. It sets a 'fall-back' position. A respondent cannot dictate what a tribunal's decision should be but can influence it. There will be a decision even if a respondent does nothing at all. That is a yardstick against which other decisions which might result from the respondent adopting different approaches can be measured.

Investigation, analysis and assessment should identify the legal options and provide some quantification of their achievability in legal terms. They will have some contribution to make in answering questions of how the pursuit of one line of legal defence may affect the viability of other lines of legal defence. They will enable some judgement to be formed about what may happen if the respondent does one thing, or another, or even does nothing. But they cannot answer the question of what *should* be done. That is a management question which needs to be answered against business criteria. The last of these three chapters regards the arrival of an originating application not as the start of an industrial tribunal case but as the raising of a management problem to which the optimum management solution must be found. It considers some of the non-legal factors which affect decision-making in this context.

Each chapter assumes that each function is undertaken by one person. The same person will, in many practical situations, perform two and maybe all three of the functions. That does not matter. What does matter is that – however they are performed and whoever performs them – there are three distinct jobs to be done.

The need for investigation

A proper decision as to whether a case should be defended at all, and if so on what grounds, and how, must rest on as good an idea as possible of what facts a tribunal would find. Those facts will depend on what evidence is put before the tribunal not only by the party making the decision but by the other party as well, and on any further evidence which the tribunal, in an inquisitorial role, may get from witnesses appearing before it. So one of the first tasks to be undertaken is factual investigation. The purpose of the investigation is not just to find evidence which might help the case of the party conducting the investigation but to consider all the evidence which might, one way or another, find its way to the tribunal.

One party cannot know, beforehand, what evidence will be given by the other party. But a careful reading of the originating application, paying attention not only to what is expressly stated but also to what is implied 'between the lines', should reveal the general areas in which evidence is likely to be produced to the tribunal by the applicant. If it does not, then an order for further particulars can be sought. An order for further particulars will still not reveal what evidence is to be given, only the facts and contentions on which the applicant intends to rely. But, having identified what facts the applicant intends to prove, or will have to prove, the respondent is in a position to decide whether to agree those facts or dispute them.

Where the respondent is willing to agree any facts, then, although any investigation may need to cover them to provide a full and rounded picture as background to the further decisions which have to be made, the investigator does not need to think too deeply about precisely what evidence is likely to be produced, from any source, in support of them. But where the respondent wishes to dispute any of the facts on which the applicant is likely to rely, account will have to be taken of all the evidence that relates to those facts. Similarly with any facts which, although they are not mentioned by the applicant, the respondent may wish to rely on. What are the applicant's witnesses likely to say? What documents will the applicant be able to produce (remembering that some of them may not yet be in the applicant's possession but may be disclosed during discovery and inspection)? What witnesses and documents can the respondent produce? What will any of the respondent's witnesses say (remembering that they are liable to be questioned, and on oath, not just by the respondent's representative but also by the applicant's representative and by the tribunal)?

When a case is actually being presented to a tribunal, objectivity can be, in some respects, a disadvantage. At the initial investigation stage objectivity is the least that is required. Scepticism is better. What matters is not what a speaker intended to say, or what the author of a document intended it to mean, but what – given the words used and any evidence which might be given about the context in which they were spoken and heard or written and read – another person might reasonably believe them to mean. What matter are not just the events and documents on which a supervisor or manager (perhaps selectively) relied in making a decision which is now being challenged by an originating application, but all events and documents, including those which the applicant may pray in aid or which an inquisitorial tribunal may bring to light.

Documents

Investigation in respect of possible documentary evidence is the easier part of the task. Here the most important things are to check all the documents that may be relevant and to read them with as open, even critical, a mind as possible. Does the personal file of an applicant dismissed for incompetence contain a glowing performance appraisal signed, by the dismissing manager, shortly before the dismissal? Does the 'final warning' say, unambiguously, that it is 'final'? Is it clear that the notice, for contravention of which the employee was dismissed, and a copy of which is on the file in the office – 'Look, here it is!' – was ever actually displayed where and when the employee could have seen it? These, and similar awkward questions, may well be asked at any tribunal hearing. The investigator must ask them first. If there are no satisfactory answers, that can be taken into account in deciding how to respond to the originating application. If there are satisfactory answers, the evidence of them can be available in case the questions are raised in a hearing.

Potential witnesses

As with possible documentary evidence, so with the evidence which may be given orally by potential witnesses. However, what documents say now is precisely what they said previously. They do not change what they say to what they intended to say or what, on reflection, they wish they had said. What they say does not depend on what questions they are asked or on how the questions are asked. Either a document is in the respondent's possession or control or otherwise obtainable by legal means, or it is not. There is no half-way house. People differ from documents in all these respects. This means that the investigation here can be more difficult but the same ground rules apply. What it needs to uncover is all the evidence, and what is said needs to be looked at objectively, even suspiciously.

The investigator needs to tread a careful path in a number of respects.

Who should be interviewed?

First, to whom does the investigation extend? Or, more particularly, how far should the investigator go in attempting to determine what evidence the applicant may produce? Industrial tribunal cases are about the employment relationship. Applicants will almost invariably be employees or former employees and respondents will be employers. The respondent's managers and supervisors are probably unlikely to give evidence voluntarily on an applicant's behalf, which means that those who can do so will often be drawn from among the applicant's colleagues or former colleagues. They may still be employees of the respondent employer and so are physically and organisationally available, through the normal channels of communication which exist between employer and employee, for questioning by an investigator.

There is no sharply defined rule of law or practice that an employer must refrain from speaking to any of its employees about a case in which the employer is the respondent and the employee may be a witness for the applicant. But there is nothing to be gained by attempting to use, expressly or by implication, the employer's authority over an employee to get confidences revealed. The employee will be a witness, if at all, as to fact: what was said, heard, seen, done. If what that employee said, heard, saw or did was relevant to the decision which is now under challenge, then the supervisor or manager who took the decision should have been aware of it when the decision was taken. Evidence about it should therefore be available to the employer without going to the employee.

Against the minor filling in of details which the questioning of any such employee might provide has to be set, at the very least, the impression that might be given that the respondent is attempting unreasonably to abuse its position as an employer. If it acts unreasonably in this way, might it not act unreasonably in other ways, too? More seriously, the victimisation provisions under the race and sex discrimination legislation apply not only to those who bring applications but also to those who give evidence or information in connection with such applications or who allege contraventions of the legislation. In the heightened emotional atmosphere which discrimination cases often engender it is not difficult to envisage a cry of 'victimisation' being raised in respect of any attempt by a respondent's investigator to interview an unwilling employee who might be thought a potential witness for an applicant.

The investigation, then, should extend only to those people who are happy freely and voluntarily to participate in it. If there is any doubt about that it is better to err on the side of caution than on the side of even well intentioned persuasion. The touchstone should be: is it already clear that the respondent would go to the extent of issuing a witness order to compel this person to give evidence for the respondent? If the answer is 'no' and the person concerned shows any reluctance to assist the investigator, that person should not be questioned any further. It has already been explained that, even if the answer is 'yes', the party obtaining a witness order has no power to compel the witness to answer any questions. Such limited power of compulsion as exists is exercised by the tribunal, not by either of the parties, and then only at the hearing itself.

How questions are asked

With the people whom the investigator does question, a careful path needs to be trodden in how they are questioned. Leading questions are just as likely to elicit convenient answers in an investigation as in a hearing. They do, however, concentrate the attention of the person being questioned on what it is the questioner needs to know – in 'yes/no' terms. Provided the investigator can be confident that what is revealed in the investigation is what will be revealed if the same matter is tested in the hearing, how it was revealed at the investigatory stage does not matter. It is a matter of judgement for the investigator how far any interviewee should learn from the investigator – by the form of any questions or otherwise – what answers might help the respondent's case and what might hinder it.

If the investigator believes that an interviewee already fully appreciates what will be important to a tribunal, as distinct from what seems personally important, there is little point in beating about the bush. The investigator may regard the interviewee as so patently honest and straightforward (or even stubborn) that however a question is asked it will get the same answer. Or the point may be so peripheral and unimportant that, while to enquire about it in a particular way may influence the result of the enquiry, the time and effort which will be saved by asking 'Did you say this?' or 'Did you do that?' rather than 'What did you say?' or 'What did you do?' more than outweigh the diminution in the value of the reply. In deciding the precise path to tread in this area what matters is not how the information is obtained but how important to the respondent's case it is and the degree of confidence the investigator has in it. Is it precisely the information that would be given at a hearing and in answer to questions not only from the respondent's representative but also from the applicant's representative and the tribunal itself?

Testing the interviewee's story

This leads to the third path that has to be trodden carefully. How far and in what way should an investigator challenge anything that is said by those interviewed? Once reluctant interviewees have been excluded the investigator and those contributing to the investigation are 'on the same side'. The investigator may have to question the same people, now as witnesses, in a tribunal hearing. It may seem that to do so effectively will be made more difficult if that very questioner has said, or even implied, in an earlier interview that a witness's answers are viewed with suspicion. Even if no hearing results, a necessary on-going relationship may be soured if the investigator says, or implies, that an interviewee's answers may not be wholly correct.

This difficulty is usually more apparent than real. If the investigator feels it necessary to query what is said by an interviewee there must be some reason for it: the crucial importance of the point, its apparent inconsistency with something else the interviewee has said or with what someone else has said, or an expectation that the point will be challenged by the applicant's representative in any tribunal hearing which does take place. The investigator perceives a problem and is seeking, with another person 'on the same side', a joint solution. Provided the interviewee understands this, the scope for ill feeling because answers are being questioned should be diminished if not completely eliminated. How the investigator makes it clear that this is the position is less important than that it should be made clear. In some circumstances, with some interviewees, it may be sufficient for the investigator to explain what is being done, and why, once at the start of the interview. In other cases it may need frequent repetition, with an explanation being given for each challenge and questions being asked in the form 'What would you say if the applicant's representative asked . . . ?'

The investigator's primary aim in querying anything that is said is, anyway, not to challenge what the interviewee is saying with a view to overturning it but to test it. It may sometimes be necessary to test the interviewee's story by comparing it directly with a contrary or inconsistent version. More often the strength of an interviewee's evidence can be sufficiently checked by questions seeking precision and clarification rather than by direct or indirect suggestions that it may be wrong.

Three points should be borne in mind. One is that what the investigator is seeking is as complete a picture as possible of what *in fact* happened. Issues of right and wrong, of reasonableness and unreasonableness, will become relevant and of crucial importance: but that is for later. What needs to be determined first is what facts can be proved. The second is that the immediate purpose of any interview is investigatory, not judgemental. It is certainly not concerned with a judgement on the 'right or wrong', 'reasonable or unreasonable' issue. Nor, even in the factual area, is it immediately concerned with judging particular evidence as better or worse than other evidence. It purpose is to collect and test the evidence. That this evidence differs from that does not make either evidence right or wrong. The third point to remember is that the role of the interviewee, for the purposes of the interview and of any tribunal hearing which may take place, is that of a witness as to fact. Why a manager took a particular decision or action is a fact about which that manager can give evidence. Whether it was or was not 'reasonable' or 'justified' is a question which the tribunal must determine. It is not one in relation to which the manager concerned is competent, as a witness as to fact, to give evidence in a tribunal hearing. It involves the formation and expression of personal opinions which, strictly, are admissible as evidence only from expert witnesses.

Facts and opinions

A statement that 'I decided to dismiss the employee because I thought it was reasonable to do so' is evidence as to the fact of the state of the manager's mind when the decision was made. 'I thought it was reasonable to do so because the employee had abused the foreman' is evidence about the fact of what had caused or contributed to that state of mind. 'I believed the employee had abused the foreman, because the foreman said so' is evidence concerning the fact of what had caused or contributed to the manager's belief in the employee's guilt. All these – although they relate to mental processes, to 'soft' facts rather than 'hard' facts – are facts about which the manager can give evidence; about which, indeed, only the manager can give direct evidence. Whether what the foreman said was sufficient to found a belief in the employee's guilt and whether, if the employee was guilty, dismissal was an appropriate response are different issues. In determining them a tribunal will take account, among many other facts, of the manager's state of mind and of what caused that state of mind. But it will not expect, or perhaps even admit, from a witness arguments as to why it was right or wrong to do this, or opinions about whether it was reasonable or unreasonable to do that. In so far as such arguments and opinions form part of an industrial tribunal case they are for representatives, or expert witnesses, to advance.

The distinction is perhaps easier to describe in theory than to recognise in practice. In hearings themselves representatives or even the tribunal will sometimes ask whether, in the light of evidence which has been produced, a witness feels, or still feels, that it was right or reasonable to do this or that. In an investigatory interview the investigator as well as the interviewee may be interested in finding the arguments through which the respondent's case can be presented in the best light as well as in collecting and testing the evidence on which that case will rest. Provided that, when argument as well as evidence is involved, the investigator recognises this, and can distinguish between them, there is no reason why an interview should not range over both.

What must be guarded against is the evidence being modified to fit the argument more neatly. The 'softer' the facts in question, the more scope there is for such modification of the evidence. The greater the interest an interviewee has in justifying an action or decision, the higher the risk that such modification will take place (however unconsciously). The more people feel threatened the more likely they are to reinterpret their previous perceptions to defend themselves and their position. While there needs to be careful testing of any evidence which is likely to be central to a case, the investigator needs to do it in as non-confrontational a way as possible. Concentration on what *in fact* happened, rather than on whether it was right or wrong, will reduce the scope for confrontation.

Although questions about motivation and mental processes cannot and should not be completely avoided, much more emphasis should be placed on the harder facts of what was said, heard, seen and done – facts about which other evidence may be available and which, if they are consistent with what the interviewee says the mental processes were, will tend to support the softer facts of what was thought and why. Questions which seek as much precise detail as possible about the physical aspects of the events which the interviewee is describing – Who sat where? Who said what? What time did it happen? What words were used? – will usually give as reliable an impression of the strength of an interviewee's evidence as asking 'Why did you do that?' or seeking a response to a suggestion that something happened differently from the way the interviewee has described.

Helping an interviewee remember
And it is through such precise, detailed questions that the fourth path is most easily trodden. This is the path between, on the one hand, failing to tap an interviewee's memory for all it really contains and, on the other, putting into an interviewee's mind things that were not there before. Some originating applications arrive within days of the events to which they relate. Many more do not arrive until weeks or even months have passed. Time limits for applications to industrial tribunals are relatively short compared with those in other courts, but they are still long enough for memories to fade. Events which are relevant to the fairness or otherwise of a dismissal, for example, can anyway have occurred long before the effective date of termination from which the time limit of three months begins to run. It is thus not unusual for an investigator to be told by an interviewee – particularly with respect to more detailed matters – 'I can't remember.'

If such really is the case then it is, and must be accepted as, the only true evidence on the point that the interviewee can give. But 'I can't remember' sometimes means in practice 'I don't remember.' With some effort and assistance the interviewee may be able to remember. When the question is first asked the memory has not been dug over deeply enough or in the appropriate place. When forced, by cross-examination at a tribunal hearing, to make additional effort and prodded, by the leading questions which a cross-examiner may ask, to dig more deeply in particular areas a witness may remember things an investigator was told had been forgotten. An important element in the investigation is therefore to see how far an interviewee's memory really does extend.

It is possible to jog the interviewee's memory by outlining other people's versions of what happened. A danger of doing this is that it may make the interviewee profess 'remembering' something which is not really remembered but which the interviewee now thinks probably happened because someone else said it did. The danger is diminished if the person who said it happened is on 'the other side', particularly if for it to have happened would be of advantage to 'the other side'. So where an investigator is aware of a specific factual allegation that is likely to be made by an applicant and an interviewee says, in relation to the area concerned, 'I can't remember,' there is not much harm in asking, 'Did so and so happen?' or even saying, 'X says that so-and-so happened. Is that right?' But even here it needs to be remembered that the strength of evidence is increased if the interviewee is not led into giving it. If there is another way of testing the interviewee's memory and evidence it is to be preferred.

One such alternative approach rests on the nature of memory. It is associative. This characteristic is heavily relied on by those who sell memory improvement programmes. They often teach their users consciously to link something less easily remembered but important with something which is more easily remembered although perhaps unimportant. Recalling the easily remembered thing leads by association to recall of the more difficult but more important one. Such links exist anyway, even without specific memory training and without conscious attempt to form them. There are few people for whom particular sights, sounds, smells or whatever do not bring back an event, often in vivid detail. An investigator can take advantage of this phenomenon to try to help an interviewee remember important points without suggesting, by the form of the questioning, what the important points may be.

The time at which a meeting took place, the room in which it took place, who stood or sat where, whether tea or coffee was served, what the participants were wearing, and so on, are all, exceptional cases apart, likely to be of no direct relevance to any issue which may have to be determined by a tribunal. But recall of any of this sort of unimportant detail may trigger recall of points which are linked with them in a particular interviewee's memory. Asking the interviewee to recall the irrelevant details may, of itself, produce those details and by association the important ones. But the interviewee may not immediately recall anything.

If this occurs and the investigator already has information about some irrelevant details from other interviewees, or from documents, giving the information to the interviewee may trigger the necessary associations and help the interviewee to remember the important points. Provided the information given to the interviewee is confined to what really is irrelevant and unimportant, there is no risk that, on the points that do matter, the interviewee will purport to 'remember' what the investigator now says happened.

A written record
Just as memories can fade in the time between an event which led to the bringing of a tribunal case and the respondent's receipt of the originating application, so they can fade in the time between an investigatory interview and tribunal hearing. The interval can be just as long. The detail as well as the broad outline of what is said in an investigatory interview will contribute to the respondent's decision about how to deal with the case: some details may be the crucial factors in that decision. It is important that the investigator gets them right and that the interviewee remembers them. It will help to fulfil both these needs if the investigator makes notes of what is said and the interviewee sees them. The interviewee can then correct any misunderstandings and has an *aide-mémoire* if called as a witness.

If a hearing does take place and the interviewee is called as a witness, a 'proof of evidence' will be needed. This is discussed in Chapter 11. The investigator may not wish to spend time and effort transcribing handwritten notes, made as an interview was taking place, into anything more formal unless and until it becomes clear that a hearing is likely and the interviewee's evidence will be needed. If there is no possibility that there has been any misunderstanding on any detail of the interviewee's evidence that may be crucial to the decisions which the respondent has to take, then delaying such transcription is the most sensible course. Where there is any possibility of misunderstanding, then the notes, at least so far as they relate to the crucial points, should be written up and agreed immediately. The additional investment will not be wasted if a hearing is not held or the interviewee is not called to give evidence. Its dividend is the greater reliability of the information on which the necessary management decision will be based.

Key points

An investigator should:

• Be at least objective. Scepticism is even better.

- Critically examine *all* documents that *might* be relevant.
- Not interview employees who are not happy to be interviewed.
- Avoid putting answers into an interviewee's mouth, particularly on important issues.
- Test what an interviewee says, in a non-confrontational way.
- Concentrate on facts, not opinions. Hard facts are better than soft facts.
- Collect evidence, not make judgements.
- Probe the interviewee's memory.
- Make notes and agree them with the interviewee.

Chapter 8
Analysis

The information produced by the investigation has to be analysed and assessed. That a respondent now knows that certain evidence can be produced tending to prove certain facts does not, of itself, contribute very much to the decision which has to be made: how to respond to the case which has been raised by an originating application. What matters is how well the evidence will match up to the task of proving the facts on which the case will turn. Being able *now* to prove, even beyond a reasonable doubt, that a dismissed employee stole from the employer is of no value to a respondent in disputing the unfairness of a dismissal if it cannot be shown, on the balance of probabilities, that at the time the dismissal decision was taken there was a genuine belief in the employee's guilt, based on reasonable grounds and after adequate enquiry.

Proving that the employee did in fact steal from the employer may still be useful, as it may lead the tribunal to reduce, even to the extent of extinguishing, any compensation the respondent has to pay if the dismissal is judged unfair. But that is a different matter. Evidence to do with that issue might merit handling in a different way from evidence relating to whether the dismissal was fair or unfair. In some cases such evidence would not be introduced until the earlier question had been determined. Any argument based on the fact of the employee's guilt would involve different statute and case law, depending on whether its object was to deny that a dismissal was unfair or to suggest that compensation should be eliminated. How the case should be handled, generally and not only in terms of a tribunal hearing, may well depend on whether it is believed the respondent can 'win' by getting a finding of fair dismissal or 'win' only by a dismissal being found to be unfair but with little or no compensation being payable.

So the broad questions that now have to be asked, in the light of the information resulting from the investigation, are 'What facts will have to be proved?' and 'How likely is it that they can be proved?'

Looking at both sides

The questions are deliberately phrased in neutral terms because they need answering, so far as the respondent can, from both the applicant's and the respondent's point of view. The person analysing the case must ask not only 'What will we need to prove, and how likely are we to be able to do so?' but also 'What will they wish to prove, and how likely are they to be able to do so?' To some extent the answers to the two sets of questions are the opposite sides of the same coin. But only to some extent. That some of the most important issues in tribunal cases are ultimately determined by the tribunal in 'yes/no' terms ('reasonable/unreasonable', 'justified/unjustified') does not mean that facts which one party has attempted to prove have been disproved by the other. Each party may have proved the detail that it set out to prove, but, taken together, the details proved by one party may be less impressive with respect to the overall question the tribunal had to answer than those proved by the other party. So it is not sufficient for the analyst simply to ask 'Can we disprove what they want to prove?' or 'Can they disprove what we want to prove?'

The very questions which a tribunal has to answer may vary from the two parties' points of view. The applicant may be concentrating attention on the fairness of a dismissal, whereas the strongest line of defence for the respondent may be that the applicant was not qualified to make an application in respect of unfair dismissal. Again it is not enough for the analyst to think only of disproving specific points expressly made by the applicant or of proving points that, in particular areas, would be enough to win the respondent's case.

Like investigation, analysis requires at least objectivity. Further than that, the analyst should be able to think what – were the analysis being conducted for the other party – its results would be: 'Were I faced as the applicant with what the investigation shows the situation to be, how would I approach it in order to win my tribunal case?'

The need to know some law

'Unstructured' presentation

Properly to answer that question, from either party's point of view, the analyst needs to understand the legal framework within which the tribunal's decision will be made. This is not to say that a party who goes to a tribunal with little detailed knowledge of the law, only a generalised sense of grievance or of righteousness, and who presents as full a picture of the facts as possible to the tribunal but without arguing how that picture produces particular answers to necessary legal questions, will not win the case. One of a tribunal's tasks is to assist parties unskilled in the law by translating their case into the necessary legal structures, implying the unstated legal arguments on which offered facts make it clear the case depends and seeking out any additional facts which those arguments make necessary. A tribunal will do this in respect of a respondent's case as much as in respect of an applicant's case. If a respondent wishes to rely on this and merely offer an unstructured presentation of all the evidence, coupled with a generalised plea that 'We did nothing wrong', it can do so.

A case presented in this way is likely to take longer to hear than one which concentrates on the points which are legally important. Any initiative which might otherwise have rested with the respondent is lost. The respondent will have less feel, before the hearing is concluded and the tribunal's decision known, for what the outcome may be and so will be less able to choose sensibly among options other than simply going through with a tribunal hearing. A crucial point that could have decided the case in the respondent's favour may get missed, for, try as it may, a tribunal cannot imply an argument the importance of which is not indicated by putting the relevant facts to it. Even if the relevant facts do emerge, a tribunal may not turn its mind unprompted to the particular rule of law which, if applied to those facts, would unequivocally decide the case in a particular way.

Although a respondent could in theory rely on an unstructured presentation of all the evidence coupled with a generalised plea that 'We did nothing wrong', no respondent is likely in practice to want to do so. And were it ostensibly to choose that approach it is unlikely that in practice its presentation would really be 'unstructured'. 'All the evidence' is a vast amount. Realistically, some selection from among *all* that is available has to be made. Any statement that 'we did nothing wrong' assumes the existence of criteria against which right and wrong can be judged. The necessary selection of evidence will almost certainly be made (perhaps unconsciously) with reference to those (perhaps unarticulated) criteria. The 'unstructured' presentation which thus results is a presentation which does in reality have a structure. But the structure may not be recognised and will probably be different from that against which the strengths and weaknesses of the case will be judged.

Which law?

So, despite the lack of technicality which is supposed to characterise industrial tribunal cases, a degree of technical analysis is necessary. How far this technical analysis can or should extend depends on a number of factors. Its outside limits should be immediately defined by the originating application itself. The analyst should know from the application whether the provisions which have to be looked at are those concerning race relations, sex discrimination, equal pay, unfair dismissal, redundancy payments, payment of wages, or whatever. If it does not appear from the originating application, there are clear grounds for seeking further particulars and, perhaps, delaying a response to the originating application – investigation, analysis, entering an appearance – until those essential particulars have been provided. This is not to say that a respondent is justified in asking for further particulars simply because an originating application does not expressly identify the legislative provision/s on which it is relying. What an originating application has to state are 'the grounds, with particulars thereof, on which relief is sought'. The courts have ruled that if the words used – whatever they may be – make this clear, it is sufficient.

In deciding at the broadest level which legislative provision/s are relevant the analyst must therefore look at the originating application as a whole and consider not just any provision which is expressly stated to be relied upon but also any provision which, on the facts alleged, might be relevant. Only rarely is this not clear. Where confusion can occur is where the facts alleged might be the basis of a complaint under more than one provision. An allegation that 'I was dismissed because I was black' may be intended to initiate a complaint under the unfair dismissal provisions, under the Race Relations Act, or under both. 'I was made redundant and did not get a redundancy payment', whilst apparently primarily a complaint specifically under section 91 of the EPCA, may also be intended to raise the issue of whether the dismissal was unfair. Confusion can also arise where different pieces of legislation interleave or even overlap in their application to particular sets of facts. The prime example is the interface between the Equal Pay Act, the Sex Discrimination Act and the provisions of European Community law. Where such confusion does exist there will be value, in procedural terms, in sorting it out as early as possible. But for analytical purposes it should put the analyst on enquiry with regard to each of the provisions that may be relevant. Rather than asking simply 'What case might be made, by each side, under this one provision?' the analyst should now be asking 'What cases might be made, by each side, under each of these provisions?'

Within the broad scope for analysis which the originating application has identified, the facts of the case, as the analyst believes they appear from both parties' points of view, will focus attention on some aspects of law and render others irrelevant. An employee aged fifty with twenty years' unbroken service submits an unfair dismissal complaint which reaches the employer within a couple of weeks of what the employer accepts was a dismissal. That is not, on the face of it, going to raise any questions about the tribunal's jurisdiction to hear the complaint or about what legally constitutes a 'dismissal'. The analysis can, it appears, begin with those provisions that concern the reason for and the reasonableness of dismissal. But if among the evidence available to the analyst there is some which shows that for fifteen of those twenty years the employee has worked abroad, the tribunal may have to consider, before it can look at the reasons for the dismissal and the question of reasonableness, the provision in section 141(2) of the EPCA that the unfair dismissal provisions 'do not apply to employment where under his contract of employment the employee ordinarily works outside Great Britain'. The particular facts of this case mean that the analysis should cover not only the provisions relating to reasons for dismissal and reasonableness but also those relating to working abroad.

The right to equal pay applies only to men and women 'in the same employment'. Where the evidence available to an analyst looking at an equal pay application includes nothing to arouse suspicion that anything other than 'the same employment' is involved it would be a waste of time and effort to delve into the technicalities of that question. But if the evidence shows that the woman works in one location and the man with whom she is claiming equality works in another, a more detailed analysis of the legislation and the case law may yield dividends.

The depth of analysis

How far should analysis be taken?

Factors which must obviously affect the breadth and depth of any analysis will be the competence of and the resources available to the analyst. The specialist labour lawyer knows, and has readily available statutes and law reports which confirm and detail, that working abroad can affect entitlement to claim unfair dismissal and that equal pay cannot be claimed across different employments. The personnel manager, or whoever else the in-house analyst may be, cannot be expected to have the same detailed knowledge of labour law or the same ready access to legal sources. But any difference is one of degree. A respondent is not going to delegate the task of analysis to someone who lacks all knowledge of labour law or who has no access to guidance on the subject. A broad understanding of the main areas of labour law has become part of the stock-in-trade of human resource specialists and managers. Books and magazines explaining and commenting on the law are available for reference by personnel departments.

Cases do arise where analysis beyond the competence and resources of an in-house analyst would be useful, and a competent in-house analyst will be able to identify them. But such cases are few and far between. This is particularly so given the availability of comprehensive and comprehensible written material explaining the intricacies of the law which tribunals apply. Ironically, it is these guides, textbooks, case digests, articles and so on which also give the impression that there are so many technicalities that the only safe course is to leave them to specialist labour lawyers. This is because the job of such books, articles, etc., is to deal with the technicalities and that is what they do. The complexities are gathered together and displayed in one place. That they arose piecemeal, and over a considerable period of time, in a large number of different cases, can tend to get forgotten. What can also be overlooked is that the cases from which the examples of technical complexity are drawn are not typical.

Law reports and real life

The vast majority will not have been ultimately determined by an industrial tribunal. Were it otherwise the decision could not be quoted as authority for the interpretation being discussed. Industrial tribunals' decisions, although they may have some persuasive effect, do not create binding precedents. That such cases have been through industrial tribunals and then on to higher courts, maybe as far as the House of Lords and/or the European Court of Justice, makes them different from the typical case in two other ways. One is that they were regarded by both parties as sufficiently important to pursue that far, with the costs that it inevitably involves. The second is that they will have involved extensive legal research and argument by highly skilled and specialist lawyers. Although the right of audience by lay representatives extends to the EAT, lawyers have to appear (unless a litigant appears 'in person', which a respondent *company* cannot do) in the higher courts.

These two points – the importance the parties attach to winning the case and the retention of external specialists to argue it – are not unconnected. They highlight another factor which will influence the breadth and depth of analysis to which a case should be subjected. Of course the applicant and the respondent both want to win. But doing so involves a cost. A cost–benefit approach to tribunal cases is discussed in the next chapter. For present purposes it is sufficient simply to recognise that from a respondent's point of view one case may differ from another in importance and that one measure of that importance is the 'cost' which a respondent is prepared to incur to improve the chances of winning. The more important a case is to a respondent, judged in this way, the more extensive the technical analysis that is justified.

Many of the cases which are quoted by commentators to illustrate the technicalities have themselves in effect created those technicalities. The parties to the cases concerned sought to win 'at any cost' and in order to do so expended the time and energy necessary to go through the statutory provisions and the previous cases with the finest of fine-tooth combs, searching for any and every word or phrase that might be turned to their advantage. Saying this implies no criticism. Given the nature of the legal system and its traditions, the approach is inevitable and necessary. It is how the law is clarified and developed. But how far it is appropriate to the in-house analysis of the typical tribunal case is another matter.

The typical tribunal case differs from those which are highlighted in the textbooks. It could not on its facts support arguments in many of the technical areas on which the textbooks concentrate. Most textbooks on unfair dismissal law will contain some discussion of the provision excluding the employee who ordinarily works outside Great Britain. Few guides on equal pay will not deal in detail with what the phrase 'in the same employment' means. The typical unfair dismissal complaint, on the other hand, is made by an employee who worked in Great Britain. The typical equal pay claim is based on comparison with a person in the same industrial or commercial unit.

Thus there is no standard intensity to which analysis should be undertaken. The legal framework within which the results of the factual investigation need to be set by the analyst will depend, as to which set of statutory provisions it is drawn from, on the nature of the complaint and, as to which detailed statutory provisions and judicial precedents it includes, on the facts of the case, on the competence and resources of the analyst and on how important winning the case is to the respondent. The purpose of the analysis is to identify, to the level which is appropriate in the light of these factors, the approaches available to the respondent in defending the case and to assess, as objectively as possible, how a tribunal might determine the case in the light of the approaches identified.

The analyst must turn if necessary, for guidance on the detail of the structure and wording of the law, to the specialist textbooks and, ideally, to the statutory provisions and reported cases themselves. In the broadest terms, though, any analysis is likely to cover four main areas.

A standard framework

Jurisdiction

First, has the industrial tribunal the power to determine the case the applicant is trying to bring? Tribunals have no general power to right wrongs and redress grievances. They derive specific jurisdictions from specific legislative provisions. With increasing acceptance that industrial tribunals have the duty to apply European law as well as the provisions of legislation, and the potential extension of their jurisdiction to hear claims for breach of contract, the limits within which they can hear cases are perhaps less easy to define than was once the case. But limits still exist. However good a case an applicant may appear to have in terms of morality or general legal principles, a tribunal has no choice but to reject it if it does not rest on a provision which the tribunal has power to apply.

Within the areas with which tribunals can deal, the legislation invariably lays down some conditions which have to be met before an application can be considered. The details vary from jurisdiction to jurisdiction but there is always some sort of time limit within which complaints must be made. The tribunals' rules themselves will include minimum requirements about the form and content of a complaint. Many employment rights extend not to all workers by only to those on contracts of service or of apprenticeship, and then often only to employees who meet conditions such as having been continuously employed for a certain length of time. The precise limits of a tribunal's jurisdiction, the conditions an applicant must meet, and who is or is not entitled to claim the right concerned, vary from case to case. But every case has the potential to raise questions in this general area, and every analysis should cover it.

The defined act

Next, each of the industrial tribunals' jurisdictions is concerned with some act (sometimes more than one) which is legislatively defined. The second general area that an analysis should invariably cover is how far what happened fits within the legal definition of the act concerned. Unless there has been a 'dismissal' there can be no 'unfair' dismissal. Where there has been no 'deduction' from 'wages' there is nothing on which the Wages Act can bite. An employee who is not 'redundant' can have no entitlement to a redundancy payment. Many of the statutory definitions require analysis in greater detail. In the race relations and sex discrimination statutes, 'discrimination' is defined with reference to 'less favourable treatment' and to the application of 'requirements' or 'conditions' which cause 'detriment'. None of those words or phrases is further defined in the statutes themselves, but their meaning has been the subject of litigation. Specialist guides and textbooks identify the factors a tribunal is likely to take account of in deciding whether what occurred amounted, within the terms of the legal definition, to 'discrimination'.

Strictly, it may be said that the whole analytical exercise is concerned with comparing the facts, as the analyst believes they might variously be presented to the tribunal by applicant and respondent, with definitions set out in the legislation and perhaps amplified by the case law. Whether a tribunal has jurisdiction to hear a complaint depends on how its jurisdiction is defined. Whether an employer acted reasonably in dismissing an employee depends on the definition of what is 'reasonable'. In deference to such a view it is worth stressing that at all stages of analysis there is value in starting from the precise words of the legislation and that, where the legislation does give a clear 'definition', the analyst should test the evidence against that definition word by word. In some areas, though, any legislative 'definition' is far too imprecise for reliance to be placed on that approach alone.

Justification/excuse

The third broad heading under which analysis is likely to be necessary, whichever of tribunals' jurisdictions is involved, is one such area. After defining an act, legislation permits it only if certain conditions are met or prohibits it unless certain conditions are met. Each area of law therefore includes one or more justifications for the act concerned and/or one or more excuses for the act concerned. Some justifications and excuses are relatively sharply defined – for instance, where direct racial or sexual discrimination has taken place. Many are couched in much looser legislative terms and require the tribunal, by balancing factors pointing different ways, to judge whether, looked at overall, the excuse or justification has been established.

Whether the application of a requirement or condition which in practice has a racially or sexually discriminatory effect is 'justifiable irrespective of the race [or sex] or the person to whom it is applied' involves balancing the severity of the discriminatory effect against the desirability, in business terms, of the objective which the requirement or condition is intended to achieve. This is the principle of proportionality. Whether a reason for dismissal is 'a sufficient reason for dismissing the employee' involves balancing, 'in the circumstances' and 'in accordance with equity and the substantial merits of the case', on the one hand the reason and on the other that dismissal should have resulted from it.

Although ultimately requiring the tribunal to interpret and apply a specific statutory formula, may such questions have expressly been held by the higher courts to be questions of fact and/or degree. A constructionist approach is inappropriate. What is 'reasonable' cannot be defined; it has to be *judged*. As it is a question of fact, different tribunals may take different views of the same issue: provided any judgement made is one that a reasonable tribunal could have made, that a different tribunal might have made a different judgement is irrelevant. But at the same time as ruling that these are matters of fact, and so for tribunals themselves to determine without interference by way of appeal on points of law, the higher courts have suggested factors which any reasonable tribunal is likely to bear in mind and tests which it is likely to apply. A tribunal which ignores these factors and tests, or which in making its factual and quantitative judgement reaches a conclusion for which there is no sufficient evidential basis, goes wrong in law.

So analysis in this area has to cover the factors and tests which a tribunal is constrained to apply, and ask in relation to each of them how both parties' evidence, as the analyst feels each may be presented, will impact on the tribunal's judgement. That one element may weigh strongly for one party is seldom sufficient; it may be outweighed by other elements which individually weigh less strongly for the other party but have greater cumulative effect. Some factors may influence the overall result more than others. If a procedure – e.g. consultation in the case of an ill-health dismissal – has been held by the higher courts to be appropriate in all but the most exceptional of circumstances and the respondent has not complied with that procedure, the analyst knows that, unless it can be shown that the circumstances were exceptional, the one factor of non-compliance with the required procedure will lead to a finding for the applicant. But in many cases no single factor will be decisive. What will matter more will be the cumulative effect of all the factors which point one way, compared with the cumulative effect of all those pointing the other way. That the wording of a warning letter was not as precise as it might have been, while not helping the respondent's case, may be outweighed by evidence that, despite any ambiguity in the letter, the applicant had been told at interviews and understood full well what the consequences of further misconduct would be.

Remedies

The fourth general area with which the analysis should deal is that of remedies. Even if a respondent has no real arguments, in relation to the tribunal's jurisdiction to hear a case, as to whether the defined act occurred, or about a justification or excuse for it, an applicant can still fall at this final hurdle. An applicant found to have been unfairly dismissed may still regard the case as 'lost' if no compensation is awarded. Financially, a respondent whose presentation persuades a tribunal to award £2,000 instead of £5,000 will have achieved more than one who persuades a tribunal that a dismissal was fair, if a finding that the dismissal was unfair would have resulted in an award of only a few hundred pounds. This is not to suggest that the size of any award is the only criterion against which relative success and failure for the applicant and the respondent can or will be judged. But it must be one factor in the equation. In order to make sensible decisions about whether and how to defend a case, a respondent needs some assessment of how the available evidence may affect the size of any award.

The analyst therefore needs to consider what remedies a tribunal has power to award in the area of law concerned, what detailed rules are laid down in the statute or have been developed by the case law for determining the form and amount of any remedies and the factors which a tribunal will take into account in fixing the level of any award. Under this main heading, as under the other three, the details vary from topic to topic. Unfair dismissal is different from redundancy payments, equal pay differs from sex discrimination. The analyst may need to seek guidance from specialist texts covering the area of law concerned. As under the other main headings, having determined the legal framework against which the issues will be decided, the analyst then needs to consider how, in the light of what is known about the evidence available, each side's case may be presented to the tribunal. Under all four headings the decisions made by the tribunal will rest on the facts that it finds, and the purpose of the analysis is to determine the areas in which facts will have to be found and to assess, in the light of what is known about the evidence, what the factual findings in those areas might be.

The investigator/analyst

Investigation and analysis have been treated as separate processes, with analysis following investigation. To some extent this may reflect what happens in practice. The criminal justice system now formally separates the functions. That of investigation is undertaken by the police, and the analysis is conducted by the Crown Prosecution Service. Even there the separation is far from complete in practice. The investigator knows, during the investigation, what points are likely to be regarded by the analyst as of more importance and so pays more attention to some areas of evidence than to others. Having considered the information so far provided, the analyst may ask the investigator to look in more detail at specified areas and/or to investigate areas so far untouched. The analogy is far from perfect but it does illustrate that, even where the functions are theoretically and formally separated, they are likely in practice to overlap and interact. Where there is no formal separation, overlapping and interaction are likely to be even greater.

When, as will often happen, the same individual from an employer's organisation is both the investigator and the analyst some analysis will be going on at the same time as the investigation. Because it seems from an analytical point of view that a particular point is likely to be important, the investigation may deal with it more thoroughly than with other points. There is nothing wrong with this. There are, however, two dangers that need to be avoided.

One is that the analytical field of view may be narrowed too early, so that the investigative objective becomes not that of collecting and testing *all* the evidence – that which may be produced by the applicant and in answer to a tribunal's questions as well as that which the respondent may find it useful to adduce – but that of finding the evidence which will best support a presentation on predetermined lines. The legal framework within which an industrial tribunal will decide a case cannot be dictated by either party. It will be determined by the tribunal in the light of the facts which emerge. Each party may feel, and perhaps argue, that some questions are relevant and that others are irrelevant in the circumstances of the case. Whatever its own views about the relevance of a particular point, each party needs to recognise that if the other party has raised that point it *is* relevant unless and until the tribunal rules, on proper legal grounds, that it is not. Similarly with importance. A party may regard one line of argument as stronger than others available to it. In the event a tribunal may reject the 'stronger' argument while still deciding in that party's favour in the light of a 'weaker' argument. The purpose of the analysis is to identify all the ways in which a case may develop and be presented. This will not be done if the analyst, whilst in an investigator's role, does not look at the case as broadly as possible.

The second danger is that the different tests which the investigator and the analyst should be applying to the same evidence may become confused. In one setting the purpose is to test evidence for its intrinsic strength: to gain some impression of how it will appear not only if introduced by the respondent but also if introduced, or questioned, by the applicant's representative or uncovered by the tribunal members themselves in an inquisitorial role. In the other setting the purpose is to determine what facts will need to be proved and to test how likely they are to be proved from the evidence available. That fact X could be proved is of little use if what has to be proved is fact Y. Discovering, as an investigator, that fact X can be proved may incline an unwary analyst to think that it is fact X that has to be proved. Or knowing, as an analyst, that it is fact X which has to be proved may lead an unwary investigator to accept, without much testing of its strength, evidence which will tend to prove fact X.

In practice a respondent's reaction to an originating application will more often than not combine the investigatory and analytical functions which have been described separately above, with the same person performing both and at the same time. Provided that person remembers that the functions are different, and that both need to be fulfilled, the proper inputs for the next stage should be produced.

Key points

An analyst should:

- Look at the case from the applicant's as well as the respondent's point of view.
- Identify the legislation and specific provisions that might be relevant, taking account of the facts as well any law which is named.
- Refer to the guides, textbooks, etc., to see what the law is, but remember that the law is what the statutes say.

- Not be afraid to call in a specialist in a special case.
- Not be frightened by the textbooks into thinking that every case is special.
- Consider:

  Jurisdiction.
  The defined act.
  Justification and excuse.
  Remedies.

- Avoid confusing the analyst's role with the investigator's.

Chapter 9
A plan of action

An originating application presents an industrial tribunal with a legal problem which, unless the application is withdrawn, it will solve using legal procedures and against legal criteria. For a respondent the arrival of an originating application poses a different problem: a management problem. Management problems need a different approach from legal problems. There is, in legal theory anyway, one 'right' answer which it is the tribunal's job to find. There is seldom one 'right' answer to a management problem. The manager's job is to identify and achieve the 'best' one. What is best depends on what the business's aims are, and may change with changing circumstances. This needs a pragmatic approach. 'Achievability' is at least as important as 'desirability'. Whether a particular solution is 'good' is of less importance than whether it is 'better' than any other solution which is realistically achievable. Desirability – what is 'good', 'better' or 'best' – is judged against business criteria, not legal ones. Any solution can be judged against any other in terms of its relative business advantages – 'benefits' – and its relative business disadvantages – 'costs'.

A cost-benefit analysis

At the simplest level, it may be possible to assess costs and benefits in straightforward cash terms. But it has to be recognised that, in cash terms anyway, 'benefits' often really means 'limitation of costs'. Tribunals do not, except in narrowly defined special circumstances, award costs. So a respondent who defends a case faces a bill whether the case is won or lost. This is seen most easily where the respondent engages an outsider – solicitor, barrister, consultant – to present the defence and then has to pay the outsider's fees and expenses. But an outsider's invoice represents only part of the true cost of defending a case. In the same way the true costs of defending a case in-house do not consist only of the salary of the staff member who prepares and presents the defence. Defending a case, using in-house or outside resources, may not be the only achievable solution. But persuading an applicant to withdraw, even without any financial inducement to do so, is also likely to involve some time and some effort which has to be paid for. Any cost–benefit analysis should recognise that, too. Each possible solution needs to be considered in terms both of what costs and/or benefits the solution itself involves and what costs and/or benefits are involved in achieving it.

The costs of the solution

What has to be paid out as a consequence of any solution comprises, directly, the amount of any award by a tribunal or of any agreed settlement. In some cases it will be a set sum, e.g. unfair dismissal compensation, but in others, particularly in equal pay cases, it may involve a continuing commitment. Sometimes the amount paid to the individual applicant represents the whole of the sum which has to be paid out by the respondent as a consequence of the solution. In others, similar sums will need to be paid out to other employees in similar positions. There may be other, less direct, financial consequences of a particular solution.

It is important to remember, when the costs and benefits of a particular solution are being considered, that although a tribunal's decision is on the face of it concerned with only one issue and between only two parties, it may in practice cover a number of issues. On any or all of those issues it may affect a large number of people. In some cases the broader implications are obvious and are formally accepted by the applicant, the respondent and the tribunal: an individual case is acknowledged to be a test case. On other occasions the broader implications may be less immediately obvious but of no less practical importance. For instance a ruling, in the context of a claim by one employee in relation to one statutory employment right, that a change in the ownership of a business did or did not preserve continuity of service (so that the applicant was or was not qualified by service for that right) might impact on the potential entitlement of the whole of the employer's work force to all other service-related statutory employment rights.

The cost of such an impact is, in broad terms, financially measurable. Calculations of the contingent liability in respect of employment rights that are faced by employers with large long-service work forces often form part of take-over or buy-out negotiations. It can be substantial. One cost of seeking to avoid liability in the individual case by arguing that continuity had been broken became, when that argument was formally rejected by a tribunal, a reduction in the price that could be obtained for the business much greater than would have been lost by settling the individual case or by trying to defend it without introducing that particular argument.

That the tribunal's ruling may not be legally definitive for the broader question is by the by. That any prospective purchaser would almost certainly have argued, even in the absence of a tribunal ruling, that continuity of employment had probably been preserved is beside the point. That had the respondent won the point on continuity the benefits could have been similarly substantial is also beside the point. The point is that the decision to raise the continuity of service defence was taken in isolation as a slightly easier means of getting rid of an irritating but quite small problem. The solution to that problem was not considered against the background of the business's overall objectives. In fact the case was won on other, more substantial grounds. But the business implications of arguing and losing the specific point were far more dramatic than the result of the individual case could ever have been. In the negotiations, which were known to be imminent when the case was fought, the seller of the business was faced with a much stronger argument that the price should be reduced, by virtue of the large contingent liability with respect to employment rights, than would have happened had the tribunal ruling not been given.

The extreme and specific nature of the example should not hide the principle it exemplifies. Apparently minor actions in one area of a business's activities can have a major impact on other areas. These are not always foreseen and sometimes are not realistically foreseeable. But the possibility of such impact should be considered. Decisions about how to react to the arrival of an originating application should be integrated with an employer's overall business strategy to the same extent as other detailed management decisions are.

The costs of achieving the solution

What any solution costs to achieve will depend on how a case proceeds. Decisions about whether or how the case should be defended will obviously be a major factor in determining the costs incurred by the respondent. Besides the fees and expenses of any outside help the respondent engages to defend the case – solicitor, barrister, other adviser or representative, expert witness – the wages, salaries and expenses of the respondent's employees involved in the defence need to be taken into account. Their other, more normal, duties are not being performed whilst employees are investigating a case or being interviewed by an investigator, or researching the law or analysing a case, or preparing for or attending a hearing, whether as a representative, a witness or just an observer. The time involved nevertheless has to be paid for. So do employees' expenses: travelling, meals, even overnight accommodation. All cases involve some paperwork: some involve a great deal. A solution which requires fewer witnesses, fewer documents, less time spent on preparing for and attending at tribunal hearings is less costly than one involving many witnesses, bulky documentation and long hearings. Less costly still is a solution involving no witnesses, no documents and no hearing.

A respondent can influence but cannot control how a case proceeds. Interlocutory applications may be made by an applicant or interlocutory orders may be made by a tribunal of its own motion. Dealing with orders for further particulars, for the discovery and inspection of documents, correspondence or hearings on other interlocutory matters all involve time and expense and so increase the immediate costs of both parties. That, should a case proceed to a full hearing, these interlocutory procedures may have reduced the total that had to be spent (by everyone involved, including the tribunal) on its resolution does not alter the fact that, whether or not the case does proceed to a full hearing, and whether or not interlocutory rulings do make it easier and cheaper to dispose of, the costs of the interlocutory proceedings have been incurred.

A respondent cannot know for certain when initially looking at a case from a cost-benefit point of view how large a part such interlocutory costs and expenses are likely to play in determining the total costs of achieving a particular solution. A respondent that deliberately sets out to hide important elements of its defence or documents which are relevant to the case can expect to face and have to deal with requests or orders for further particulars or discovery of documents. A respondent that plans a defence along lines that depend on particular tribunal procedures must recognise that making applications and putting forward arguments for those procedures to be followed will involve some expense. Beyond that, the respondent may gain some feel for how likely it is that interlocutory costs will occur by considering what is known about the applicant and the applicant's advisers and resources.

A single unrepresented applicant complaining about an issue which affects no one else, and who is unsupported by any organisation, is generally less likely to initiate or engender protracted interlocutory procedures than are lawyers funded by a trade union or the EOC or CRE in a case which raises an important principle or has a direct effect on a large number of the respondent's employees. There will be exceptions to this general rule of thumb. Some litigants in person are more, not less, likely than lawyers to attempt to explore all nooks and crannies of the law, procedural as well as substantive. Given that the applicant will probably be or have been an employee, the respondent should have some idea whether the applicant is likely to fall into this category.

The other, and even greater, influence on the costs that achieving a particular solution will involve but over which the respondent has very little control is whether any decision reached by an industrial tribunal will actually mark the end of the case: whether it will be a 'solution'. However substantial the costs of appearing at an industrial tribunal may be, they will probably be less than those involved in appearing at the EAT. They will pale into insignificance beside those involved in appearing before the Court of Appeal, the House of Lords or the European Court of Justice. Nor will a respondent know for certain, when initially considering the costs and benefits of different solutions to the problem raised by an originating application, whether an appeal will be made against a tribunal's decision. But some cases are much more likely to engender appeals than others. A respondent's decision how to react to an originating application should not be based only on costs that may be incurred in a tribunal hearing if it seems likely that the costs may also have to include those of an appeal hearing, perhaps at more than one level.

Factors which will affect the likelihood, even before a tribunal reaches its decision, that there will be an appeal against it include those which affect the likelihood of interlocutory procedures occurring: the psychology and motivation of the applicant, the nature and extent of any support the applicant has in bringing the case, the importance of the case in terms of principle or in terms of its practical knock-on effects. But the single most important factor is the extent to which a tribunal's decision will rest on rulings on points of law as opposed to findings on matters of fact. This is a factor which the respondent can influence. Achieving a solution which rests on a new interpretation of a statutory provision, or which requires an otherwise binding precedent to be distinguished, is more likely to involve the additional costs that arise from appearing at appeal courts than one which rests only on certain facts being found in the respondent's favour.

In industrial tribunals and before the EAT the costs normally lie where they fall. Those incurred by the respondent have to be met by the respondent; those incurred by the applicant, by the applicant. Exceptionally, as has been discussed, an order may require one party to pay the other party's costs. In practice, such orders are seldom made and when they are an applicant is unlikely to be ordered to reimburse the respondent with anything like the amount of expenditure that the respondent has actually incurred. For the purposes of a cost–benefit assessment, the wisest and simplest course is usually for a respondent simply to forget the theoretical possibility of recouping costs from the applicant. The possibility of the respondent being ordered to pay the applicant's costs, however, should not be overlooked; nor should the normal practice of the Court of Appeal and the House of Lords of ordering the loser to pay the winner's costs.

When all these items are added up the total can be substantial. It is not unusual for it to exceed by a considerable amount the sum for which the case could be settled out of court or which would be awarded to an applicant were the complaint successful. Where that would occur there is obviously an argument, in the simplest financial terms, for the respondent to pay the lower sum to settle the case; or even to leave the case undefended and pay the lower sum by way of an award. It would be cheaper than paying the higher sum involved in defending the case and, possibly, an award as well if the defence is unsuccessful.

The real-life equation is not as simple. The figures appearing on either side of the equation are difficult, sometimes impossible, to calculate, particularly when an originating application first reaches the respondent. Until the case has been investigated and analysed it is not known who might be involved, as possible witnesses, in defending it. How long a hearing and preparation for it might take are unclear. A case which, on the face of it, is short and simple can become time-consuming and complicated by interlocutory applications or appeals. What an applicant may have in mind as a settlement figure, or what a tribunal might award if the complaint were to succeed, may be undefined.

Non-financial costs and benefits

More important, perhaps, to look at costs and benefits only in cash terms is to ignore factors which, although difficult to put a money value on, may be more significant to the company. This point is often made by saying, 'To buy off this applicant now may make short-term economic sense, but what message will that approach send out to other employees?' The implication is that 'we must fight this case or it will be thought we are an easy touch'. The implication is valid – sometimes. But not always. Rather than relying on such a generalised assumption and using it to make an 'either/or' decision – settle or fight – the respondent should attempt consciously to assess costs and benefits, including non-cash items, for each of the options available.

This type of 'image' issue often assumes much importance in decision-making about how to react to originating applications. What will our employees, our managers, the public, our competitors think? It is true that, exceptional circumstances apart, industrial tribunal hearings are held in public and can be reported in the media. The details of solutions which do not involve tribunal hearings, settlements, can also become public property through the grapevine. Issues of image should not be ignored, but they should be as carefully inspected and as critically judged as any other factors in business contexts.

A message to employees

There may be some truth in a manager's assertion that a settlement in a particular case will lead members of a work force to think that anyone who takes the trouble to submit an originating application will be offered a sum of money in settlement. But some work forces also believe, for example, that in order to be promoted an employee has to support the same football team as the boss. The latter belief will probably be untrue, arising perhaps out of the quotation by leaders of workforce opinion of odd instances that could be interpreted as support for the belief and silence about any that could not. Its existence and the extent to which it might be strengthened or diminished are unlikely to be a major consideration in actual promotion decisions. In so far as such a belief does become troublesome in real terms, management is likely to take steps to counter it. Efforts will be made, through formal or informal channels of communication, to publicise instances which prove it to be untrue; the real factors affecting promotion decisions in general, or a particular promotion decision, are highlighted.

The analogy is not perfect but it does illustrate three important points which can be overlooked:

- What matters is not so much what the work force might believe as how true the belief is.
- An employer has considerable control over the message that any action or decision conveys to employees. Where an action or decision, looked at on its own, may give the 'wrong' impression, steps can be taken to correct that impression by paying attention to when, how and by whom the action or decision is made known and to what other information is also made known.
- Dealing with an industrial tribunal case is no more, or less, likely to affect the image that employees have of their employer than any other of the employer's actions and decisions. There is no reason why the image factor should loom any larger, or any less large, in this context than in any other.

None of this is intended to suggest that the 'message' that any solution might convey to employees is not important. It is possible to envisage circumstances in which, in business terms, it may be the most important single factor in determining what the best solution would be. Faced with a high level of intermittent absence which it has proved impossible to reduce by encouragement, exhortation or minor disciplinary action, an employer may feel that dismissal – unchallenged or found to be fair by an industrial tribunal – is necessary *pour encourager les autres*.

Any such dismissal would have to be justified on its own account. But one of the employer's main objectives in dismissing the employee and defending a case which it engendered would be to send a particular message to the rest of the employees. To settle such a case, even for a few pounds, would indeed send the wrong message, although it would be much cheaper in straightforward financial terms than appearing before a tribunal. Were the case to be won on a technicality, rather than it being held that dismissal for persistent intermittent absence was justified, the message would be weakened. To lose such a case would send totally the wrong message. Whether and how the case should be defended and what it is worth spending on the defence will all be properly conditioned, in terms of overall business objectives, by the image factor.

Company image and personal image

Assessing issues of image in terms of costs and benefits is not easy. Inevitably it involves a large measure of subjective judgement. This raises a particular problem. The 'employer' or the 'respondent' whose image is in question usually has no *real* existence. It is a legal person and it may, for many purposes, have a corporate image created and fostered by advertising, liveries, logos and other PR paraphernalia. But to employees it is more often 'management'; or this or that individual manager or supervisor; or just the ubiquitous 'they'. The decision which any originating application is challenging will, while *legally* being that of the company, *actually* have been taken or confirmed by one or more individual managers. They may thus have a personal interest, and not only a company interest, in defending the decision and in the image which rests on that decision being found to be justified. Any discussion about 'the company's image' will sometimes really be primarily concerned with, and usually have some (perhaps unspoken) relevance to, the self-image of one or more individual managers or supervisors.

To say this is not to imply that the effect which a particular solution may have on how individual managers and supervisors are seen by others and see themselves is not a relevant factor in any cost/benefit review. It can be relevant; it can be important. But individuals' images are not synonymous with the image of the company, and care needs to be taken that they are not assumed to be. This is particularly so when the person who must decide whether and how a respondent should react to an originating application is the person, or one of the people, who personally made or confirmed the decision that the originating application is challenging. Given that most originating applications allege unfair dismissal and that most employers' dismissal procedures provide for dismissals to be internally considered, either initially or on appeal, by senior levels of management in employers' organisations, this is a situation which often arises. The decision-maker in such a situation needs to ask, deliberately and critically, and as objectively as possible, whether any concern about the company's image would be as strong had it been another manager's decision that was being challenged.

A message to supervisors and managers

But even that is not enough. Just as employees often see the employer as 'management' or 'them', so managers often see the work force as 'them' and management generally as 'us'. The need to support more junior individual managers and supervisors in decisions and actions taken in good faith in their managerial and supervisory roles, even where the decisions and actions were not quite the best that might have been taken, will often influence the subsequent decisions and actions of more senior managers. Such considerations may, when consciously weighed and in the right circumstances, be perfectly proper, relevant and important. But there is no intrinsic reason why they should be given any more weight in considering possible solutions to the problem posed by the arrival of an originating application than they should be in dealing with any other management problem. And such factors should certainly not be seen as synonymous with, or determining, the image of the company *vis-à-vis* its employees.

In the effect that it has on one or more supervisors or managers, a particular solution will indeed send some message to the work force. It will also send a message to the supervisors and managers. What needs to be considered is what those messages will be; can and should the employer do anything to influence how they are received and interpreted; and how do the costs and benefits of the messages being sent balance with the other factors that are relevant, in business terms, to finding the best solution to the problem faced by management. The best message is not always 'My manager, right or wrong.' It is not inconceivable that a better message might, in a particular case and with a particular manager or supervisor, be 'Look what a fine mess you've got us into.' The balance of business advantage may even lie in a company defending a case which it expects to lose. That might provide an experience by which a supervisor or manager can learn, more tellingly and cheaply than on any training course, how uncomfortable a witness attempting to defend an untenable position in a tribunal can be and what a bad decision can cost the company in terms of compensation.

Public image

The image of the company in a broader context, 'public relations', may be affected by a case. Some tribunal cases are reported in the media, particularly local papers. Most, however, are not, and the impact of a few lines in a local paper should be assessed by the same criteria, and with the same objectivity, as decisions made in other areas. One cannot help wondering on some occasions why, given the impact which a manager claims to expect from a short, one-off news item in a local paper, the same manager will argue the necessity of spending thousands on a long-term national advertising campaign to keep the company name and its product at the forefront of the public mind. Questions of public image can be relevant and important in deciding how to deal with an originating application. But such factors, like all the others, need to be looked at as objectively as possible and properly weighted in the light of the needs of the business rather than providing a welcome rationalisation for a decision which is really based on other considerations.

A shifting balance

Costs and benefits are relative. As circumstances change so do the desirability and achievability of options. Although the overall decision which a manager has to make is not simply 'settle or fight', a choice between those options will have to be made at least once in relation to any case and a number of times in relation to many. A tribunal asks and answers questions (e.g. jurisdiction, defined act, justification/excuse, remedies) in series, sometimes at different hearings, and the balance of costs and benefits among remaining options may shift after each answer has been given. The possibility of answers either way is known at the start, so how costs and benefits may change in the event of different answers can also be estimated at the start. The precise effect that any legal answer has had on the achievability of subsequent options and on their relative costs and benefits may not be wholly ascertainable until the precise terms of that answer are known, but that there will be an effect, and in general terms what it will be, can be foreseen. This means that, in deciding how to react to an originating application, a respondent can and should consider the costs and benefits not only of options which are immediately available but also of those which may become available; and that steps taken now should be judged in the light not only of their immediate effects but also of those they will have on steps that it may become desirable, in the light of the changing balance of costs and benefits, to take in the future.

Example 1. A generous offer

A respondent who has not entered an appearance may still be a party to an out-of-court settlement. In practice this is most likely to occur where attempts to reach a settlement are already being made and appear to be nearing success when the originating application is put in. Despite any such negotiations an applicant may decide to start the case in the tribunal – perhaps because the time limit for doing so is near, or to put negotiating pressure on the employer. ACAS may become involved, at the suit of either of the parties, before an application has been made to an industrial tribunal. Once any such application has been made the tribunal will, in most jurisdictions, refer it to ACAS, who may get in touch with the named respondent before an appearance has been entered. But unless the respondent genuinely believes that a settlement will be achieved, with or without ACAS's help, before the latest date for submission of a notice of appearance, it is almost invariably better for an appearance to be entered. If it is not and there is no settlement the respondent will have lost any opportunity that might otherwise have existed for influencing the tribunal's decision in the case. The cost involved just in submitting a notice of appearance is minimal. The option of settlement remains.

A possible exception to this general rule occurs when there is no defence that the respondent wishes to mount under any heading but a settlement is impossible because the applicant is seeking a sum of money, or other conditions, which exceed what a tribunal could or would award. Imagine a respondent prepared to pay a dismissed employee as much as or more than the total of a basic award, appropriate to the applicant's age and length of service, the maximum compensatory award and the maximum additional award. Imagine also an applicant who, for whatever reason, will not accept that sum. For the respondent to defend the case even to the extent of entering an appearance increases the costs, however marginally, without attracting any obvious benefit. Whatever happens at the tribunal, the award cannot be more than the respondent is offering. In such a case – and they do infrequently occur – a respondent might seriously consider not entering an appearance.

Even in such a case the wiser course will usually be to enter an appearance. Although it has been said that 'there is no defence that the respondent wishes to mount under any heading' there is clearly an issue on which the applicant and the respondent cannot agree: namely, the remedy. The respondent's view is that this should not be more than the maximum the tribunal has power to award. That seems incontestable. But, in view of the applicant's disagreement, it is a view that has to be 'defended'. Even if the dismissal is outrageously unfair, provided the defence goes no further than supporting that view, it cannot be said that the respondent is acting 'frivolously, vexatiously or otherwise unreasonably' in mounting it. Rather, it is the applicant that may be held to be acting 'frivolously, vexatiously or otherwise unreasonably' in contesting it. Such a limited defence does not, in the absence of any disagreement about rates of pay, length of service or age, involve any disputes of fact and so can be resolved without contested evidence being called. Nor does it involve complex legal argument. It can be put forward to its full extent in a notice of appearance which will be considered by a tribunal at any hearing without any need for the respondent to be present.

In such circumstances the immediate and obvious cost, simply of preparing and submitting a notice of appearance, is minimal. What are the benefits? And are there other costs? One benefit enjoyed by all those who enter an appearance and not enjoyed by those who do not is that the right to be informed of the progress of the case and to participate in it is maintained. More specifically to these circumstances, a notice of appearance in the terms outlined may help to persuade an applicant that there is nothing to gain by pursuing the case through the tribunal and so make speedy disposal of it by settlement more likely. Even if the applicant does not personally see that pressing on to a hearing will produce no more than is now on offer, except more expense, a notice of appearance in these terms might strengthen any suggestions that the applicant's advisers, conciliation officers or even the industrial tribunal may wish to make that this is so.

The 'cost' to the respondent, over and above that 'simply of preparing and submitting a notice of appearance' in the terms outlined above, is that it may be seen as a formal admission of 'guilt'. Even whilst offering a substantial sum of money to someone who may otherwise take action before an industrial tribunal, an employer will often hold to the view that the offer is being made purely out of the goodness of the company's heart and not because anything has been done with which the company should reproach itself – or for which anyone else should reproach the company. That view becomes more difficult to sustain if, when the aggrieved person effectively says, formally on an originating application, 'You have treated me unfairly,' the employer effectively says, formally on a notice of appearance, 'Yes, but . . .'

Having identified the benefits and costs of this situation, even though they are not quantified in precise financial terms, a decision has to be made, against business criteria, as to which outweighs the other. How important to the company is the maintenance of the stance that 'we did nothing wrong'? How much time, effort and money will it cost to mount the fullest possible defence of the case at an industrial tribunal hearing? How likely does the respondent judge it to be, in the light of the factual investigation and the legal analysis which have been undertaken, that any such defence will result in a finding that the company 'did nothing wrong'? Would an express finding by a tribunal that the company *did* do something wrong, which would result if a full defence were mounted and failed, be more damaging than a concession, for the purposes of argument and so that the amount of compensation can be fixed, that it *may* have done something wrong? Does the respondent believe, in the light of what is known about the psychology and motivation of the applicant, and about who is advising the applicant, that entry of an appearance in the terms proposed will affect the applicant's willingness to settle for the sum offered? And so on.

Example 2. A reasonable offer

The example assumes that what the employer was offering was at least equal to the theoretical maximum an industrial tribunal had the power to award. In practice, tribunals seldom come anywhere near the theoretical maxima in making financial awards. Additional awards are applicable only in unfair dismissal cases where an order for reinstatement or re-engagement has been made and unjustifiably not complied with by the respondent. In practice such orders are made in only a small percentage of cases. A maximum compensatory award will arise only in a case where the level of the applicant's loss is high and/or it is held by a tribunal to be likely to continue for a long time. A respondent would have some idea, from investigation and analysis under the remedies heading, what the practical limits of a tribunal's likely financial award might be and may have pitched any offer to settle a case with reference to those limits rather than to the theoretical limits on which the example was initially based.

The example also assumed that 'there is no defence that the respondent wishes to mount under any heading'. That may have been because the respondent felt that there was no good defence. But it could have been that, despite the existence of a good defence, the respondent felt that the balance of business advantage lay in paying out a certain amount by way of settlement rather than actually mounting that defence. The financial costs of mounting the defence may be high. The nature of the evidence involved may make the respondent reluctant to have it heard in public. The best defence may be on a technicality, and the respondent may not wish to be seen to be relying on a technical knock-out in its dealings with an employee or former employee. Although able legally to justify a dismissal as 100 per cent 'fair' an employer – in a case of incapability through illness, for instance – may be genuinely sympathetic with an employee's personal predicament and wish, as a good employer, to cushion the blow of dismissal by a generous severance payment. A vast range of factors might initially lead a respondent to take this view. But the balance of business advantage will inevitably change as the overall cost of achieving a solution changes.

With the example modified to take account of these two factors, a notice of appearance dealing only and briefly with the question of compensation, while still an option, becomes less attractive. On the issue of the remedy itself there will now be the necessity for some evidence and argument on whether an order for reinstatement or re-engagement should be made. Such orders are seldom made, because the conditions in which they can be made are seldom found to have been met. But where unfair dismissal is found, or conceded, the tribunal is required to consider whether an order for reinstatement or re-engagement should be made. If there is no evidence that re-employment would not be practicable or just, there may be no grounds on which a tribunal could deal with the issue other than by making an order. The reason for the levels of financial compensation that are awarded in practice is that the tribunals find, as a fact, that they properly reflect the losses suffered by successful applicants. Again, in the absence of evidence from the respondent, or at least the testing of the applicant's evidence by the respondent, on the crucial factual issues with reference to which compensation levels are set, a tribunal may be limited in the amount that it awards, in the light of the facts that it finds, only by the statutory maximum.

So although the respondent may genuinely prefer to settle the case at what it regards as a reasonable, even generous, sum, it may be necessary to work towards that settlement or to provide for the possibility that such a settlement cannot be reached voluntarily by entering an appearance on which a more detailed and vigorous case on the issue of remedies can be based. A notice of appearance setting out such a case may persuade, or help others to persuade, the applicant that the employer's offer is indeed 'reasonable, even generous'. If it does not, it allows the respondent at a tribunal hearing to present evidence and argument on the question of remedies. Tribunals will normally exclude evidence that an offer has been made and refused and about any amount offered. But the evidence and argument that led the respondent to fix the size of the offer would be precisely the evidence and argument which will lead the tribunal to set any award within the limit of what was actually offered.

The notice of appearance might go further. It might set out defences with respect to jurisdiction, the defined act and/or justification and/or excuses. Even though at this stage the respondent does not really wish to rely on those points, making it clear that they are available may make the applicant more inclined to accept the respondent's offer to settle the case. Should the applicant persist in pursuing the case, so causing the respondent to start incurring the costs involved in preparation for a hearing and maybe in appearing at the hearing itself, the balance of business advantage may change so as to lie in actively defending the case rather than settling it, at least at the amount initially envisaged.

The example has assumed that an offer to settle the case was already 'on the table' when the originating application was received by the respondent. Although this does sometimes happen, any steps with a view to settlement will often not be taken until after the originating application has been received and a notice of appearance has been entered. But this does not mean that, in deciding its approach, the respondent should not even consider the option of settlement until after the notice of appearance has been put in.

Example 3. Fight first, offer later

Say that the factual investigation and legal analysis have led a respondent to believe that there is a reasonably good chance that an originating application will be held to have been submitted out of time but that, if it is held to have been in time, there is little likelihood of any other defence succeeding. This issue of jurisdiction will be determined first, and almost certainly in a preliminary hearing just on that point, and the respondent may feel that the point should be argued as strongly as possible. The costs of fighting it are likely to be relatively limited and the benefits of winning, namely the avoidance of any finding on the substantive issue and of any remedy, relatively high. If the point is lost, and attention will have to be turned to more complex and time-consuming issues in the main hearing, the costs of fighting those points may begin to outweigh those of settling the case, particularly given that the benefits that might come from winning the case on these other points seem unlikely to arise. So the respondent may plan – if, and only if, the initial point is lost – then to direct a major effort towards settling the case.

This does not mean that the notice of appearance which is entered should deal only with the question of jurisdiction. As discussed above, any notice of appearance will need to preserve the respondent's options should a settlement not be achievable. But, as also discussed above, what is said on a notice of appearance may also affect the course of negotiations. A notice of appearance drafted with this scenario in mind may be different from one that was drafted with the real object of fighting the case through to the bitter end. A further difference may arise from the importance in this scenario of the jurisdictional point being heard at a preliminary hearing. The notice of appearance must include or be accompanied by an application that such a preliminary hearing should be held.

Example 4. Fight now, but how?

Whether an originating application was in time or out of time will not usually involve a great deal of evidence or complex legal argument. Other questions of jurisdiction may. Although the benefits to a respondent of winning a case on a preliminary point remain the avoidance of having to argue subsequent points and of an adverse award being made, the costs of doing so can be out of all proportion to those benefits. A respondent may feel confident that, with much time, effort and expense, it will be able to dispose of a case at a preliminary stage by demonstrating that a woman claiming equal pay with a man was not in the same employment as that man. If the respondent believes there is an equally good chance of winning the case, while spending much less time, effort and money, by demonstrating a material difference other than sex between the woman's case and the man's, it may decide to ignore the preliminary point or deal with it relatively cursorily.

Whether a respondent will be willing in this way to forgo a good defence because of the costs of mounting it will depend on its view of the costs and benefits of following that course as compared with those of following other courses. Were the woman the only one in the position concerned, and were the difference between her pay and that of the chosen male comparator small, the costs of her winning might be small compared with those of fighting the case on even the simplest grounds. If the pay difference in question is larger the balance of advantage may shift. What might be lost by reliance only on the less complex defence is now such that, despite the increased cost involved in doing so, it becomes worthwhile to bring the more complex defence into play. If the woman is a member of a group of similar female workers, so that any decision in her case will impact on their pay as well, the cost of pursuing the more complex preliminary defence and all defences which may, however improbably, lead to a finding in the respondent's favour, with leading and junior counsel and days' worth of evidence and argument, may pale into insignificance beside the cost of losing the case.

Desirable v. achievable

Enough examples have been given to illustrate how legal and business considerations interact both substantively and procedurally. In deciding what is achievable a respondent should take account of what investigation, analysis and assessment have found. In deciding what is desirable it should take account of costs and benefits. In deciding how to react to the arrival of an originating application it must balance achievability with desirability.

The substance of the law the industrial tribunals apply and the procedures they follow provide the inescapable backdrop against which such decisions have to be made. The respondent will have an opportunity to influence a tribunal's decisions on both substance and procedure. The ways in which they might be influenced; the arguments which might exercise most influence; the likelihood of those arguments' success; the benefits of them succeeding or the costs of them failing; the costs of advancing them whether they win or lose – all are questions that need some legal input to answer. But the crucial decision on what, in the light of the answers to these questions, is the course which should be followed is not a legal decision: it is a business decision.

Key points

The respondent's action plan should:

- Be drawn up before any action is taken to respond formally to an originating application.
- Be based on the results of investigation and analysis.
- Be based on a cost–benefit assessment which

Covers both direct and indirect costs and benefits.
Covers both cash and non-cash costs and benefits.
Assesses costs and benefits objectively and against business, not personal, criteria.
Looks at all available options.

- Identify, in order of priority, desired solutions.
- Assess the achievability of each desired solution.
- Recognise that the balance between the desirability and achievability of each solution may change, and assess how the respondent's own actions may affect it.
- Select that action which offers the best balance of desirability, current achievability and the maintenance or improvement of all options' future achievability.
- Outline alternative action to be taken as foreseeable changes occur in the balance between the desirability and achievability of all solutions.

Chapter 10
Presenting a case

Achieving any of the solutions desired by the respondent will require persuasion. The applicant will need persuading to withdraw, or the tribunal will need persuading to dismiss the case or to award a minimum remedy. What will be persuasive, in substance and in form, for one of these purposes may be less so for the other.

Two communication systems

Conciliation system and decision system

There are, in effect, two communication systems. Both involve the applicant and respondent. That apart, they are in most respects different. The objective of one is settlement of the case without the need for a hearing and substantive decision by an industrial tribunal. A third party in this system may be a conciliation officer, so call this the 'conciliation system' or 'C system'. But it will not always be so: many cases are withdrawn, with or without money changing hands, with no involvement by ACAS. Where the third party is involved its primary role within this system is to facilitate communication between the other two. The third party in the other system is the industrial tribunal, and the objective in that system is to decide the case. Call this the 'decision system' or 'D system'. An outcome is achieved by the applicant and respondent communicating not with each other but with the tribunal.

Any solution achieved under the C system is the result of a joint decision: an agreement between the applicant and the respondent which is reached in private. Each can set, and change, the criteria by which its contribution to the joint decision is made. Those criteria are likely to contain pragmatic elements. The process of persuasion here is concerned as much with getting the other party to change its decision criteria as with suggesting that any proposal meets those criteria. In the D system the decision is made by the third party, the tribunal, and the process is public. Persuasion here rests more on demonstrating that the proposed solution, the decision which the party wants, meets criteria which are externally imposed and are based on principle. Under the C system the parties have similar status and power. Each threatens the other that non-co-operation will lead to a hearing, resulting not only in the case being decided by a tribunal but also in all the cost, inconvenience, etc., that will involve. When, under the C system, a party advances arguments about the legal strengths of its own case and the weaknesses of the other party's the purpose is not to settle the legal question but to improve the persuasive effectiveness of that threat. Under the D system the parties remain equal but in the sense that neither has much status or power as against the tribunal.

The periods at which the two systems operate overlap but the emphasis between them shifts with time. In general terms the emphasis will start in the C system and only if that fails will it shift to the D system. But settlement can occur at any time: before an originating application is submitted, well before any hearing takes place, 'at the door of the court' or after any part of the case has been heard. A solution produced by the C system is total: the whole case is disposed of as a single entity and at one time. The D system adopts, always in terms of analysis and often in terms of procedure, a staged approach. The first stage may be a decision on a jurisdictional point. If the applicant loses that point the solution is, appeals apart, total: the whole case is dismissed. But if the applicant wins on that point the solution is not total: further hearing/s will be necessary. Thus solution by the C system precludes further use of the D system, but a solution from the D system may permit or even encourage further use of the C system.

The C system is interactive in that each party can, and to be effective will, adjust what it says in response to what the other has said. The system provides immediate and continuing feedback. If it seems the desired message is not getting through, its content or form can be changed. In the D system there is little feedback within each stage or, where all issues are dealt with at one hearing, between stages. A party does not know, until a presentation has been completed and it is too late to alter it, whether it is having the desired effect. Whatever impression tribunal members may give during the course of a hearing, the decision is not given until all evidence and argument is complete.

Given that the C system involves communication between applicant and respondent, it may build on the employment relationship that probably existed or still exists between them. Either party may know something of the other's psychology or motivation and design or adapt approaches in the light of such knowledge. Both parties may draw on common experience and traditions so that certain things 'go without saying'. But there is no prior relationship between either party and the tribunal on which to build in the D system. Any knowledge or understanding which may be common to the applicant and the respondent is not shared by the tribunal with whom, and not each other, each has to communicate.

Their interaction

The systems are different and separate. But both operate at the same time, and with the applicant and respondent as parties in both of them. Some communications are specific to one system or to particular participants within one system. What a party says to a conciliation officer cannot be repeated in a tribunal hearing, and what one party tells a conciliation officer will not necessarily be repeated to the other party. Tribunals will not admit, or will ignore, details of negotiations 'without prejudice' between the parties. Thus what is said within the C system does not carry over into the D system, although it may influence a party's aims and how it presents its case within that other system. But whatever is said in the D system does carry over into the C system and becomes part of the material with which that system is concerned. When the respondent is communicating with the tribunal the communications are also received by the applicant. If by the time that happens any possibility of the case being resolved by withdrawal has been abandoned the effect on the applicant does not matter. Where, on the other hand, withdrawal is still an aim and a possibility, the effect on the applicant, within the C system, as well as on the tribunal, within the D system, has to be considered.

A notice of appearance is a communication addressed by the respondent to the tribunal. Unless it raises some preliminary issue or includes or is accompanied by some interlocutory application it will simply be put on the case file. It will have no immediate impact on any decision which a tribunal may have to make, except perhaps in procedural terms. The same notice of appearance is going to be seen, when it is first entered or very shortly after, by the applicant, the applicant's advisers and ACAS.

Each will see it in a different light. All will assess the strengths and weaknesses of the defence it outlines. ACAS's assessment may well be the most objective, and ACAS will expressly be looking for settlement possibilities. The applicant's advisers will probably also attempt to look at it objectively, first to identify more sharply what will be the important issues at any hearing and, second, in the light of this, to reassess the likelihood of success should the case proceed to hearing. Besides making an objective assessment the applicant's advisers will, if the applicant is not given or does not accept advice to withdraw, also be using the notice of appearance subjectively: to decide and refine the strategy and presentation which will best achieve the applicant's objectives. The applicant's own assessment may be highly subjective but no less important for that. A mention of a particular aspect of a case may make one applicant, with a particular motivation and psychological make-up, more determined to proceed to a hearing, whereas it may incline another applicant, with different motivation and psychology, to settle.

So before the notice of appearance serves the communication purpose for which it is ostensibly prepared, and in relation to the tribunal to which it is expressly addressed, it is communicating between the respondent and other audiences. Those other audiences can – and, for it to serve any useful purpose so far as the respondent is concerned, would have to – react to the communication before it serves its ostensible purpose in relation to the addressee. It is obviously sensible that, so far as is consistent with its ostensible purpose and addressee, it should be presented with its other audiences and purposes in mind. Depending on the respondent's strategy, it may even be that its form and content should be determined with reference more to its effect on the applicant, etc., than to its effect on the tribunal.

The notice of appearance will be on the case file and available when any interlocutory decisions are made. Shortly before any hearing does take place the notice of appearance will be given to tribunal members. It is bound to define, at least to some extent, the areas with which the tribunal will allow the respondent to deal, and it will pre-condition the tribunal, to some extent, to direct its own attention to particular factual and legal questions. Well before then the situation with regard to disposal of the case by withdrawal will have developed. If the notice of appearance which was drafted with more of an eye to persuading the applicant to withdraw than to persuading the tribunal to dismiss it now looks inadequate for the latter purpose, the respondent can seek leave to amend it. Provided that is done timeously and without causing injustice or appearing to be an abuse of process, leave is unlikely to be refused.

The notice of appearance has been used as an example because it is the first formal communication from the respondent to the tribunal and because it is when it is drafted that the largest range of options are likely to exist and may need to be kept open. The same principles apply to all other communications while disposal by withdrawal remains an aim and a possibility. The further through the hearing process a case progresses the more options are closed, but even a respondent's closing address to the tribunal on the issue of liability could be affected: its terms could influence the sum for which an applicant will settle if the tribunal finds the employer liable but invites the parties to agree on remedies.

Identity and role of the presenter

The presentation of a respondent's case to a tribunal is not confined to what happens at the hearing. It encompasses all stages from the notice of appearance to the closing address on the issue of remedies. It needs to be planned with that in mind. One person will obviously have to act as presenter in any tribunal hearing, and it is preferable if that person plans and handles all stages of presentation as a coherent whole. The person may self-select by virtue of position and function within the respondent's organisation. Where there is a choice, a person who has played no direct part in the events leading up to the case is to be preferred to one who has taken part in them. The presenter's role is then less likely to become confused with that of a witness as to fact. Presentational skills are obviously valuable, but thorough preparation contributes more to success than eloquence. The presenter needs to have or be given sufficient authority to commit the respondent to a negotiated solution within the terms of the respondent's action plan and sufficient personal authority to be able to question, as an advocate in charge of a witness, the most senior person who may be required to give evidence. If the person who conducted the investigation, analysis and assessment also undertakes the presentation time and effort will be saved. Similar tasks will not have to be done twice by two people. But it is not essential. The tasks are similar but different.

There can be confusion about the role of the person who is presenting a respondent's case to a tribunal. The nature of a tribunal hearing, with its emphases on the questioning of witnesses and the development of argument, can make it appear that what is involved is a search after truth and the 'right' answer in legal terms. That is not wholly wrong, but once a case has reached a tribunal hearing each party has a view about what is true and what the correct legal answers are. The job of the presenter is to put those views as effectively as possible and to convince the tribunal that they are right. The purpose of questioning witnesses is not to discover what they will say but to use the evidence they can give in the way that will best support the party's case. The purpose of argument is not to construct a theorem which can always be used to prove any given legal principle but to persuade a tribunal that a particular desired result is right in this particular case.

This does not mean that a presentation should be based on untruths or that it should ignore evidence which does not support a party's case. A presenter has to acknowledge that the touchstone for the tribunal in its findings of fact will be 'the truth, the whole truth and nothing but the truth'. A case which is or appears to be based on falsehood or which overlooks inconvenient but true facts is unlikely to be convincing. To that extent a presenter is concerned with truth. But the search for truth is secondary. It is pursued not because it is the end in itself but because it is, or appears to be, the most effective way of achieving the real goal. The goal is to persuade the tribunal to reach the decision which the party is seeking.

An argument which will serve as a general proof in relation to a legal principle will be more effective than one which smacks of special pleading. For that reason a presenter might make great play of the universal validity and general applicability of a line of argument which is being advanced. That a point is right 'in principle' will make it more likely to be persuasive in the context of a particular case. To that extent a presenter is concerned with 'principle'. But the concern arises not because it is, of itself, desirable, only because of the contribution it will make towards the real objective: getting the desired answer from the tribunal.

The need for objectivity, even scepticism, in investigation, analysis and assessment has been stressed. The dangers of too subjective an approach to deciding how an employer should respond to the arrival of an originating application have been discussed. In the context of presentation, however, too objective an approach can be harmful. There must be objective consideration of a case, to identify its weaknesses as well as its strengths, but once decisions have been made about the preferred solution and strategy, and the case has begun to be presented, the presenter needs to become a partisan campaigner for the respondent rather than an objective investigator, analyst or assessor. Each action and decision about what the respondent says and does in connection with the case should be judged against the test of whether it will help or hinder the achievement of the chosen solution. Each piece of evidence and each line of argument must be looked at afresh in the light not of how strong it is but of how it can best be used, or countered, in achieving that solution.

How strong objective investigation and analysis have revealed evidence or argument to be will be an important factor in deciding how it should be used. A case which is presented in an 'objective' fashion will usually be more persuasive than one which is clearly a partisan campaign. Objectivity should not be abandoned. But, like 'truth' and 'principle', 'objectivity' becomes, when the presentation stage is reached, something to be used as is most appropriate for the purpose of achieving the respondent's goal rather than being sought for its own value.

What preparation involves

Working back from the objectives to the evidence

Preparing to present a respondent's case to a tribunal mirrors, in some respects, the process by which the respondent decided whether, and if so how, the case should be defended at a tribunal. Investigation, the collection of evidence, was followed by analysis of the evidence within the framework of legal rules that it brought into play. The ways in which the case might be resolved by a tribunal or otherwise were then assessed. In the light of their probability of success, and of their costs and benefits in overall business terms, an action plan or strategy was chosen. Almost invariably that strategy would include – even if only on a contingency basis, to cope with the possibility that the applicant would not settle at any price – a presentation of some case to a tribunal. Exceptionally the case may be concerned with no more than whether the tribunal can award more than the statutory maximum that the respondent had been offering for a voluntary settlement. More often it will involve more substantial questions. Its general lines, and whether the respondent should aim for or expect different aspects of the case to be decided at separate hearings, will be part of the strategy.

The presenter now has to work back, from the objectives set by the strategy in relation to the tribunal case, through the framework of legal rules which will bear on the achievement of that objective, to the facts which will be necessary for those legal rules to operate in the way desired, and thence to the evidence that will have to be adduced to prove those facts. At the same time the presenter has to remember that the applicant will also be putting a case to the tribunal. The presenter must prepare to meet it to the extent that is necessary for the respondent's objectives to be achieved.

That the mental process of preparation is 'backwards' in this way does not require the physical processes of preparation to be tackled in the same order. But there is advantage if they are. An early step in actually preparing to present a case might therefore be the drafting of the address to the tribunal. Although this will be the last stage of presentation it is the stage at which the respondent's arguments are fully articulated. It is the stage when it can be explained why this legal rule is applicable rather than that; why this interpretation of the law is to be preferred to that; why, because of this evidence and that evidence, these are the true facts; and why – in the light of this law and these facts – this is the right decision. Preparation of a full address to the tribunal focuses the mind of the presenter on precisely what law and facts will make the strongest case for the respondent and thus on the evidence which is needed to prove those facts.

How to organise the evidence

When the evidence which is needed has been identified, and its relative importance has been assessed, then, and only then, can it properly be decided how best it can be adduced. Deciding what witnesses should be called and what documents should be put in should follow, not precede, the decision about how the case will ultimately, in the closing address, be argued to the tribunal. A fact which may be disputed and which is crucial to the success of a presenter's argument needs the strongest possible evidence; corroboration from more than one witness, perhaps, and any available documentary support. A fact which may be disputed but which is unimportant to the argument on which the respondent's presenter is relying may be ignored or dealt with, *en passant*, by a witness called for another purpose. A fact which may not be disputed but on which, nevertheless, the address to the tribunal will rest should be supported by some evidence.

Identifying what witnesses to call and what documents to put in is only part of the decision about how the necessary evidence can best be adduced. Witnesses will have to be questioned. The presenter must decide in what order, what about, and how. And the decisions on 'what about' and 'how' need to be made in relation to the applicant's likely witnesses as well as any called by the respondent. Documents will be retained by the tribunal until the decision has been made but this does not mean that the tribunal will necessarily and automatically identify what the respondent believes to be the important parts of them or interpret them in the same way as the respondent. The presenter needs to decide, in the light of the importance that points resting on documentary evidence will have to the address to the tribunal, whether and how they need highlighting or reinforcing by other evidence. Documents are not normally put in as evidence until a hearing has actually begun. A document attached to a notice of appearance will accompany it when it goes to tribunal members. Where a short document plays a crucial part in a respondent's defence, a presenter may decide to draft the notice of appearance specifically so that it can include that document in the hope of emphasising it in the tribunal members' minds.

The decisions about which witnesses and documents to use, and how to use them, interrelate. Similar evidence may be available from more than one source. It may be felt to be stronger and likely to be given more weight by the tribunal if given by one witness rather than another – whether because of those witnesses' roles in relation to the event concerned or because of the way each 'comes over'. One witness may be able to give evidence on two or three crucial facts, whereas to cover the same ground without that witness would require two or three witnesses. One witness may, although able to give evidence of value to the respondent, be felt likely also, if subjected to particular lines of cross-examination, to give damaging evidence. The advantage of calling that witness may be outweighed by the possible disadvantage. Similarly, a document may do more harm than good if it contains, besides that which the respondent is relying on, evidence which will help the applicant even more.

The criterion on which the presenter takes these decisions is how helpful or harmful the witness or document will be, overall, to the case which the respondent is putting. They are, first of all, partisan decisions. The presenter is under no duty, in preparing and presenting the respondent's case, to make the applicant's task any easier. The decisions have, secondly, to be made at a considerable level of detail. What matters is not simply 'Should this witness be called?' What matters is 'What will this witness say if asked that question?' This means that, thirdly, the decisions can be properly taken only in the light of the detailed structure of the case which the presenter intends to base on the evidence which has been given.

The notice of appearance

Similar arguments might support a proposition that the preparation of the address to the tribunal should even precede the preparation of the notice of appearance. It is, after all, the first formal step in the presentation of the respondent's case to the tribunal. Ideally that may be so. In practical terms it is seldom likely to happen. The respondent should submit a notice of appearance within fourteen days of receipt of the originating application. That relatively short time scale is likely to be fully occupied by investigation, analysis and strategic decision-making, without trying to crowd full and detailed preparation for a case's presentation into it, too. There will be a longer period – a few weeks at least, maybe a few months – between the entry of the respondent's appearance and any hearing.

The notice of appearance is not only the first formal step in the D system, in the presentation of the respondent's case to the tribunal. It will also play some part in the C system, in seeking to dispose of the case without it being heard. Work which is undertaken specifically with a hearing in mind will have been wasted if the applicant withdraws the case before hearing. That may be unavoidable. If a case is not settled or withdrawn until shortly before the date for which a hearing has been listed, or even 'at the door of the court', the respondent's presenter will have had to prepare fully, but the full presentation will not be made. The likelihood of such waste can, however, be minimised by the major effort on preparation being delayed until it is seen whether the case is, in practice, likely to be heard or until, given the hearing date and the amount of work which is involved, its start cannot safely be put off any longer.

Also, although the notice of appearance can include as much detail as the respondent wishes, it is not required by the tribunal's rules to do more than outline the respondent's defence in general terms, 'stating whether or not [the respondent] intends to resist the application and, if so, setting out sufficient particulars to show on what grounds'. The strategic decisions already taken about whether and if so how to defend the case provide all the information necessary to complete the notice of appearance. The presenter's starting point was described above as 'the objectives set by the strategy in relation to the tribunal case'. Drafting the notice of appearance involves extracting from the overall strategic decision about the case as a management problem those elements which relate to it as a tribunal case, and expressing them in terms appropriate to a tribunal's involvement. As much as being the first step in a respondent's presentation to the tribunal, therefore, it is a useful first step for the presenter in preparing the respondent's presentation.

A programme for preparation

In summary, then, what preparation involves is as follows. The notice of appearance is drafted. This document crystallises, from the overall strategy, the presenter's objectives in relation to the tribunal hearing: what main questions the respondent wishes the tribunal to decide and how it wishes the tribunal to decide them. The precise form of its drafting should bear in mind any influence that it may have on the chances of the case being withdrawn as well as its role in the context of the tribunal hearing.

Where particular interlocutory steps play a part in the respondent's strategy, they need to be set in train. Applications connected with them also need to be drafted consistently with the respondent's aims in relation to settlement as well as to the possibility of a hearing, taking account of those aims and how achievable they appear at the time such applications are submitted. The need for such steps, particularly in connection with discovery of documents or witness orders, may not become apparent until the detailed arguments on which the respondent wishes to rely are precisely defined by the address to the tribunal being drafted. Where such a development seems at all possible, then such drafting, at least as far as is necessary to decide whether interlocutory applications need to be made, should take place as soon as possible. Otherwise, and normally, further preparation may be delayed until it becomes clearer that a hearing is indeed likely to take place.

When the next step does take place it is the drafting of the address to the tribunal: setting out in detail the facts and the law on which the respondent will rely in persuading the tribunal to answer the necessary questions in the desired way and, where necessary, the arguments as to why these facts are the true ones and/or this law should be applied in this way. The drafting of the address is followed by the selection of the evidence which is needed to support the argument contained in the address and by a decision as to how that evidence should be put before the tribunal. Plans for the examination or cross-examination of witnesses need to be prepared. Documents need to be collected into a bundle and decisions made about how they are to be used in the hearing. The next two chapters are concerned with the evidential aspects of this process: Chapter 11 with the people and Chapter 12 with the paper. The remainder of this chapter is concerned with argument: the purpose and structure of the address to the tribunal.

The address to the tribunal

The purpose of the address is to explain the party's view of why, given the evidence that has been put before it, the tribunal should decide disputed questions of fact one way rather than another and how correct application of the law to the facts produces this answer rather than that. Precisely what the respondent's address should contain cannot be decided until the moment it is delivered. It has to deal with the situation that exists then. Any commentary must be on evidence that has actually been given, not on what the presenter expected would be given. An anticipated argument from the applicant which has not actually been advanced may not need to be countered.

A party is entitled to address the tribunal, but is not bound to do so. The ground which presentation of any address covers and the detail into which it goes should depend on how much explanation is necessary. Where facts are not disputed, there is no need for explanation of how the evidence leads to the finding of those facts. If the finding of a fact one way or the other would have no effect on the outcome of the case, explaining why it should be found one way rather than the other, or indeed mentioning it at all (apart, perhaps, from explaining that it is irrelevant), is unnecessary. Where the weight of the evidence on a particular factual point has been overwhelmingly in favour of the party making the address little argument about that fact is needed – although a presenter should be cautious about assessing too optimistically how the tribunal will view the relative weight of conflicting evidence, particularly where a fact is of crucial importance to the case being made.

Which facts are irrelevant and which are of crucial importance depends on the relevant law. Where this is well established and clear there is no need for extensive argument about it, although reference to the words of the relevant statutory provision usually provides the best structure for an address.

If everything has gone well throughout the hearing there may be no need for any address at all. In practice that will seldom happen, and it will never be possible to say beforehand when it will. The presenter therefore needs to prepare to argue the case to the fullest foreseeable extent. Elements of the planned address that events render irrelevant can then be discarded. This is preferable to having to advance arguments which have not been prepared.

Matching preparation to presentation

The physical form which preparation takes must be a matter of personal choice. A system which works well for one presenter may be disastrous for another. Some people make do with headline notes and find more detail distracting; others lack confidence without a virtually full script. To some the layout of any notes provides the best means of reminding the presenter of what needs to be said, in what order and how. Others use underlining or bold capitals or fluorescent highlighters or other textual marking devices. A diagram, such as a flow chart or decision tree, may help a particular presenter more than any textual approach. Some are happier with one piece of paper; others with one for each main point they wish to make. Others can competently cross-refer between two or more documents without losing their place. Where a presenter intends to include a direct quotation from a statute or a law report, most would find it convenient to read it from the statute or the law report concerned. But where it is short the presenter's flow may be better preserved if the precise quotation is included in any notes. There is then no need to bring out a book, open it, turn to the page and find the right place on it.

In deciding the physical form which preparation will take the presenter should remember the circumstances in which the presentation will eventually be made. A full script, particularly if it is intended to be repeated word for word (or even to be read out, although that should be avoided unless the presenter feels unable to work in any other way), can be difficult to edit to take account of developments which occur during the hearing. Even where a full script is prepared, it will probably be necessary to accompany it by headlines or marginal notes or some other means of helping the presenter to distinguish relevant parts from irrelevant ones, without losing the flow of the presentation, when the address is actually being made.

In presenting the address it may be desirable to refer to the precise answers actually given by witnesses and to build them into the argument. The precise answers will not have been given when preparation is being undertaken but the desirability of doing so may be foreseen. A form of preparation which allows the answers, when given, to be slotted into the appropriate place is helpful. A specific gap may be left in the script or notes, or more general provision might be made by leaving wide margins, or even by using only half of each sheet. The margins or other half-sheet are then available for further manuscript notes to be added, at the appropriate places, as the hearing proceeds. How preparation achieves its objective is of less importance than that the objective – the presentation of a relevant and coherent argument of the strength necessary to secure the best possible result – is achieved.

Relevance

Relevance is determined, in outline and at the preparation stage, by the legal rules which apply to the case concerned: those identified at the earlier analytical stage. If the interpretation of the rules is in question, argument about their meaning is relevant. The legal rules require certain facts to be proved: this determines which facts are relevant. If different interpretations of the rules are being argued, each interpretation may, if it is accepted, bring different facts into the frame of relevance. The evidence on which reliance is placed to prove or disprove relevant facts, and how its weight should be assessed, are relevant. Where it is necessary to infer essential findings of fact because of the absence of direct evidence, the arguments which support the inferences are relevant. Other points have little relevance and, except as necessary background, should not clutter up the address to the tribunal, either in preparation or presentation. What is actually relevant when the address to the tribunal is delivered will almost certainly have been considerably refined from what, at the preparation stage, might have been relevant. But preparation should cover all foreseeable possibilities.

Structure

The coherence of an argument derives from its structure and the clarity of its expression. The latter may be assisted by its presentation but really depends on the clarity of thought which lies behind it. The presenter should look for an overall structure in which one point leads easily to the next and, within that, for sub-structures in which the same thing happens at a greater level of detail. If necessary such a structure can be specially constructed. Should how it makes a coherent whole not be immediately self-evident, that can be explained. By and large, though, it will be more sensible to use the ready-made structure which the law provides and which dictates the framework within which the case will be decided.

> This is a case of unfair dismissal. The respondents have admitted dismissing the applicant. So we have to prove the reason for the dismissal and that it was one of the reasons permitted by the Act. If we do prove that, the dismissal will be fair, provided it was reasonable for the respondents to treat that as a sufficient reason for dismissal.

Similar words can be heard on most days in tribunals throughout the country. They set out a clear and appropriate overall structure for the address which follows it. The reason for dismissal can be demonstrated and, if necessary, which is not very often, whether it fits into one of the permitted categories can then be argued. The meat of the case is likely to be the question of reasonableness, but the necessary sub-structure for that will probably be provided by one or more of the leading cases.

> The applicant was dismissed for gross misconduct. For a dismissal to be reasonable the respondent has to have had a genuine belief that the

employee was guilty of the misconduct alleged. That belief has to be based on reasonable grounds and to be formed after reasonable investigation.

This not only sets out the relevant law, it also outlines a structure under which the address can deal coherently with the genuineness of the belief, the grounds on which it was formed and the investigation which took place. On any of these points a further sub-structure might be useful. For instance, discussion of the investigation might be in two parts: first what took place, for which a chronological approach might be most effective, and then whether that was 'reasonable'. Further levels of sub-structure might follow.

The number of levels at which sub-structures of this sort are needed depends on what has to be proved and the detail of the argument necessary to prove it. The aim in terms of presentation should be simplicity: as few levels as possible. An argument which appears simple from its presentation is more likely to be understood, and so accepted, than an argument which appears complex and difficult to understand. But the desire for simplicity of presentation should not override the need for every point in the argument to gain its full weight in support of the argument. If the number of points which have to be made is large, or if the chain of reasoning which leads from a particular point to the overall conclusion is long, a device is needed which groups the points in some understandable way and clearly reveals the links in the chain of reasoning. It may be better to subdivide the argument more, to introduce another level of sub-structure, than to deal with too many detailed points under the same general heading or to leave it unclear how establishment of this point leads logically to that point being true. Where a particularly complex structure with many levels of sub-structure seems necessary, the prior submission of a written skeleton argument, explaining that structure, might be valuable.

When an argument has been deconstructed in this way it needs to be reconstructed. Signposts around the geography of the structures and sub-structures should be used. A presenter may have said that three main topics will be discussed and then gone into detail on the first of them. Within that topic four sub-headings may have been used. When all four have been dealt with it needs to be made clear not only how they relate to the first main topic but also that, having now finished with that topic, the presenter is moving on to the second.

Language and grammar

The clarity of an address to the tribunal is also influenced by the words in which it is couched and by how they are put together. Simplicity is again the aim. Simple words are better than complex words. 'Saw' is better than 'observed', for instance. Short sentences are better than long ones. It may take a number of short sentences to do the work of one long one, and the total number of words used may be greater, but clarity and comprehensibility can be vastly increased. It has to be remembered that, although it may be prepared in written form, the address to the tribunal will be presented orally. A reader who finds a word or sentence confusing can re-read it. A listener cannot. What may be appropriate, even better, for a written presentation may be wrong for an oral one. Examples, analogies, similies and metaphors can help – provided they are simple, expressed in simple words and sentences, and the link between the point being made and the illustration is direct and clear.

Jargon – words or phrases which have a special meaning in a particular context but no meaning, or a different meaning, in more general use – should not be used; or its meaning should be explained. From their shared experience, applicant and respondent may understand them. The tribunal may not. Words with a high emotional content should be avoided unless they are deliberately being used precisely because of their content, and that should seldom happen. To say that a witness's statement is 'ludicrous' means that the person saying it does not believe the witness and implies, perhaps, some of the reasons for that disbelief. What is really needed is an express explanation of those reasons and how they support the disbelief. The choice of the word 'ludicrous' does nothing to meet that objective.

Logical strength

The strongest argument is that which leads logically and inevitably from given points to its stated conclusion. Here the given points are the evidence and the law. The evidence leads to the facts. Comparison of the facts with the law determines whether its requirements have been met. If they have, one result follows. If they have not, the result is different.

Were it really that simple, industrial tribunals would not be necessary. A first-generation computer, given the evidence and the law, could trace the path which logic dictated and spew out the inevitable result. In practice few things are as straightforwardly black-and-white as that analysis requires. Tribunals have to make judgements between shades of grey: whether this is more white or more black than that, whether adding this amount of white to that amount of black produces something that is nearer black than white. Some elements of that judgement cannot be other than purely subjective: later generations of computers may be able to distinguish between shades of grey, but that was only an illustration.

The ideal, of an argument that leads logically and inevitably from the evidence and the law to the conclusion desired by the respondent, may not be attainable, but it remains what the presenter should aim for. That logic does not determine an answer does not mean that it does not contribute substantially to its determination. Some subjective judgement is unavoidable, but the greater the area which can be logically covered, the smaller the area that is left in which the answer could go either way, depending on who is making the decision. Subjective decisions may anyway be influenced by the logic of a presentation's argument. That points A, B, C and D have been logically proved by a respondent may lead a tribunal to accept more readily that the respondent's assertion in relation to point E is correct, even though it has not been logically proved.

The address to the tribunal should therefore attempt to forge any necessary logical links between evidence and facts, between the words of the statute and the legal interpretation being proposed, and between facts and law. Which links actually need to be forged depends, as discussed above, on what has happened at the hearing. But which links *may* need to be forged should be clear when the address is being prepared. Forging each link involves explaining how acceptance of this point and this point leads to that point. 'The evidence of witness A must be preferred to the conflicting evidence of witness B because A was there and B was not': 'because' is the crucial word.

In analytical terms the acceptance that, first, the weight of evidence can be affected by directness and, second, that B's evidence is less direct than A's leads to the conclusion that A's evidence has more weight. The first term – that weight of evidence can be affected by directness – was implied by the word 'because' rather than being expressly stated. To take an argument to unnecessary depths of analytical detail is as irrelevant as to cover points which have no bearing on the case. Where the necessary implication is likely to be understood and accepted the first term will often be 'taken as read', but it is still there, and the conclusion depends upon its acceptance. Where there is any likelihood of it being misunderstood or rejected it needs to be articulated and its effect, in conjunction with the second term, demonstrated. The end of the necessary path of analysis has been reached when it can confidently be said that the applicant, the tribunal and the respondent would each, in response to a statement in the form '. . . because . . .', not ask 'Why?' The end of the path that is possible has been reached when, if the respondent is asked 'Why?' in response to a statement in that form, there is no answer other than 'Because I say so.' Presenters with young children will recognise this point.

Arguing in the alternative

As a presenter does not know before the hearing precisely what evidence will be given or what arguments may be advanced by the other party, preparation may, besides including arguments which may simply be discarded if they prove unnecessary, include alternative arguments. If things go this way, this argument will be used; if they go a different way, that other argument will take its place. But the hearing, although it may remove uncertainties about precisely what evidence is given and precisely what arguments the applicant is relying on, does not remove all uncertainties. Some remain until the decision is given. If, in the light of what takes place at the hearing, the one decision which the respondent desires could be achieved in more than one way, the address to the tribunal needs to advance the most persuasive case possible in relation to each of those ways. That a respondent has argued strongly that the applicant was not dismissed does not mean that the respondent cannot go on to argue just as strongly that, if the applicant was dismissed, the dismissal was not unfair. Nor does advancing the second weaken the first, or the existence of the first argument weaken the second.

Similarly, of the range of decisions which are open to a tribunal, the respondent may regard one as most desirable and a second, although not as desirable as the first, as far more desirable than the third. In those circumstances the address to the tribunal should also advance both the alternative arguments. 'The dismissal was not unfair but, if it was, the compensation should be reduced to nil because . . .' Again, each of the arguments should be advanced as strongly as possible. The presenter does not need to, nor should, choose between them. There is, in theory, one 'right' answer. If one of two or more arguments advanced by the respondent is accepted that is because it is the 'right' one and not because it happens to be the one the respondent prefers. Advancing an argument less strongly because it leads to a less desirable solution does nothing to increase the strength of the argument on which the more desirable solution has been sought. All it does is make it less likely that, if the most desirable solution is not forthcoming, the second best solution will be.

Key points

The presenter should:

- Be in tactical control of the case, within the strategy set by the action plan.
- Remember the interaction of the conciliation and decision systems.
- Use 'truth', 'principle' and 'objectivity' to serve the respondent's cause.
- Work backwards from objectives to argument to facts to evidence.
- Prepare an address to the tribunal covering all foreseeable developments, in a form which will aid oral presentation.
- Present an address to the tribunal which

Is relevant in the light of what happens at the hearing.
Has a coherent structure.
Is clear and simple to understand.
Concentrates on logical argument.
Where necessary, argues alternatives.

Chapter 11
Witnesses

Having identified the facts that need to be proved and the evidence which will be required to prove them, the presenter must decide how that evidence is to be put before the tribunal. Some cases require only documentary evidence, which is the subject of the next chapter. Most require the calling of at least one witness.

Whom to call

It is important to remember that that is the proper sequence of decision-making. A witness is called because particular evidence is needed. The evidence to be given should not be determined by which witness is called. Once called, though, the other party or the tribunal may ask a witness to give evidence other than that for which the witness was called. So the decision on which witnesses to call must take account not only of what evidence the presenter's case needs to support it but also of the totality of the evidence relevant to the case which the witnesses could give. Some of it will be of value to the presenter's case; if it were not, the witness would not be called. A lot of it will be neutral. Some of it may be damaging. Any disadvantage which exposure of the damaging evidence may cause has to be balanced against the need for the valuable evidence. The balance of advantage will sometimes lie in forgoing the best evidence on an important fact to avoid the risks that calling a particular witness might involve. More often the balance will lie the other way. A witness's evidence contains nothing damaging; its positive effect is much greater than any negative effect it might have; or, although it has the potential to be damaging, the likelihood of the damaging questions being asked is considered small enough to be worth the risk.

A proof of evidence

In order to make decisions on these matters the presenter needs to know the witness's story in all areas into which the hearing may probe or stray. The medium through which this is achieved is the 'proof of evidence'. In some legal circumstances the term may be used as a term of art, with specific connotations as to content and form. Here it simply means any written statement of what a witness would say, if asked the relevant questions, at a tribunal hearing. It need not be signed, although often it will be. It may be a full textual narrative or consist of a series of short headline statements. It may have been written out by the witness personally. Equally, it may have been prepared by the initial investigator, by the presenter or even by someone else in the light of discussion or interview with the witness. What is important is that it should accurately reflect what the witness genuinely remembers, 'warts and all'. Its purpose is not only to confirm the evidence which is helpful to the respondent's case but also to forewarn the presenter of any pitfalls. If they are known about in advance steps can be taken to avoid them or to deal with them. Hiding them from the presenter will not guarantee that they are not exposed in the hearing, by the presenter stumbling unaware into them as much as by the applicant or the tribunal expressly seeking them. By then it may be too late to repair any damage.

So it is important where a proof is not drafted personally by a witness that the witness fully understands that whoever has drafted it is not, by doing so, suggesting what the witness ought to be saying. The draft is no more than an attempt by the drafter to reflect what the witness has already said. If it is wrong, or the witness feels uncomfortable with it in any respect, it must be changed so that, in its final version and whoever physically prepared it, the witness wholeheartedly accepts it as his or her own.

What will often happen in practice is that the person who conducts the initial investigation will make notes during any interviews and the notes will form the basis from which proofs of evidence are drafted. This is particularly likely where the investigator and presenter are the same person. There may be a time lapse between the note-taking and the drafting of the proofs. Proofs will be needed only if the case proceeds to a hearing. Any time and effort involved in preparing them will be wasted if withdrawal of the case can be achieved. As with other preparatory work, it is sensible to delay the drafting and agreeing of proofs until a real likelihood of the need for them becomes apparent. They do, however, contribute to other preparatory work and so cannot be left until the day before the hearing.

Examination

Preparation

Knowing what evidence is needed and what evidence the chosen witnesses can give, the presenter needs to prepare to match the two. As with the address to the tribunal, the physical form of any such preparation must be that with which the presenter will personally be most comfortable. However it is achieved in physical terms, what the presenter needs is some means of checking that all necessary points in a witness's evidence are covered in a hearing in the amount of detail and with the weight that the address to the tribunal relies on. The questioning of witnesses is an interactive process, and it can be counterproductive to attempt to pre-programme such a process in too much detail. A particular reaction may differ in content or form from that which was expected and make subsequent steps in the planned programme inappropriate. That the evidence *is* given is more important than *when*, during the total time the witness is at the witness table, it is given. The precise form in which the evidence is given matters only if it affects its weight. Even so, besides some means of checking what points need to be covered, a presenter will often find it useful to consider the order in which points should be tackled and even in some instances the precise form of particular questions to be asked.

Most witnesses, however confident they appear and profess to be, find giving evidence somewhat daunting. They need time to settle down in the unaccustomed atmosphere not only of the industrial tribunal but also and specifically of the witness table itself. To give them time to do so, a presenter may plan to deal first with relatively unimportant matters or those with which the witness is most familiar and confident, even if they would not be tackled first under a strictly chronological approach. A presenter may know that one witness is likely to be garrulous, and so plan to ask abrupt and restrictive questions, whereas another may be taciturn and need to be drawn out with a more leisurely and open approach. A presenter might be concerned about inadvertently leading witnesses on points where it is vital that their evidence has maximum weight. If so, the precise wording of questions which do not lead in the areas of concern might be worked out in advance.

Decisions on matters like these mean that the presenter needs to take account not only of what the witness will say but also of how the witness is likely to say it. It is not the written proof that is giving the evidence: it is the witness as a person. Where a tribunal case is being handled in-house the presenter is likely to have some personal knowledge of the witness anyway, but it is still valuable if they meet specifically to establish their respective roles in the forthcoming hearing and to go through the witness's evidence. It is worth stressing again that it should be no purpose of any such meeting to suggest what the witness's evidence should be. Its purpose should be to clarify and confirm what the witness's own story is and to explain what is likely to happen at the hearing – the physical layout, the general procedure, the order of questioning, and so on. The witness may be given general advice: 'Short and simple answers are better than long and complex ones,' 'If you don't know, say so,' 'Answer the question. Leave any argument to me,' 'The other party is likely to ask about so-and-so.' But there should be no rehearsal in the sense of the witness being taken through the series of questions which the presenter intends to ask and the answers which the witness is expected to give. It is usually apparent when a witness's evidence is really a dramatic duologue, and it detracts considerably from its weight. It also means that the witness has had no practice, when the other party starts to ask questions, in giving unrehearsed evidence.

Questions and answers

The general rule is that each question should be as short and as simply phrased as possible, and that it should seek an answer which is short and simple. The presenter knows the witness and will adapt the style and approach accordingly. Usually the first evidence will be brought out point by point, each point by one simple question and one simple answer. As the process of questioning proceeds, and depending on how important to the presenter's case a particular point is, and how strongly it is likely to be disputed, the level of generality of the questions may be changed.

There are some witnesses who may be relied on to cover all the relevant ground and none that is irrelevant, clearly and in all necessary detail, in response to one simple question: 'What happened?' They are the exceptions. Even with them the presenter will probably need to ask some more detailed questions. There are likely to be some points, of the evidence or of the facts to which it relates, that are particularly important and need highlighting. This is best achieved by the presenter asking specific questions to highlight them rather than the witness voluntarily placing particular emphasis on them. The witness is a witness as to fact and is more likely to be believed if seen to be restricted to that role rather than appearing to be trying, from the witness table, to 'make a case'. The presenter is the one who is 'making the case'. The presenter has a duty, and will be expected, to take the 'neutral' evidence which a witness has given and show how it serves a partisan cause.

At the hearing the presenter is in control of the questioning of the witness, subject to any directions or rulings by the tribunal. The presenter decides what questions to ask, in what form, and in what order. The witness is not there to volunteer information, or to answer questions which are not asked, or to debate the issues with the presenter or with the tribunal. In so far as the witness oath requires 'the whole truth' it is for the presenters and the tribunal to decide the areas in which 'the whole truth' lies and not for the witness to decide which points are important and must be covered in evidence. If by specifically responding to selective questioning by one representative a witness is led to give an incomplete and therefore misleading picture, it is the job of the other presenter or the tribunal to correct that by asking for amplification. That is the theory. In practice, of course, many witnesses do feel they have a particular story to tell and will try to tell it whatever questions they are asked. Under cross-examination, particularly, witnesses will often avoid direct questions, answering 'Yes, *but* . . .' or 'No, *but* . . .' or 'Perhaps . . .' or 'It's not that simple . . .' instead of 'Yes,' or 'No,' or 'I don't know.'

What the presenter has to do here is judge the balance of advantage between interrupting and letting the witness amplify the specific reply the question was seeking. With a party's own witness a courteous interruption is sometimes best, particularly if the evidence being given is of little relevance to the case. Often there is not much to be gained and possibly something to be lost by a presenter trying to stop a witness answering as fully as s/he wishes. If one side's presenter attempts to stop a witness qualifying an answer by interrupting, it highlights the fact that the witness has more to say on the point at issue and invites the other party or the tribunal to explore the highlighted area at a subsequent stage in the witness's evidence. But if a witness does respond 'at large' to specific questions the presenter should ensure that the specific answer required has been given. This may have been done as part of the general answer which has already been given. In that case the witness might be asked to identify the relevant part, or the specific question may need to be asked again.

If a specific question has been asked it is likely that it was because a specific answer was needed. This will not invariably be so. The presenter has identified some points as of crucial importance to the argument that will be put in the address to the tribunal. There may be many; often there will be very few. That a point is not crucial does not make it irrelevant. Although at the end of the day a case may turn, in factual terms, on how one or two disputed facts are decided, it does not mean that those facts can be studied in isolation. They have to be looked at in context. The context will, indeed, determine which are the crucial facts. The tribunal will therefore expect the evidence as a whole to give a full picture of the events which gave rise to the case. Such a full picture will not need to be given by each witness in turn. If a part of the overall picture has been painted by one witness and it is not disputed, then there is no need for it to be gone over again by another (although some repetition may be necessary to put the second witness's own evidence into context). Where the purpose of a question, although asked in a specific form, was really to fill in the general background there may be no need to insist on it being answered specifically.

Making notes

The presenter's preparation has to be based on evidence which it is antici-pated that witnesses will give – with perhaps contingency plans for variations which it is thought may occur. Part of the presenter's job in questioning witnesses is to try to elicit from them the evidence which was anticipated and on which the preparation was based. But it is important that the presentation rests ultimately on the evidence which has actually been given, not on what the presenter thought beforehand would be given. This makes it important for the presenter to pay careful attention to what is actually said: first, to check that it accords with what was expected and, if it does not, to see whether by further questioning it can be made to; second, where it does not so accord and cannot be made to, so that the presentation can be adjusted as necessary. This is one reason why there is tremendous benefit in a presenter making notes of evidence as it is actually given. A presenter is much more likely to detect differences between expectation and actuality by writing down the words actually used by witnesses than by just listening to them or by ticking off a pre-written checklist of points.

Of course it is unrealistic to expect a presenter to make a verbatim record of all the evidence given by all the witnesses, particularly at the same time as assessing what is said, deciding what lines of questioning to pursue and framing individual questions. But note-taking to that extent is not what is required. Much of what is said, even by a hostile witness, will not be particularly contentious and/or will not be particularly relevant to the case the presenter is putting forward. For such evidence a cryptic note of its gist is sufficient. But some points are recognisably crucial. It is in respect of such points that as detailed and accurate a note as possible needs to be made.

Tribunal proceedings are not recorded. No shorthand note is taken. But the legally qualified chair is under a duty to make a note of the evidence given and may be required, in some appeal cases, to produce that note. This is one factor which affects the pace at which tribunal hearings are conducted. If things are happening too fast for adequate notes to be taken a request will be made that they should be slowed down. By dint of long practice legally qualified chairs are skilled at note-taking; many have devised personal shorthand or abbreviation systems. But the fact that they are taking notes should give the presenter some time to do so, on particularly important points, and will mean that the tribunal will look reasonably sympathetically at pauses in the process of questioning witnesses if it is clear that the pauses are caused by the presenter making a note of precisely what has been said.

Coming up to proof

When a presenter calls a witness the presenter knows from the proof of evidence what the witness has previously said about particular issues. A witness's recollection of an incident or event has been recounted in the proof. The presenter is now asking that the witness should recall the incident or event again. The presenter expects and hopes that it will be recounted in the same way. It is on the basis of how it was recounted in the proof that decisions were made about how to respond to the originating application and that the presenter has prepared the presentation for the hearing. But the evidence which has to be given is not about the proof. The question is not 'What did you say when you were previously asked what happened on such-and-such occasion?' but 'What happened on such-and-such occasion?'

The proof of evidence will be available to the presenter who is asking the questions but not to the witness who is answering them. The witness will probably have re-read it shortly beforehand to refresh his or her memory, but the tribunal will not normally allow a witness to refer to a proof or witness statement or notes whilst actually giving evidence. In some cases this will make no difference. The witness is clear and firm about what happened, and whenever and in whatever circumstances and in whatever form questions are asked about it they will always elicit the same replies. Other witnesses may react differently when answering questions in a tribunal from how they did when answering the questions of a colleague investigating a case or when preparing a proof of evidence. What was remembered in a witness's own workplace by dint of reference to a diary or looking through a file may be forgotten or remembered differently in a tribunal.

One thing a presenter can do where it seems that a witness may give oral evidence less clear and firm than it was in the proof is attempt to reproduce, at the hearing, some of the conditions under which the proof was composed. If there is a diary or there are papers on a file which jogged the witness's memory at the initial investigation or when the proof was being prepared, then thought should be given to putting that diary or those papers in as evidence. It may not be appropriate to do so. They may not be contemporaneous notes but may have been specifically prepared as memory-joggers for the initial investigation, or they may contain more that is harmful than is helpful. But the prohibition is on a witness referring to a proof when giving evidence. It does not extend to reference to any document which has been put in evidence.

In this situation, but more generally as well, besides being of value for their own evidential weight documents can be valuable as providing prompts and *aide-mémoires* for witnesses. It is not up to the witness, in answering questions, to root through the documents to see whether they contain the 'right' answer or some guidance as to what the 'right' answer might be. But it is open to a presenter to say, 'Will you now have a look at page 13 in the bundle?' 'Did you write that letter?' or 'Were you at the meeting that that memo mentions?' and then to ask 'What happened to cause that letter to be written?' or 'What happened at that meeting?'

How far this technique can be taken depends on what documents are in evidence. The reciprocal is that the decision about what documents should be put in evidence ought to take account of their value not only in direct terms but also as signposts for the giving of oral evidence.

How far the technique should be taken depends on how necessary it is. Where a presenter believes that a witness will 'come up to proof' without being led through the bundle of documents it will usually be quicker and more effective to elicit the evidence by a few open-ended questions – 'What happened next?' 'Then what happened?' 'Then what did you do?' – and referring the witness to corroborative or relevant documents in response to the replies. Where a presenter fears that such an open-ended approach is likely to produce irrelevant or confused answers, or even to cause a witness to say things which may contradict the proof of evidence, using documentary evidence as a framework for questioning can assist in ensuring that the evidence which is given is that on which the presenter's case relies. It is often easier than attempting, without any such framework, to construct the series of more detailed but non-leading questions which might otherwise be required to deal with the situation.

Leading a witness

It is clear that this approach involves leading the witness. It has been repeatedly stressed that no party should lead its own witness. Is there not some inconsistency here? First, although the presenter should not lead a witness in respect of the substance of the evidence which is given, it is expressly the presenter's function to lead the witness through the process of giving evidence. Second, the prohibition on leading is not formal, or absolute. There is nothing wrong, and it will save a lot of everyone's time, if non-contentious points are brought out by leading questions: 'Was that on such-and-such a date?' where the date is not disputed but it is important to establish what it was so that the chronological development of events can be seen, or 'Did you write to him about it?' when the letter bearing the witness's signature is in evidence before the tribunal. It is on important issues of fact which have been or may be challenged that a presenter should try to avoid leading the witness. Third, the reason for not leading a witness in contentious areas is that, as we have already seen, to do so is likely to reduce the weight of the evidence that is given. A balance has to be struck. If the only real options appear to be the 'wrong' evidence with more weight or the 'right' evidence with less weight the latter may be better. Fourth, faced with that sort of option, the less blatant any leading is the less likely it is to reduce the evidence's weight. There is less likelihood that leading by reference to a document will reduce the weight of the evidence than there is that a straightforward leading question will. It is usually possible to find some reason, other than just to point to the desirability of a particular answer, for such a reference to be made.

As a rule of thumb (although not an exhaustive test) any question which can be answered by 'yes' or 'no' is a leading question. Questions which ask 'who?', 'what?', 'where?' or 'when?' are unlikely to lead. 'How?' and 'why?' are also unlikely to lead: they are, however, concerned with causation. Where the link between what happened and 'how' or 'why' it happened is nothing more than the operation of some physical or mechanical law – for instance, the bottle fell over because it was tilted beyond its centre of gravity – asking such questions does not invite expressions of opinion. But when human reactions and motivation are involved – perhaps those of the witnesses themselves – simply asking 'how' and 'why' questions may lead to too much opinion and too little fact, larded with a considerable amount of self-justification.

Facts and opinions

Some witnesses' thought processes and opinions at the time decisions in question were made can be important facts and, ultimately, it may be necessary for such witnesses to say in their own words how and why the decisions were reached. But the tests which a tribunal will be applying in these areas are concerned with the physical and mental processes which led to the making of the decision; with the facts or factors which contributed to the making of the decision, and with whether inferences which were drawn from those facts and factors were validly drawn. It will often be better for such issues to be approached at first by looking at the harder facts of what was done and what was taken into account rather than by immediately asking how or why a particular decision was reached or a particular view formed. Thus a witness might be asked at large 'What factors did you have in mind when deciding what to do in this case?' or, where a presenter judges that a more detailed approach will be more likely to produce the 'right' answers, taken step by step through the process by which the factors were identified. 'What questions did you ask?' 'What did this person say?' 'What did that person say?' 'What papers did you read?' 'What did each of them say?' Then, only after the hard facts have been identified, the witness may be asked 'What conclusion did you reach?' and 'Why?' or 'How did you balance this against that?'

To facilitate such a process the presenter may link each succeeding question with the answer to the last or to one or more earlier questions by the form of the question – 'What did you say in response to that?' or 'What happened next?' – or by prefacing the question with some comment: 'You have already said that you took account of A and B and C. What else did you have in mind?' Although this technique can give a useful structure to questioning and help to put a witness at ease, it needs to be used with caution. It can sometimes amount to leading the witness to an extent which would downgrade the value of the reply. And where any prefacing comment is more than a few words it can confuse rather than reassure the witness.

Cross-examination

Preparation

The respondent's presenter's questioning of the applicant's and the respondent's witnesses is in many respects similar, and much of what is said above applies in 'cross-examination' (questioning the other party's witnesses) as much as in 'examination in chief' (questioning one's own). So, for instance, the prohibition on leading witnesses does not apply to cross-examination. Some leading questions are probably inevitable, particularly given the need to put opposing evidence to the witness. But it remains true that the weight given to a witness's evidence will be affected by how that evidence is elicited. A respondent's presenter should try, where possible, to put non-leading questions to the applicant's witnesses, too.

One important difference is that the respondent's presenter knows from the proofs of evidence how the respondent's own witnesses are likely to answer any questions that they may be asked, whereas when the respondent's presenter asks a question of an applicant's witness there can be far less confidence about what the answer will be. Some such questions have to be asked, if what the witness has said in evidence has been or is likely to be directly challenged by the evidence of other witnesses. But there are other such questions which do not have to be asked. If such a question is asked and the 'right' answer is given, it may provide valuable support for the respondent's case. If it is asked and the 'wrong' answer is given, it could be more damaging to the respondent's case than if the question had not been asked at all. It can be a difficult judgement to make, and it will not always be correctly made, but what should guide the presenter is the question 'Will asking the question be more, or less, likely to lead to the decision I am seeking?'

Another difference is that, not knowing in detail what the applicant's witnesses will say (or perhaps even who they will be), the presenter cannot prepare in the same level of detail for cross-examination as for examination. What the presenter can do beforehand is identify the areas in which the evidence is likely to be of vital importance and prepare, if it proves necessary in the light of the evidence they actually give, to cross-examine the applicant's witnesses in those areas. If the applicant's pleadings expressly or by necessary implication allege facts that the respondent needs to disprove, there will have to be evidence of those facts, and that evidence will have to be challenged, however and by whomever it may be given. If the applicant's pleadings expressly or by implication deny facts on which the respondent is relying, the applicant will have to bring evidence to contradict what the respondent puts forward, and that in turn will have to be challenged by the respondent.

Whether to cross-examine

At the hearing, in the areas thus identified, the presenter knows what facts have to be established to provide the necessary basis for the overall case which is to be argued to the tribunal and knows the evidence about those facts that has been or will be given by the respondent's witnesses. Having heard an applicant's witness giving evidence in chief, the respondent's presenter can decide whether any, and if so what, points in that evidence may lead the tribunal to decide against the respondent on crucial factual issues. If there is none there is no need to cross-examine. Any temptation to subject an applicant's witnesses to questioning just 'because they are there' should be avoided. Even when it is genuinely believed that an applicant's witness has given incorrect evidence there is no value in challenging it if total acceptance of that evidence by the tribunal will do no harm to the respondent's case.

That general statement needs two provisos. Witnesses sometimes make statements which allege or imply conduct – of a company or by an individual – so outrageous that they require immediate rebuttal even though they have no relevance to the case being heard. If they are not rebutted they may, although not affecting the outcome of the case, affect the reputation of the person against whom the allegation is made, generally or particularly among those who are following the case – the respondent's other employees, for instance. The respondent's presenter may feel bound to cross-examine an applicant's witness simply so as to challenge a statement of this nature. Where that does happen, particularly if it provides the only reason for cross-examination, the issue should be dealt with as shortly and sharply as possible: 'I put it to you that what you have said is totally false/without foundation.' In this way the respondent's rebuttal becomes part of the evidential record. That the point, although being formally rebutted, was not further pursued because it was seen as irrelevant can be explained during the address to the tribunal.

The second situation in which a respondent's presenter may wish to cross-examine an applicant's witness, even though the witness' evidence has done no harm to the respondent's substantive case, is where the witness has by implication attacked the reliability of another witness on whose evidence the respondent is relying. Imagine that A. has given evidence as to X and Y. X is a crucial point, Y is not. B. gives evidence as to Y and Z. Z is a crucial point on which the respondent accepts B.'s evidence. B.'s evidence about Y contradicts that given by A. As Y is not crucial, there is no substantive need for the respondent's presenter to challenge B.'s evidence about it. But accepting that B.'s evidence on that point is correct means that A.'s evidence on that point must have been wrong. Of itself, that does not matter. What does matter is the suspicion it raises that if A.'s evidence was wrong on point Y it may also be wrong with respect to point X. So, although whichever way point Y is decided by the tribunal will not affect the outcome of the case, the respondent's presenter may need to challenge B.'s evidence about it. Not in order directly to establish that Y happened as A., rather than as B., described it but with the more general purpose of protecting the credibility of A.

The need to put opposing evidence

There are two main ways in which a witness's evidence can be weakened by the other party. One is by setting against it contradictory evidence, from other witnesses or in documents. The other is to show that the witness's evidence is of itself wrong, or more likely than not to be wrong. These approaches are not mutually exclusive. Simply getting C. to tell a different story from D. does not mean that C.'s story will be preferred to D.'s. C.'s evidence has to be, as well, more credible than D.'s. Simply showing that a witness's evidence seems flawed – because of internal inconsistencies, sheer improbability or obvious bias – will not necessarily lead to its rejection: there must be a more believable alternative on offer.

Where the evidence about a relevant and important fact given by an applicant's witness conflicts with that of a respondent's witnesses or documents the respondent's presenter must draw that conflict to the attention of the applicant's witness. There are two reasons. First, it helps to meet the respondent's aim of weakening the applicant's evidence by setting the contrary evidence against it. Second, it recognises the broader aim of the tribunal. The respondent's presenter's objective is to present a particular case, not to search at large for the 'truth'. The tribunal, on the other hand, is seeking 'the truth', and if any witness is able to give evidence about a point touched upon by another witness it will expect to be able to compare their stories and test them against each other where they differ.

Witness A. tells the tribunal that 'X happened'; witness B. was present on the same occasion. Unless witness B. denies to the tribunal that 'X happened' it will be bound to hold that X did happen. Where one party's witnesses have already all given their evidence the other party's witnesses, unless they were excluded from or absent during the earlier part of the hearing, will have heard what they had to say by the time they come to give their own evidence. B. will have heard A. say that 'X happened'. If B. agrees with A.'s version of events, B.'s evidence need not cover the point again or, if it does, it will not conflict with what A. has said. But if B. disagrees with what A. has said, B.'s evidence will differ from what A. has said: B. is effectively saying that A. is wrong. A. has already given evidence and will have no opportunity, other than by being recalled, to react to that challenge. B.'s differing version will need to be outlined, even though B. has not yet given the evidence concerned, during cross-examination so that A. has a chance to react to it.

A. may, often will, do no more than repeat that 'X did happen', which may appear to do little to further the presenter's aims of weakening A.'s evidence. But if A. has not been given the opportunity expressly to defend the evidence by being told when it was being given that it would be challenged at a later stage in the proceedings, the tribunal will be more inclined to accept it as correct, both when it was given and when arriving at its findings. That it was challenged to A.'s face and at the time when it was given will, even if the challenge was rebutted by a straightforward rejection, put the tribunal on warning that the question has not been settled just by A.'s evidence and ensure that it keeps an open mind until B.'s evidence has been given. And A. may say, 'Now you mention it, I remember more clearly. In fact what happened was Y.'

An indirect approach

The more abruptly and directly a witness's evidence is challenged the more the witness will be inclined to take an entrenched position and simply repeat that it is correct. Sometimes no other approach is available. But where a less direct approach is available it may be more productive.

Imagine that A., an applicant, has said in evidence that s/he was not aware that particular conduct would lead to dismissal. The respondent admits that there is no written warning addressed to the applicant or any express statement in the works rules, but argues that A. nevertheless must have known the offence concerned was 'dismissable' because it had been discussed in a staff meeting and it was common knowledge that B., another employee, had been dismissed for it. If A. is immediately asked at the start of cross-examination, 'Were you aware of this?' the answer is likely to be 'No.' That answer having been given, it is likely to colour all subsequent replies on related issues. But if the first questions are about the meeting, A. may acknowledge having been at the meeting; then that the subject may have been touched upon during it; then that words might have been used which could have been understood as indicating that such conduct would not be tolerated. Or, if first asked about

B., A. may indicate awareness of the incident, and of what B. had done, and of what the consequence had been. If A.'s earlier answers are as suggested, it will be much harder for A. – if ultimately asked 'Were you aware of this?' – to answer, simply, 'No.'

It needs to be remembered that cross-examination is concerned with adducing and testing evidence rather than with advancing argument. What the respondent's presenter is attempting to do in the process described above is to get witness A. to make some statements which can be shown to weaken others. The purpose of doing so is to convince the tribunal that A.'s evidence is wrong on the crucial point, not to convince A. that it is wrong. If A. admits that it is wrong, so much the better, but that is not essential. It may sometimes be better to stop short of directly asking whether, in the light of what has been said in cross-examination, A. now wishes to retract the statement made in examination in chief. Where it seems likely that A. will retract the statement the question should be asked. It should also be asked if, whatever A. now says, that the earlier answer is wrong will remain clear. Where it may be dangerous to ask it is where the process has produced material which the respondent's presenter can use in the address to the tribunal to cast doubt on A.'s earlier evidence but where further questioning or highlighting of the issue might produce, from the witness, explanations of any apparent inconsistencies on which the presenter's argument will need to rely. The worst sin in cross-examination is to ask one question too many. That is less true in industrial tribunals, whose members are more awake to the tricks of the advocate's trade than juries are, but it remains a useful motto.

Imagine that A.'s own words at one point in giving evidence were 'I did not know that the offence was regarded so seriously as to warrant dismissal' and at another point 'I thought I would not be dismissed because of my long service and excellent performance.' How far length of service and excellence of performance should influence a dismissal decision is a relevant consideration. But the point at issue here is not that. It is whether A. knew the offence was 'dismissable'. On that issue the two statements are, on the face of it, inconsistent. The former implies that dismissal is inappropriate because the offence was not, when it was committed, known to be sufficiently serious. In the latter the implication is that, although dismissal is known to be generally appropriate to an offence of the seriousness concerned, it should not occur here because of the particular circumstances. The statements can be reconciled by A. explaining that 'It was not until I learned, at the disciplinary interview, that the offence was regarded as dismissable that I thought I would not be dismissed because of my long service and excellent performance.' For the respondent's presenter to push the point too far during cross-examination, rather than simply highlighting the statements to be made use of later in argument, is tantamount to inviting A. to offer that easy explanation – whether it is true or not.

Re-examination

After cross-examination the party calling the witness has a chance to ask further questions – to 're-examine'. The tribunal may ask questions before or after any re-examination. If it is after, and any new points are raised, the tribunal should give the parties a further opportunity to cross-examine or re-examine on, but only on, the new points. Re-examination is not intended to bring in new evidence but to clarify any evidence which has already been given. If cross-examination has not left any issues which require clarification, re-examination is not necessary. Simply getting a witness to repeat what has been said before adds nothing and wastes time. Re-examination is necessary where a witness has been encouraged by leading questions to adopt phraseology which may be ambiguous or apparently inconsistent with some other evidence or has been led by restrictive and selective questioning into giving only a misleading part of the whole story on the issue concerned.

Detailed preparation for re-examination is even less possible than it is for cross-examination. All the presenter can do is keep firmly in mind what it is that has to be proved and that it will be proved by weighing all the evidence. And remember that the applicant's presenter will be trying, during cross-examination, to do the same in relation to the respondent's witnesses as the respondent's presenter will try, during cross-examination, to do in relation to the applicant's. For a presenter to ask 'How, if I were on the other side, would I attack this witness?' will often provide the best guide to any defence that can be prepared.

Key points

A presenter should:

- Have a proof of evidence for each potential witness.
- Decide what witnesses to call by identifying evidence which is needed, not vice versa, and by balancing the advantages and disadvantages of calling each witness.
- Prepare a plan for each witness's examination, identifying the essential evidence, and make sure each point is covered.
- Adapt a style of questioning to suit the witness and the circumstances.
- Make detailed notes of important evidence.
- Use documentary evidence as an aid to questioning.

- Avoid leading witnesses on important points.
- Seek facts, not opinions.
- Cross-examine only where necessary.
- Put opposing evidence to the other side's witnesses.
- Prefer demonstration of inconsistencies to direct challenges.
- Know when to stop cross-examining.
- Use re-examination to clarify previous evidence, not to introduce new evidence or simply repeat previous evidence.

Chapter 12
Documents

Paper plays an extremely important part in tribunal proceedings. It can be divided into five main sorts (besides any personal papers which the presenter may use as an aid to presentation).

Five sorts of paper

There are papers which had an existence independently of the proceedings and which are now relied on by either or both parties as showing that 'this was said' or 'that happened'. They may include, for example, letters offering an appointment or giving a warning, written particulars of terms of employment, an advertisement or notice, notes or minutes of a meeting, time sheets or attendance records, a doctor's report, and so on. The term *documentary evidence* will be used to distinguish such papers from the other sorts.

Written evidence as the term is used here is different. Whilst it is still relied upon by a party as showing that 'this was said' or 'that happened', it was brought into being for that specific purpose. It had no existence independently of the proceedings. It may include a witness statement or affidavit (that is, a sworn statement); an agreed statement of facts, in a case, for instance, where the facts are not disputed but the law is, and the parties have agreed and the tribunal has directed that there is no need for witnesses to be called; a schedule or summary of relevant factual information, such as might be used, rather than large numbers of individual records being produced, to show comparative qualifications of different job applicants where race or sex discrimination is being alleged, or of sickness absence where a dismissal is being challenged as unfair; and so on.

Representations in writing are also bought into being for the specific purpose of the proceedings, but for a broader purpose. They are concerned not just to establish that 'this was said' or 'that happened' but to argue that the case, or a particular substantive or procedural point within it, should be decided in this way or in that. They thus cover the 'pleadings' – the originating application, the notice of appearance, answers giving further particulars, etc. A party may decide to write to the tribunal, setting out the case rather than attending a hearing; if complex legal

points are involved parties may submit written 'skeleton arguments' outlining the logical structure of the case that they intend to present; and so
on.

Legal sources set out the substantive and procedural rules which the
tribunal has to apply. The term obviously covers both the legislation –
statutes, orders, regulations, directives – and the case law – which may
be included in law reports such as *Industrial Relations Law Reports* or
Industrial Cases Reports or may be only in transcripts of unreported
decisions – by which the tribunal is (or it is argued that it is) bound. But
the term is used here to cover also such other written material as the tribunal is entitled (or a party may attempt to persuade a tribunal) to use in
reaching its decisions on points of law. It may include a code of practice,
a parliamentary paper or report of parliamentary proceedings, a legal
textbook or commentary, a summary of a case in a digest such as the
Industrial Relations Legal Information Bulletin or the Incomes Data
Services *IDS Briefs*, and so on.

Finally, there are *decisions*. The case law just referred to consists of
decisions, but the term is used here not in that more general sense. It
applies here specifically to decisions made by a tribunal in the context of
and for the purpose of the particular case. Ultimately the result of tribunal proceedings will be a written decision. But well before that stage
has been reached other decisions will often have been made by the tribunal – granting orders for discovery or further particulars, about
whether there should be a single or a split hearing, giving an opinion in
the light of a pre-hearing assessment – each of which will have resulted
in at least one piece of paper. Those will be relevant to and may need to
be referred to during the course of a tribunal hearing.

The terms used above are terms of convenience, not terms of art. It is
not always clear whether a particular document falls into one category or
another. 'Representations in writing' will often include 'written evidence' in that they rely on facts which are stated nowhere else and of
which the only *evidence*, therefore, is what the *representations* say. An
advocate who argues that a textbook is a 'legal source', of at least persuasive authority, may find that argument rejected and so treat the textbook instead as 'written evidence' of how informed legal thinkers view
the issue in point and/or adopt it as expressing, in 'representations in
writing', the argument which is being advanced. Generally, nothing turns
on the terminology.

Representations in writing and the seven-day rule

The one ostensible exception to this is that, under rule 7(3):

> if a party shall desire to submit representations in writing for consideration by a tribunal at the hearing of the originating application that party shall present such representations to the Secretary of the Tribunals not less than seven days before the hearing and shall at the same time send a copy to the other party or parties.

In practice this rule operates not so much to exclude 'representations in writing' as defined above, on the grounds that the seven-day rule has not been complied with, as to allow 'written evidence' to be introduced without challenge as to its admissibility by being classified as, or included with, 'representations in writing', which are submitted at least seven days beforehand.

Although, under rule 8(1), a tribunal

> shall not be bound by any enactment or rule of law relating to the admissibility of evidence in proceedings before the courts of law

it retains the discretion to refuse to admit evidence if it views its weight as so low as to make it virtually worthless. It is not *bound* to reject a written statement from a witness in favour of the witness being called to give oral evidence, as may be the case in other courts of law, but it *may* do so. Where at a hearing a party attempts to introduce such a statement, the other party may object and/or the tribunal, of its own motion, may rule that it should not be admitted. But if the statement has been sent to the tribunal and copied to the other party at least seven days before the hearing, it will, in accordance with a practice that has been reviewed and not disapproved of by the higher courts, be regarded as complying with rule 7(3) and be admitted. This does nothing to increase its evidential value. As its author is not available for cross-examination on any disputed points the evidence on those points may continue to carry very little weight, but at least it is there.

Some of these papers – the main general legal sources, the pleadings and any decisions generated by the tribunal itself – will be available to the tribunal and the other party as a matter of course. Even so, where a party intends to rely on an unreported case or on one which has only been reported or noted in other than the main law reports, the tribunal should at least be forewarned so that a copy of the report can be available at the hearing. Alternatively the party may decide to provide copies of the transcript or report.

Bundles

Agreeing a bundle

Other papers to which a party may wish to refer the tribunal will somehow have to be placed before it by that party. This is usually done by means of a 'bundle'. The letter which the tribunal sends to parties or their representatives setting the date of the hearing will contain a request that each party should notify the other and the tribunal, well in advance of the hearing, of papers on which it intends to rely. The other party can then ask to see or have a copy of any papers on the list. 'Professional advisers' are expressly asked to prepare a bundle – and told that if possible there should be an agreed bundle which includes both parties' papers. Even where the person who is presenting a case at a tribunal on a respondent's behalf is a member of the respondent's staff, and not a 'professional adviser' in the same sense as an external solicitor, barrister or consultant, the request should still be complied with.

Agreeing a bundle does not mean that both parties accept that every piece of paper in the bundle is relevant and true. It simply means that they have consolidated the papers that each wishes to put to the tribunal and agreed the order in which they should appear in the bundle. This means that there is only one set of papers, rather than two different sets that may duplicate each other in some respects. It makes reference by both parties and the tribunal to particular papers easier.

The existence of an agreed bundle does not limit the documents that can be put before a tribunal to those included in it. If extra documents are introduced the 'one set of papers' advantage is diminished. If any new document is irrelevant or of no probative value the tribunal will not admit it. It is less likely to do so if the document is part of an agreed bundle. If the tribunal believes that its introduction has taken the other party by surprise – a possibility which may be increased if there was an agreed bundle – an adjournment may be granted so that the other party can study it. The costs of any such adjournment can be awarded against the party which made it necessary.

Agreeing a bundle is concerned with the efficiency of the tribunal proceedings and not with their substance. It should be only where one party objects on grounds of admissibility to the inclusion of a particular document proposed by the other that there will be disagreement. Even then it should be possible to agree the rest of the bundle. The disputed document can then be submitted separately by the party that wishes to introduce it, the objecting party can argue against it and the tribunal can rule on the question of its admissibility.

Questions of admissibility are concerned with evidence: documentary evidence and written evidence as described above. Representations in writing are not 'admissible' or 'inadmissible' in the same sense, but they are subject to the seven-day rule outlined above. Although a bundle, whether agreed or not, is primarily intended to include evidence, it is often convenient if it also includes those representations in writing that have become common property by the time of the hearing – that is, the pleadings and any decisions already made in the case. It is unusual for the bundle itself to contain other representations in writing, such as skeleton arguments, or for it to include extracts from or copies of legal sources. If a party does wish to submit such other documents to the tribunal it should, unless (like transcripts of relevant higher court judgements) they will clearly be accepted if introduced at the hearing, do so separately, at least seven days before the hearing date, with a copy to the other party.

Agreeing a bundle is often part of an on-going process of procedural dealings between the parties or their representatives. This process may include requests for further particulars and/or discovery and inspection of documents on a voluntary basis, discussion of convenient hearing dates, whether joint application might be made for a particular procedure to be followed, and so on. Such dealings may be being carried on at the same time as negotiations of a possible settlement are taking place. So each party may have more than one aim: to seek a satisfactory settlement, to prepare to make the best possible case at a tribunal, to ensure that any hearing is conducted as efficiently as possible. Both parties should have the last of these aims in common. Although it is unrealistic to suggest that they will forget their conflicting aims in the other areas, or ignore any impact which agreement in this area might have on the achievement of their aims in other areas, co-operation in agreeing a bundle should not be difficult.

What normally happens is that one party sends the other a list of what it proposes to submit as part of a joint bundle and perhaps encloses copies of any documents which it thinks the other may not yet have seen. The recipient responds with a list, and perhaps copies, of any additional documents and any objection to the inclusion of anything on the other party's list. If the original party still wishes to include a document to which the other party objects, or itself objects to a document proposed by the other party, discussion, by letter or phone, may follow until all questions of inclusion or exclusion have been settled. If they cannot be settled the parties may decide to put in completely separate bundles or jointly to submit an agreed bundle which excludes any disputed documents. It will then be up to the interested party to submit the latter separately. Once the contents of any bundle/s, whether joint or separate, have been decided they can be made up and copied. Six identical sets of papers will be required: one for each of the two parties, one for each of the three tribunal members and one for the witness table.

Preparing a bundle

Papers should be put in some sort of logical order. It will usually be chronological order but occasionally some other order may be better. For instance, if two or more applicants' cases are to be heard together with the same representatives a bundle may include papers common to all applicants in one section and follow it with a separate section for each applicant, the papers in each section being in chronological order. Each sheet should be numbered, with the numbering running consecutively from the front to the back of the bundle. It may sometimes be appropriate to use a two, or more, level numbering system; for example decimally, with each document being given a new number 1, 2, and so on, and each page within a document being numbered by a suffix 1.1, 1.2, and so on. The prime aim, though, is to make it easy for presenters, tribunal members and witnesses to find their way around the bundle, and a simple numerical page numbering system is usually easiest to follow. A contents sheet or index is helpful, particularly if the bundle contains a large number of documents. So too are devices such as tags at any break points between sections.

While shoddy presentation should be avoided, the bundle's importance depends on how helpful it is and how easy it is to use, not on how professional it looks. The use of devices such as tags has to be balanced against the need for six copies to be made. Photocopying is largely an automated process nowadays. Making five copies involves not much more labour, although quite a bit more money, than making one. Sticking tags on dividers is labour-intensive and doing it six times takes nearly six times as long as doing it once. Copies of papers need to be clear and easily legible. If a handwritten document is important and the handwriting is difficult to decipher its author may be asked to prepare a typewritten transcript. The original should still be included in case of any dispute about the accuracy of the transcription. The author would base any oral evidence on the original rather than on the transcript. But reference by the presenters, the tribunal and other witnesses to the precise contents of the note would be made easier by the transcript. Photocopies of photocopies of photocopies can lose their legibility; faxes can fade. Each page of a bundle should be in the clearest, most legible form possible. The 'best evidence' rule – that a copy of a document will not be admitted if the original is available – does not formally apply in tribunals. But it is worth bearing it in mind for purposes of legibility when compiling bundles.

The collation of bundles should be checked. Little is more disruptive to a presentation's flow than someone interrupting to say that a document referred to is not in the place to which reference was made. And the bundles need to be joined together in such a way that their contents will retain their numbered order but can easily be read individually and in their entirety. Staples or punch holes through crucial words and figures do not help. Nor does a struggle to hold a bundle open in order to read a particular paper.

Either party may initiate the process of agreeing a bundle. If a joint bundle is to be submitted, which party undertakes the task and assumes the cost of its preparation is a matter for agreement. As a matter of practice, given that employers usually have more resources than employees or ex-employees, and that they usually have possession or control of the majority of relevant papers, the respondent will often do it. But there is no reason why, particularly if the applicant wishes to include numerous documents in which the respondent has no interest, the respondent should foot the whole bill. If in these circumstances the applicant will not agree to meet an appropriate part of the cost the respondent can simply refuse to agree a bundle and save expense by submitting one separately, leaving the applicant to prepare and pay for the production of another one.

The normal practice in England and Wales is for bundles to be produced at the start of a hearing. There is no prohibition on submitting them earlier but, in the absence of directions that they should be, there is no guarantee that doing so will lead the members of the tribunal to study them before the hearing begins. There is, as already mentioned, a general request in the letter setting the date of the hearing that parties should inform each other and the tribunal, by list, of the documents they may wish to refer to. Where bundle/s have been prepared, whether joint or separate, the party preparing the bundle should send a copy of the contents or index sheet to the tribunal as soon as possible. If it reveals an extensive or complex bundle it may generate a request from the tribunal for its submission prior to the hearing. If no such request is received there is little to be gained by earlier submission unless a party needs to rely on the seven-day rule to ensure the admission of representations in writing.

Referring to documents

Simply getting papers in front of the tribunal is not enough. Their weight as evidence has to be established. A particular document, although included in its entirety to show its provenance, may contain irrelevances which, were it a witness giving oral evidence, would be skipped over. So a whole rule book and disciplinary procedure might be included in a bundle although the points at issue might be concerned with one particular sort of alleged offence and/or whether one particular procedural step was properly taken. A word or phrase which seems ambiguous if looked at in isolation may be revealed in the light of other parts of the same document or other written or oral evidence to have a very specific meaning. A note of a meeting, particularly one written as the meeting was actually taking place, may be very strong evidence of what took place at the meeting but it cannot of itself be conclusive. The author of the note may have misheard or miswritten what was said or may, deliberately or unconsciously, have failed to note some of the things that were said or done or misinterpreted what was going on.

Getting a witness along to a tribunal is not enough. The witness has to be questioned by the presenters and the tribunal to bring out those things which are relevant, to clarify points which may be obscure and to test any evidence which is contradicted. Paper cannot be questioned, but its relevance still needs to be highlighted. Ambiguities and obscurities still need to be clarified. Its accuracy and validity still need to be tested if what it says is contradicted by other evidence. Precisely how this should be done needs planning with the same care and attention as is devoted to planning how witnesses evidence should be adduced.

The pattern of tribunal hearings is that evidence is adduced and then, when – and only when – all the evidence from both sides has been given, the parties argue their cases. So documentary and written evidence ought to be brought out during the earlier, evidence-adducing, stage rather than being first mentioned when reliance is placed on it in a closing address. On the other hand, once it is before the tribunal, paper can be read or reread at any time. If a witness has not been asked a question when at the witness table, then, short of recalling the witness, the question must remain unasked and unanswered. But a question in relation to a document can be answered by scrutiny of the document whenever that question arises, up to and including the formulation by the tribunal of its decision.

In so far as an address to the tribunal refers to a document only to illustrate or confirm a non-contentious point, there will be little objection if that document, provided it has been put before the tribunal as part of the bundle, has not previously been expressly mentioned. But it will often be valuable for the contents and meaning even of non-contentious documents to be highlighted at the evidence-adducing stage. When formulating their decision tribunal members will have any bundle or bundles with them and they will be able to refer to them if necessary. Whether they feel it necessary will depend, among other things, on the points which have been expressly drawn to their attention by the parties during both parts of the hearing, evidence-adducing and argument. A document which has featured specifically in the evidence 'given' at the hearing is more likely to be remembered and reviewed than one that is simply there in the bundle, even if it has been mentioned in argument.

Exposing documents to challenge

Where a party wishes to use a document expressly to support its case that a disputed point should be decided in a particular way, the tribunal will expect the document and the relevant part of it to have been exposed to some evidential scrutiny and testing before reliance is placed on it in argument.

This is particularly important when the very validity of the document is being challenged. One party may claim, for instance, that notes which the other has submitted as being a contemporaneous record of a meeting were not in fact made at or immediately after the meeting but were composed later and for the specific purpose of being used as evidence at the hearing. In that case the first issue the tribunal must decide in relation to these notes is what, in fact, they are. If they are contemporaneous notes their evidential value will be high. If they are not, they may not even be admitted. Simply including the document in a bundle does nothing to answer that essential preliminary question. Other evidence about it, possibly extensive evidence, will be necessary.

More often the parties disagree not about the validity of a document but about its accuracy. Both parties accept that document A consists of notes or minutes of a meeting, but one party alleges that they do not correctly record what went on at the meeting. Document A says that 'X happened'; witness B. says that 'X did not happen'. The tribunal will have to assess the comparative strength of the conflicting evidence. The presenter may argue in general terms that, for instance, a document's memory does not fade as a witness's might. But witness B. could have been asked to look at document A and explain the discrepancy. If that was not done the tribunal may be inclined to regard such a general argument as insufficient to outweigh witness B.'s evidence. The witness's evidence was, or could have been, tested by cross-examination. The paper itself could not be cross-examined; nor was the document's evidence tested by being expressly exposed to comment by the witness. Of the two conflicting pieces of evidence – that of the document and that of the witness – the latter has been tested and the former has not. Merely on those grounds the witness is to be preferred. The issue will not be settled 'merely on those grounds': credibility, consistency and possible bias will also influence a decision on the point. But failure to highlight and test the document at the evidence-adducing stage could be what tilts the balance the wrong way.

The same applies when there is no dispute about what a document says but there are conflicting views about what the words in it mean. In interpreting some documents – for instance, written contracts – courts are supposed to disregard all else than the written words themselves. It is seldom that a tribunal is faced with such a restrictive task. If it is, it is unlikely to refuse to admit extraneous evidence, although it may ignore it. C., a witness for the applicant, gives evidence that the words in document D were understood as meaning Y. The respondent's case is that they meant Z. If C.'s attention is not drawn specifically to the possibility that the words meant Z the evidential foundation of the respondent's eventual argument that they did is weakened, whatever its strength may be in terms of grammatical correctness and syntactical analysis.

Generally it will be possible to draw the tribunal's attention to papers and to expose their contents to any necessary evidential testing at the same time as witnesses are being questioned. So oral evidence may cover a witness's authorship or receipt of a letter; what reference the witness made to a sickness absence record in making a dismissal decision; what steps the witness took to follow a written procedure; and so on.

Reading documents aloud

Exceptionally, a presenter may wish to draw the tribunal's specific attention at the evidence-adducing stage to a document which is not directly relevant to or covered by any witness's oral evidence. This should rarely happen as there will be few documents which will contain evidence sufficiently important to merit highlighting in this way while being insufficiently important to need corroboration by oral testimony and/or to need testing against conflicting evidence. Where it does happen the presenter should tell the tribunal that the document concerned is regarded as particularly important evidence and offer to 'read it into the record'. When any such offer should be made will depend on what the document is and how reference to it fits in with the overall structure of the party's presentation. Generally it will precede the calling of any of the party's witnesses or follow after all of them have been called, rather than coming between the calling of two witnesses, but there may be exceptions. For instance, if a party wishes to present evidence from witnesses A., B. and C., in that order, and it has been accepted that witness B.'s evidence is to be given in writing rather than orally, the presenter will obviously make any necessary reference to B.'s written evidence after A.'s evidence is complete and before C. is called as a witness.

Tribunals, each of which is in control of its own procedure, vary in their view of how useful it is for documents which have been put in as evidence to be read out at the hearing. Some, in response to an offer from the presenter, will ask for a document to be read. Others will note the importance the presenter ascribes to it but say that the members will read it for themselves. A presenter who is concerned that the importance of particular parts may be overlooked unless they are highlighted by being read out will have an opportunity to stress the specific points in the address to the tribunal. Once a tribunal has said that it will itself assimilate the whole of the evidence in the document concerned it cannot be suggested that the whole of that evidence has not been 'given'. For the presenter to stress the points, even by quoting from the document, in the closing address is doing no more than selecting, from among all the evidence which has been given, particular points for emphasis.

Whether documents, or large parts of them, should be read out loud is a matter of *how* documentary and written evidence should be drawn to a tribunal's attention. The more important question is *whether* they should be brought to a tribunal's specific attention. That rests on their significance in the context of the overall case which the presenter wishes to make.

Key points

A presenter should:

- Use the seven-day rule to submit any document the admissibility of which may be challenged.
- Attempt to agree a bundle with the other party, but not agree to inclusion of otherwise inadmissible documents.
- Ensure that any bundle is tidy, well ordered and legible and that six copies are available.
- Ensure that all important documents are brought to the tribunal's attention as evidence.
- Ensure that all documents relating to disputed facts are exposed to evidential challenge.
- Offer to read documents aloud if they have not otherwise been covered in oral evidence.

Chapter 13
A management review

Most tribunal cases, whatever their costs may turn out to be, will have one benefit: that of experience. In the euphoria of 'winning' or the despondency of 'losing' this can be overlooked. It should not be. Whether the case was won or lost, there were reasons. Identifying and reacting to those reasons can improve the chances of winning and/or decrease the chances of losing the next case. And there could be a 'next case'. It is the applicant, not the respondent, who decides that.

How a case is handled at a tribunal does not have very much effect on whether it is won or lost, although it has some. A substantively hopeless case is unlikely to be won by excellent presentation. A substantively superb case will probably not be lost by poor presentation. The main determinant of the result of a case is what actually happened. If a tribunal's decison says that an employer's action or decision was wrong the likelihood is that that is true. It was 'wrong' judged against the criteria that tribunals apply, even if it was 'right' in business terms. This does not mean that what is right in legal terms has to become right for business purposes. But it does mean that, in deciding what is right, the business has to take account of the legal criteria. The next analogous business decision has to balance not only the criteria that the former decision did: it now needs to add the tribunal's criteria into the reckoning. The result may be the same, but it is better informed and consciously taken.

The result may not be the same. There are many instances of management decisions which were right in management terms, and which could have been right in legal terms too, being held to be wrong because they were taken too hastily or because of some procedural hiccup. From an employer's point of view, pernickety details of timing and procedure may seem unimportant when set against broader company objectives. They may still initially be rejected as unimportant when a tribunal decision turns on them: 'We would have won but for that silly point about . . .' But if 'that silly point about . . .' makes the difference between the substantial costs of fighting and losing a tribunal case and no case being brought, or any case which is brought being easily and cheaply winnable, it becomes more important. A minor change in management behaviour may make a major difference in potential management costs. So it is worth looking at a tribunal's decision, however distasteful its overall message may be, to see whether the respondent's procedures and practices can be improved.

Some management decisions are held to be wrong because it could not be proved that they were right. The supervisor or manager may have used very precise words in explaining the disciplinary procedure or the consequences of further misconduct to an employee. But if the employee denies it, and the manager cannot positively remember, the weight of evidence before a tribunal will be that such precise words were not used. And that there could have been a misunderstanding on the matter may tilt the balance against the respondent. That the employer is convinced the employee's denial is false does not matter. That 'everybody knows,' or that the words would have been used 'because I always do so', is not enough. A note made at the time, or a confirmatiory letter, could have made a crucial difference in evidential weight and in the outcome of the case. Any changes that a tribunal decision identifies as desirable may not be ones of substance or procedure. If a case has gone against a respondent because the tribunal has found the 'wrong' facts, it may be that a minor change in administrative practices would vastly improve a respondent's chances of avoiding, or winning, any future cases.

A respondent may have failed to prove its case not because there was insufficient evidence but because the balance of business advantage had been felt to lie in not using particular evidence. A note that did exist may have been, in content or in form, such that the employer did not want to expose it to public view despite its evidential weight. It may have contained unjustified and irrelevant personal comments as well as recording what actually happened. An internal memo may have mentioned factors - perhaps an employee's ethnic origin, or a previous warning which was supposed to have been cleared from the record - that the respondent did not wish it to be thought had been taken into account. The factors may not have influenced the decision, but mention of them in any evidence might give the impression that they had. Had any such document been drafted in the awareness that it might have some future evidential value, it might have been worded differently. In some cases a similar point has even more force. It is not unknown for a respondent to settle a case simply to avoid the exposure of one or more documents to discovery.

The presentation of the case, as well as its substance, should be reviewed. It is never possible to be sure what the result of a different approach to a witness or of advancing a different argument or of putting the same argument in different words would have been, but a tribunal's decision may give some impression of what worked well and what less well. A respondent's presenter and a respondent's witness, particularly if they are colleagues, might usefully discuss how they each fulfilled their respective roles in the eyes of the other. An investigator who found evidence being given at a tribunal different from that given in an investigatory interview should consider how and why the discrepancy occurred.

How good was the analysis? How accurate the assessment of the chances of success on this point or that? These functions may not need to be performed again for a long time, or perhaps at all. But, if they do, their performance next time might be improved by a conscious and deliberate attempt to discover and learn any lessons that experience in this case can provide.

And what did the costs and benefits, in business terms, turn out to be? This may be as difficult to gauge after the event as it was to forecast when the action plan was being decided. It is no more possible to quantify precisely the effect a particular outcome has actually had on a company's image than it is to quantify precisely the effect it might be expected to have. But an attempt to compare actuality with expectations, at least in broad terms, should be made. It may make it easier on any future occasion to balance the relative importance of the various factors and to assess what the real impact of different courses of action on different factors might be.

Appendix
The Industrial Tribunals (Rules of Procedure)
Regulations 1985, SI No. 16

Citation, commencement and revocation

1. (1) These Regulations may be cited as the Industrial Tribunals (Rules of Procedure) Regulations 1985 (and the Rules of Procedure contained in Schedules 1 and 2 to these Regulations may be referred to as the Industrial Tribunals Rules of Procedure 1985 and the Industrial Tribunals Complementary Rules of Procedure 1985 respectively). They shall come into operation on 1 March 1985.

(2) The Industrial Tribunals (Rules of Procedure) Regulations 1980 and the Industrial Tribunals (Rules of Procedure) (Equal Value Amendment) Regulations 1983 shall cease to have effect on 1 March 1985 except in relation to proceedings instituted before that date.

Interpretation

2. In these Regulations, unless the context otherwise requires, the following expressions have the meanings hereby assigned to them respectively, that is to say:

'the 1966 Act' means the Docks and Harbours Act 1966;

'the 1978 Act' means the Employment Protection (Consolidation) Act 1978;

'applicant' means a person who in pursuance of Rule 1 has presented an originating application to the Secretary of the Tribunals for a decision of a tribunal and includes:

    (*a*) the Secretary of State, the Board or a licensing authority,

    (*b*) a claimant or complainant,

    (*c*) in the case of proceedings under section 51 of the 1966 Act, a person on whose behalf an originating application has been sent by a trade union, and

    (*d*) in relation to interlocutory applications under these Rules, a person who seeks any relief;

'the Board' means the National Dock Labour Board as reconstituted under the Dock Work Regulation Act 1976;

'the clerk to the tribunal' means the person appointed by the Secretary of the Tribunals or an Assistant Secretary to act in that capacity at one or more hearings;

'court' means a magistrates' court or the Crown Court;

'decision' in relation to a tribunal includes a declaration, an order (other than an interlocutory order), a recommendation or an award of the tribunal but does not include an opinion given pursuant to a pre-hearing assessment held under Rule 6;

'the Equal Pay Act' means the Equal Pay Act 1970;

'equal value claim' means a claim by an applicant which rests upon entitlement to the benefit of an equality clause by virtue of the operation of section 1(2)(c) of the Equal Pay Act;

'hearing' means a sitting of a tribunal duly constituted for the purpose of receiving evidence, hearing addresses and witnesses or doing anything lawfully requisite to enable the tribunal to reach a decision on any question;

'licensing authority' means a body having the function of issuing licences under the 1966 Act;

'the Office of the Tribunals' means the Central Office of the Industrial Tribunals (England and Wales);

'the panel of chairmen' means the panel of persons, being barristers or solicitors of not less than seven years' standing, appointed by the Lord Chancellor in pursuance of Regulation 5(2) of the Industrial Tribunals (England and Wales) Regulations 1965;

'party' in relation to proceedings under section 51 of the 1966 Act means the applicant and the Board or the licensing authority with which or (as the case may be) any person with whom it appears to the applicant that he is in dispute about a question to which that section applies and, in a case where such a question is referred to a tribunal by a court, any party to the proceedings before the court in which the question arose;

'person entitled to appear' in relation to proceedings under section 51 of the 1966 Act means a party and any person who, under subsection (5) of that section, is entitled to appear and be heard before a tribunal in such proceedings;

'the President' means the President of the Industrial Tribunals (England and Wales) or the person nominated by the Lord Chancellor to discharge for the time being the functions of the President;

'the Race Relations Act' means the Race Relations Act 1976;

'Regional Chairman' means the chairman appointed by the President to take charge of the due administration of justice by tribunals in an area specified by the President, or a person nominated either by the President or the Regional Chairman to discharge for the time being the functions of the Regional Chairman;

'Regional Office of the Industrial Tribunals' means a regional office which has been established under the Office of the Tribunals for an area specified by the President;

'Register' means the Register of Applications and Decisions kept in pursuance of these Regulations;

'report' means a report required by a tribunal to be prepared by an expert, pursuant to section 2A(1)(b) of the Equal Pay Act;

'respondent' means a party to the proceedings before a tribunal other than the applicant, and other than the Secretary of State in proceedings under Parts III and VI of the 1978 Act in which he is not cited as the person against whom relief is sought;

'Rule' means, in Schedule 1 to these Regulations, a Rule of Procedure contained in that Schedule, and, in Schedule 2 to these Regulations, a Rule of Procedure contained in Schedule 1 or Schedule 2 as appropriate;

'the Secretary of the Tribunals' and 'an Assistant Secretary of the Tribunals' mean respectively the persons for the time being acting as the Secretary of the Office of the Tribunals and as Assistant Secretary of a Regional Office of the Industrial Tribunals;

'the Sex Discrimination Act' means the Sex Discrimination Act 1975;

'tribunal' means an industrial tribunal (England and Wales) established in pursuance of the Industrial Tribunals (England and Wales) Regulations 1965 and in relation to any proceedings means the tribunal to which the proceedings have been referred by the President or a Regional Chairman.

Proceedings of tribunals

3. (1) Except where separate Rules of Procedure made under the provisions of any enactment are applicable and subject to paragraph (2) of this Regulation, the Rules of Procedure contained in Schedule 1 to these Regulations shall have effect in relation to al proceedings before a tribunal where:

(a) the respondent or one of the respondents resides or carries on business in England or Wales; or

(b) had the remedy been by way of action in the county court, the cause of action would have arisen wholly or in part in England or Wales; or

(c) the proceedings are to determine a question which as been referred to the tribunal by a court in England or Wales; or

(d) in proceedings under the 1966 Act they are in relation to a port in England or Wales.

(2) In any such proceedings before a tribunal involving an equal value claim the Rules of Procedure contained in Schedule 2 to these Regulations (including Rule 7A) shall replace Rules 4, 8, 9, 11, 12 and 17 in Schedule 1.

Proof of decisions of tribunals

4. The production in any proceedings in any court of a document purporting to be certified by the Secretary of the Tribunals to be a true copy of an entry of a decision in the Register shall, unless the contrary is proved, be sufficient evidence of the document and of the facts stated therein.

Regulation 3(1)   SCHEDULE 1
                                        RULES OF PROCEDURE

Originating application

1. (1) Proceedings for the determination of any matter by a tribunal shall be instituted by the applicant (or, where applicable, by a court) presenting to the Secretary of the Tribunals an originating application, which shall be in writing and shall set out:

(a) the name and address of the applicant; and

(b) the names and addresses of the person or persons against whom relief is sought or (where applicable) of the parties to the proceedings before the court; and

(c) the grounds, with particulars thereof, on which relief is sought, or in proceedings under section 51 of the 1966 Act the question for determination and (except where the question is referred by a court) the grounds on which relief is sought.

(2) Where the Secretary of the Tribunals is of the opinion that the originating application does not seek or on the facts stated therein cannot entitle the applicant to a relief which a tribunal has power to give, he may give notice to that effect to the applicant stating the reasons for his opinion and informing him that the application will not be registered unless he states in writing that he wishes to proceed with it.

(3) An application as respects which a notice has been given in pursuance of the preceding paragraph shall not be treated as having been received for the purposes of Rule 2 unless the applicant intimates in writing to the Secretary of the Tribunals that he wishes to proceed with it; and upon receipt of such an intimation the Secretary of the Tribunals shall proceed in accordance with that Rule.

Action upon receipt of originating application

2. Upon receiving an originating application the Secretary of the Tribunals shall enter particulars of it in the Register and shall forthwith send a copy of it to the respondent and inform the parties in writing of the case number of the originating application entered in the Register (which shall thereafter constitute the title of the proceedings) and of the address to which notices and other communications to the Secretary of the Tribunals shall be sent. Every copy of the originating application sent by the Secretary of the Tribunals under this Rule shall be accompanied by a written notice which shall include information, as appropriate to the case, about the means and time for entering an appearance, the consequences of failure to do so, and the right to receive a copy of the decision. The Secretary of the Tribunals shall also notify the parties that in all cases under the provisions of any enactment providing for conciliation the services of a conciliation officer are available to them.

Appearance by respondent

3. (1) A respondent shall within fourteen days of receiving the copy originating application enter an appearance to the proceedings by presenting to the Secretary of the Tribunals a written notice of appearance setting out his full name and the address and stating whether or not he intends to resist the application and, if so, setting out sufficient particulars to show on what grounds. Upon receipt of a notice of appearance the Secretary of the Tribunals shall forthwith send a copy of it to any other party.

(2) A respondent who has not entered an appearance shall not be entitled to take any part in the proceedings except:

(i) to apply under Rule 13(1) for an extension of the time appointed by this Rule for entering an appearance;

(ii) to make an application under Rule 4(1) (i);

(iii) to make an application under Rule 10(2) in respect of Rule 10(1)(b);

(iv) to be called as a witness by another person;

(v) to be sent a copy of a document or corrected entry in pursuance of Rule 9(6), 9(10) or 10(5).

(3) A notice of appearance which is presented to the Secretary of the Tribunals after the time appointed by this Rule for entering appearances shall be deemed to include an application under Rule 13(1) (by the respondent who has presented the notice of appearance) for an extension of the time so appointed. Without prejudice to Rule 13(4), if the tribunal grants the application (which it may do notwithstanding that the grounds of the application are not stated) the Secretary of the Tribunals shall forthwith send a copy of the notice of appearance to any other party. The tribunal shall not refuse an extension of time under this Rule unless it has sent notice to the person wishing to enter an appearance giving him an opportunity to show cause why the extension should be granted.

Power to require further particulars and attendance of witnesses and to grant discovery

4. (1) A tribunal may:

(*a*) subject to Rule 3(2), on the application of a party to the proceedings made either by notice to the Secretary of the Tribunals or at the hearing of the originating application, or

(*b*) in relation to sub-paragraph (i) of this paragraph, if it thinks fit, of its own motion:

(i) require a party to furnish in writing to the person specified by the tribunal further particulars of the grounds on which he or it relies and of any facts and contentions relevant thereto;

(ii) grant to the person making the application such discovery or inspection (including the taking of copies) of documents as might be granted by a county court; and

(iii) require the attendance of any person (including a party to the proceedings) as a witness, wherever such person may be within Great Britain, and may, if it does so require the attendance of a person, require him to produce any document relating to the matter to be determined;

and may appoint the time at or within or the place at which any act required in pursuance of this Rule is to be done.

(2) A party on whom a requirement has been made under paragraph (1)(i) or (1)(ii) of this Rule on an *ex parte* application, or (in relation to a requirement under paragraph (1)(i)) on the tribunal's own motion, and a person on whom a requirement has been made under paragraph (1)(iii) may apply to the tribunal by notice to the Secretary of the Tribunals before the appointed time at or within which the requirement is to be complied with to vary or set aside a requirement. Notice of an application under this paragraph to vary or set aside a requirement shall be given to the parties (other than the party making the application) and, where appropriate, in proceedings which may involve payments out of the

Redundancy Fund or Maternity Pay Fund, the Secretary of State if not a party.

(3) Every document containing a requirement under paragraph (1)(ii) or (1)(iii) of this Rule shall contain a reference to the fact that, under paragraph 1(7) of Schedule 9 to the 1978 Act, any person who without reasonable excuse fails to comply with any such requirement shall be liable on summary conviction to a fine, and the document shall state the amount of the current maximum fine.

(4) If the requirement under paragraph (1)(i) or (1)(ii) of this Rule is not complied with, a tribunal, before or at the hearing, may dismiss the whole or part of the originating application, or, as the case may be, strike out the whole or part of the notice of appearance, and, where appropriate, direct that a respondent shall be debarred from defending altogether. Provided that a tribunal shall not so dismiss or strike out or give such a direction unless it has sent notice to the party who has not complied with the requirement, giving him an opportunity to show cause why such should not be done.

Time and place of hearing and appointment of assessor

5. (1) The President or a Regional Chairman shall fix the date, time and place of the hearing of the originating application and the Secretary of the Tribunals shall (subject to Rule 3(2)) not less than fourteen days (or such shorter time as may be agreed by him with the parties) before the date so fixed send to each party a notice of hearing which shall include information and guidance as to attendance at the hearing, witnesses and the bringing of documents (if any), representation by another person and written representations.

(2) In any proceedings under the 1966 Act in which the President or a Regional Chairman so directs, the Secretary of the Tribunals shall also take such of the following steps as may be so directed, namely:

    (*a*) publish in one or more newspapers circulating in the locality in which the port in question is situated notice of the hearing;

    (*b*) send notice of the hearing to such persons as may be directed;

    (*c*) post notices of the hearing in a conspicuous place or conspicuous places in or near the port in question;

but the requirement as to the period of notice contained in paragraph (1) of this Rule shall not apply to any such notices.

(3) Where in the case of any proceedings it is provided for one or more assessors to be appointed, the President or a Regional Chairman may, if he thinks fit, appoint a person or persons having special knowledge or experience in relation to the subject matter of the originating application to sit with the tribunal as assessor or assessors.

Pre-hearing assessment

6. (1) A tribunal may at any time before the hearing (either, subject to Rule 3(2), on the application of a party to the proceedings made by notice to the Secretary of the Tribunals or of its own motion) consider, by way of a pre-hearing assessment, the contents of the originating application and entry of appearance, any representations in writing which have been submitted and any oral argument advanced by or on behalf of a party.

(2) If, upon a pre-hearing assessment, the tribunal considers that the originating application or the contentions or any particular contention of a party appear or, as the case may be, appears to have no reasonable prospect of success, it may indicate that in its opinion, if the originating application shall not be withdrawn or the contentions or contention of the party shall be persisted in up to or at the hearing, the party in question may have an order for costs made against him at the hearing under the provisions of Rule 11. A pre-hearing assessment shall not take place unless the tribunal has sent notice to the parties to the proceedings giving them (and, where appropriate, in proceedings which may involve payments out of the Redundancy Fund or Maternity Pay Fund, the Secretary of State, if not a party) an opportunity to submit representations in writing and to advance oral argument at the pre-hearing assessment if they so wish.

(3) Any indication of opinion made in accordance with paragraph (2) of this Rule shall be recorded in a document signed by the chairman, a copy of which shall be sent to the parties to the proceedings and a copy of which shall be available to the tribunal at the hearing.

(4) Where a tribunal has indicated its opinion in accordance with paragraph (2) of this Rule no member thereof shall be a member of the tribunal at the hearing.

The hearing

7. (1) Any hearing of or in connection with an originating application shall take place in public unless in the opinion of the tribunal a private hearing is appropriate for the purpose of hearing evidence which relates to matters of such a nature that it would be against the interests of national security to allow the evidence to be given in public or hearing evidence from any person which in the opinion of the tribunal is likely to consist of:

(a) information which he could not disclose without contravening a prohibition imposed by or under any enactment; or

(b) any information which has been communicated to him in confidence, or which he has otherwise obtained in consequence of the confidence reposed in him by another person; or

(c) information the disclosure of which would cause substantial injury to any undertaking of his or any undertaking in which he works for reasons other than its effect on negotiations with respect to any of the matters mentioned in section 29(1) of the Trade Union and Labour Relations Act 1974.

(2) A member of the Council on Tribunals shall be entitled to attend any hearing taking place in private in his capacity as such member.

(3) Subject to Rule 3(2), if a party shall desire to submit representations in writing for consideration by a tribunal at the hearing of the originating application that party shall present such reprentations to the Secretary of the Tribunals not less than seven days before the hearing and shall at the same time send a copy to the other party or parties.

(4) Where a party has failed to attend or be represented at the hearing (whether or not he has sent any representations in writing) the contents of his originating application or, as the case may be, of his entry of appearance may be treated by a tribunal as representations in writing.

(5) The Secretary of State if he so elects shall be entitled to apply under Rule 4(1), 13(1) and (2), 15 and 16(1) and to appear as if he were a party and be heard at any hearing of or in connection with an orginating application in proceedings in which he is not a party which may involve payments out of the Redundancy Fund or Maternity Pay Fund.

(6) Subject to Rule 3(2), at any hearing of or in connection with an originating application a party and any person entitled to appear may appear before the tribunal and may be heard in person or be represented by counsel or by a solicitor or by a representative of a trade union or an employer's association or by any other person whom he desires to represent him.

Procedure at hearing

8. (1) The tribunal shall conduct the hearing in such manner as it considers most suitable to the clarification of the issues before it and generally to the just handling of the proceedings; it shall so far as appears to it appropriate seek to avoid formality in its proceedings and it shall not be bound by any enactment or rule of law relating to the admissibility of evidence in proceedings before the courts of law.

(2) Subject to paragraph (1) of this Rule, at the hearing of the originating application a party (unless disentitled by virtue of Rule 3(2)), the Secretary of State (if, not being a party, he elects to appear as provided in Rule 7(5)) and any other person entitled to appear shall be entitled to give evidence, to call witnesses, to question any witnesses and to address the tribunal.

(3) If a party shall fail to appear or to be represented at the time and place fixed for the hearing, the tribunal may, if that party is an applicant, dismiss or, in any case, dispose of the application in the absence of that party or may adjourn the hearing to a later date: Provided that before deciding to dismiss or disposing of any application in the absence of a party the tribunal shall consider any representations submitted by that party in pursuance of Rule 7(3).

(4) A tribunal may require any witness to give evidence on oath or affirmation and for that purpose there may be administered an oath or affirmation in due form.

Decision of tribunal

9. (1) A decision of a tribunal may be taken by a majority thereof and, if the tribunal shall be constituted of two members only, the chairman shall have a second or casting vote.

(2) The decision of a tribunal, which may be given orally at the end of a hearing or reserved, shall be recorded in a document signed by the chairman.

(3) A tribunal shall give reasons, which may be in full or in summary form, for its decision.

(4) The reasons for the decision of the tribunal shall be recorded in a docu-

ment signed by the chairman, which shall also contain a statement as to whether the reasons are in full or in summary form.

(5) Where:

(a) the proceedings before the tribunal involved the determination of an issue arising under or relating to section 51 of the 1966 Act, the Equal Pay Act, the Sex Discrimination Act, the Race Relations Act, sections 23, 58, 59(a) or 77 of the 1978 Act, or sections 4 or 5 of the Employment Act 1980; or

(b) the reasons have been given in summary form and it appears at any time to the tribunal that the reasons should be given in full; or

(c) a request that the reasons be given in full is made orally at the hearing by a party or by a person entitled to appear who did so appear; or

(d) such a request is made in writing within twenty-one days of the date on which the document recording the reasons in summary form was sent to the parties;

the reasons shall be recorded in full in a document signed by the chairman.

(6) The clerk to the tribunal shall transmit any document referred to in paragraphs (2), (4) and (5) of this Rule to the Secretary of the Tribunals who shall as soon as may be enter it in the Register and shall send a copy of the entry to each of the parties and to the persons entitled to appear who did so appear and, where the originating application was sent to a tribunal by a court, to that court.

(7) Any document referred to in paragraphs (4) and (5) of this Rule shall be omitted from the Register in any case in which evidence has been heard in private and the tribunal so directs and in that event any such document shall be sent to the parties and to any superior court in any proceedings relating to such decision together with the copy of the entry.

(8) The Register shall be kept at the Office of the Tribunals and shall be open to the inspection of any person without charge at all reasonable hours.

(9) Clerical mistakes in any document referred to in paragraphs (2), (4) and (5) of this Rule, or errors arising in such a document from an accidental slip or omission, may at any time be corrected by the chairman by certificate under his hand.

(10) The clerk to the tribunal shall send a copy of any document so corrected and the certificate of the chairmen to the Secretary of the Tribunals who shall as soon as may be make such correction as may be necessary in the Register and shall send a copy of any corrected entry or of any corrected document containing reasons for the tribunal's decision, as the case may be, to each of the parties and, in the case of a corrected entry, to the persons entitled to appear who did so appear and, where the originating application was sent to the tribunal by a court, to that court.

(11) If any decision is:

(a) corrected under paragraph (9) of this Rule,

(b) reviewed, revoked or varied under Rule 10, or

(c) altered in any way by order of a superior court,

the Secretary of the Tribunals shall enter the entry in the Register to conform with any such certificate or order and shall send a copy of the new entry to each of the parties and to the parties and to the persons entitled to appear who did so appear and, where the originating application was sent to the tribunal by a court, to that court.

(12) Where, by this Rule, a document is required to be signed by the chairman but by reason of death or incapacity the chairman is unable to sign such document it shall be signed by the other members of the tribunal, who shall certify that the chairman is unable to sign.

Review of tribunal's decision

10. (1) A tribunal shall have power to review and to revoke or vary by certificate under the chairman's hand any decision on the grounds that:

(a) the decision was wrongly made as a result of an error on the part of the tribunal staff; or

(b) a party did not receive notice of the proceedings leading to the decision; or

(c) the decision was made in the absence of a party or person entitled to be heard; or

(d) new evidence has become available since the conclusion of the hearing to which the decision relates, provided that its existence could not have been reasonably known of or foreseen; or

(e) the interests of justice require such a review.

(2) An application for the purposes of paragraph (1) of this Rule may be made at the hearing. If the application is not made at the hearing, such application shall be made to the Secretary of the Tribunals at any time from the date of the hearing until fourteen days after the date on which the decision was sent to the parties and must be in writing stating the grounds in full.

(3) An application for the purposes of paragraph (1) of this Rule may be refused by the President or by the chairman of the tribunal which decided the case or by a Regional Chairman if in his opinion it has no reasonable prospect of success.

(4) If such an application is not refused under paragraph (3) of this Rule it shall be heard by the tribunal which decided the case, or

(a) where it it not practicable for it to be heard by that tribunal, or

(b) where the decision was made by a chairman acting alone under rule 12(4),

by a tribunal appointed either by the President or a Regional Chairman, and if the application is granted the tribunal shall proceed to a review of the decision and, having reviewed it, may confirm, vary or revoke that decision, and if the tribunal revokes the decision it shall order a re-hearing before either the same or a differently constituted tribunal.

(5) The clerk to the tribunal shall send to the Secretary of the Tribunals the certificate of the chairman as to any revocation or variation of the tribunal's decision under this Rule. The Secretary of the Tribunals shall as soon as may be make such correction as may be necessary in the Register and shall send a copy of the entry to each of the parties and to the persons entitled to appear who did so appear and where the originating application was sent to a tribunal by a court, to that court.

Costs

11. (1) Subject to paragraphs (2), (3) and (4) of this Rule, a tribunal shall not normally make an award in respect of the costs or expenses incurred by a party to the proceedings but where in its opinion a party (and, if he is a respondent, whether or not he has entered an appearance) has in bringing or conducting the proceedings acted frivolously, vexatiously or otherwise unreasonably the tribunal may make:

(*a*) an order that that party shall pay to another party (or to the Secretary of State if, not being a party, he has acted as provided in Rule &(5)) either a specified sum in respect of the costs or expenses incurred by that other party (or, as the case may be, by the Secretary of State) or the whole or part of those costs or expenses as taxed (if not otherwise agreed);

(*b*) an order that that party shall pay to the Secretary of State the whole, or any part, of any allowances (other than allowances paid to members of tribunals or assessors) paid by the Secretary of State under paragraph 10 of Schedule 9 to the 1978 Act to any person for the purposes of, or in connection with, his attendance at the tribunal.

(2) Where the tribunal has on the application of a party to the proceedings postponed the day or time fixed for or adjourned the hearing, the tribunal may make orders against or, as the case may require, in favour of that party as at paragraph (1)(a) and (b) of this Rule as respects any costs or expenses incurred or any allowances paid as a result of the postponement or adjournment.

(3) Where, on a complaint of unfair dismissal in respect of which:

(i) the applicant has expressed a wish to be reinstated or re-engaged which has been communicated to the respondent at least seven days before the hearing of the complaint, or

(ii) the proceedings arise out of the respondent's failure to permit the applicant to return to work after an absence due to pregnancy or confinement.

any postponement or adjournment of the hearing has been caused by the respondent's failure, without a special reason, to adduce reasonable evidence as to the availability of the job from which the applicant was dismissed, or, as the case may be, which she held before her absence, or of comparable or suitable employment, the tribunal shall make orders against that respondent as at paragraph (1)(a) and (b) of this Rule as respects any costs or expenses incurred or any allowances paid as a result of the postponement or adjournment.

(4) In any proceedings under the 1966 Act a tribunal may make:

(*a*) an order that a party, or any other person entitled to appear who did so appear, shall pay to another party or such person either a specified sum in respect of the costs or expenses incurred by that other party or person or the whole or part of those costs or expenses as taxed (if not otherwise agreed);

(*b*) an order that a party, or any other person entitled to appear who did so appear, shall pay to the Secretary of State a specified sum in respect of the whole, or any part, of any allowances (other than allowances paid to members of tribunals) paid by the Secretary of State under paragraph 10 of Schedule 9 to the 1978 Act to any person for the purposes of, or in connection with, his attendance at the tribunal.

(5) Any costs required by an order under this Rule to be taxed may be taxed in the county court according to such of the scales prescribed by the county court rules for proceedings in the county court as shall be directed by the order.

Miscellaneous powers of tribunal

12. (1) Subject to the provisions of these Rules, a tribunal may regulate its own procedure.

(2) A tribunal may, if it thinks fit:

(*a*) extend the time appointed by or under these Rules for doing any act notwithstanding that the time appointed may have expired;

(*b*) postpone the day or time fixed for, or adjourn, any hearing (particularly as respects cases under the provisions of any enactment providing for conciliation for the purposes of giving an opportunity for the complaint to be settled by way of conciliation and withdrawn);

(*c*) if the applicant shall at any time give notice of the withdrawal of his originating application, dismiss the proceedings;

(*d*) except in proceedings under the 1966 Act, if both or all the parties (and the Secretary of State, if, not being a party, he has acted as provided in Rule 7(5)) agree in writing upon the terms of a decision to be made by the tribunal, decide accordingly;

(*e*) subject to the Proviso below, at any stage of the proceedings order to be struck out or amended any originating application or notice of appearance or anything in such application or notice of appearance on the grounds that it is scandalous, frivolous or vexatious;

(*f*) subject to the Proviso below, on the application of the respondent, or of its own motion, order to be struck out any originating application for want of prosecution;

Provided that before making any order under (e) or (f) above the tribunal shall send notice to the party against whom it is proposed that any such order should be made giving him an opportunity to show cause why such an order should not be made.

(3) Subject to Rule 4(2), a tribunal may, if it thinks fit, before granting an application under Rule 4 or Rule 13 require the party (or, as the case may be, the Secretary of State) making the application to give notice of it to the other party or parties. The notice shall give particulars of the application and indicate the address to which and the time within which any objection to the application shall be made, being an address and time specified for the purposes of the application by the tribunal.

(4) Any act other than the holding of a pre-hearing assessment under Rule 6, the hearing of an originating application or the making of an order under Rule 10(1), required or authorised by these Rules to be done by a tribunal may be done by, or on the direction of, the President or the chairman of the tribunal or

any chairman being a member of the panel of chairmen.

(5) Rule 11 shall apply to an order dismissing proceedings under paragraph (2)(c) of this Rule.

(6) Any functions of the Secretary of the Tribunals other than that mentioned in Rule 1(2) may be performed by an Assistant Secretary of the Tribunals.

Extension of time and directions

13. (1) An application to a tribunal for an extension of the time appointed by these Rules for doing any act may be made by a party either before or after the expiration of any time so appointed.

(2) Subject to Rule 3(2), a party may at any time apply to a tribunal for directions on any matter arising in connection with the proceedings.

(3) An application under the foregoing provisions of this Rule shall be made by presenting to the Secretary of the Tribunals a notice of application, which shall state the title of the proceedings and shall set out the grounds of the application.

(4) The Secretary of the Tribunals shall give notice to both or all the parties (subject to Rule 3(2)) of any extension of time granted under Rule 12(2)(a) or any direction given in pursuance of this Rule.

Joinder and representative respondents

14. (1) A tribunal may at any time either upon the application of any person or, where appropriate, of its own motion, direct any person against whom any relief is sought to be joined as a party to the proceedings, and give such consequential directions as it considers necessary.

(2) A tribunal may likewise, either upon such application or of its own motion, order that any respondent named in the originating application or subsequently added, who shall appear to the tribunal not to have been, or to have ceased to be, directly interested in the subject of the originating application, be dismissed from the proceedings.

(3) Where there are numerous persons having the same interest in an originating application, one or more of them may be cited as the person or persons against whom relief is sought, or may be authorised by the tribunal, before or at the hearing, to defend on behalf of all the persons so interested.

Consolidation of proceedings

15. Where there are pending before the industrial tribunals two or more originating applications, then, if at any time upon the application of a party or of its own motion it appears to a tribunal that:

(a) some common question of law or fact arises in both or all the originating applications, or

(b) the relief claimed therein is in respect of or arises out of the same set of facts, or

(c) for some other reason it is desirable to make an order under this Rule, the tribunal may order that some (as specified in the order) or all of the originating applications shall be considered together, and may give such consequential directions as may be necessary: provided that the tribunal shall not make an order under this Rule without sending notice to all parties concerned giving them the opportunity to show cause why such an order should not be made.

Transfer of proceedings

16. (1) Where there is pending before the industrial tribunals an originating application in respect of which it appears to the President or a Regional Chairman that the proceedings could be determined in an industrial tribunal (Scotland) established in pursuance of the Industrial Tribunals (Scotland) Regulations 1965 and that the originating application would more conveniently be determined by such a tribunal, the President or a Regional Chairman may, at any time upon the application of a party or of his own motion, with the consent of the President of the Industrial Tribunals (Scotland), direct that the said proceedings be transferred to the Office of the Industrial Tribunals (Scotland): Provided that no such directions shall be made unless notice has been sent to all parties concerned, giving them an opportunity to show cause why such a direction should not be made.

(2) Where proceedings have been transferred to the Office of the Industrial Tribunals (England and Wales) under Rule 16(1) of the Industrial (Rules of Procedure) (Scotland) Regulations 1985 they shall be treated as if in all respects they had been commenced by an originating application pursuant to Rule 1.

Notices, etc.

17. (1) Any notice given under these Rules shall be in writing.

(2) All notices and documents required by these Rules to be presented to the Secretary of the Tribunals may be presented at the Office of the Tribunals or such other office as may be notified by the Secretary of the Tribunals to the parties.

(3) All notices and documents required or authorised by these Rules to be sent or given to any person hereinafter mentioned may be sent by post (subject to paragraph (5) of this Rule) or delivered to or at:

(*a*) in the case of a notice or document directed to the Secretary of State in proceedings to which he is not a party, the offices of the Department of Employment at Caxton Hall, Tothill Street, London SW1H 9NF, or such other office as may be notified by the Secretary of State;

(*b*) in the case of a notice or document directed to the Board, the principal office of the Board;

(*c*) in the case of a notice or document directed to a court, the office of the clerk of the court;

(*d*) in the case of a notice or document directed to a party:

(i) his address for service specified in the originating application or in a notice of appearance or in a notice under paragraph (4) of this Rule; or

(ii) if no address for service has been so specified, his last known address or place of business in the United Kingdom or, if the party is a corporation, the corporation's registered or principal office in the United Kingdon, or, in any case, such address or place outside the United Kingdom as the President or a Regional Chairman may allow;

(*e*) in the case of a notice or document directed to any person (other than a person specified in the foregoing provisions of this paragraph), his address or place of business in the United Kingdom, or, if such a person is a corporation, the corporation's registered or principal office in the United Kingdom;

and if sent or given to the authorised representative of a party shall be deemed to have been sent or given to that party.

(4) A party may at any time by notice to the Secretary of the Tribunals and to the other party or parties (and, where appropriate, to the appropriate conciliation officer) change his address for service under these Rules.

(5) The recorded delivery service shall be used instead of the ordinary post:

(*a*) when a second set of documents or notices is to be sent to a respondent who has not entered an appearance under Rule 3(1);

(*b*) for service of an order made under Rule 4(1)(iii) requiring the attendance of a witness.

(6) Where for any sufficient reason service of any document or notice cannot be effected in the manner prescribed under this Rule, the President or a Regional Chairman may make an order for substituted service in such manner as he may deem fit and such service shall have the same effect as service in the manner prescribed under this Rule.

(7) In proceedings brought under the provisions of any enactment providing for conciliation the Secretary of the Tribunals shall send copies of all documents and notices to a conciliation officer who in the opinion of the Secretary is an appropriate officer to receive them.

(8) In proceedings which may involve payments out of the Redundancy Fund or Maternity Pay Fund, the Secretary of the Tribunals shall, where appropriate, send copies of all documents and notices to the Secretary of State notwithstanding the fact that he may not be a party to such proceedings.

(9) In proceedings under the Equal Pay Act, the Sex Discrimination Act or the Race Relations Act the Secretary of the Tribunals shall send to the Equal Opportunities Commission or, as the case may be, the Commission for Racial Equality copies of all documents sent to the parties under Rule 9(6), (10) and (11) and Rule 10(5).

Regulation 3(2)   SCHEDULE 2

COMPLEMENTARY RULES OF PROCEDURE

For use only in proceedings involving an equal value claim

Power to require further particulars and attendance of witnesses and to grant discovery

4. (1) A tribunal may:

(*a*) subject to Rule 3(2), on the application of a party to the proceedings made either by notice to the Secretary of the Tribunals or at the hearing of the originating application, or

(*b*) in relation to sub-paragraph (i) of this paragraph, if it thinks fit, of its own motion:

    (i) require a party to furnish in writing to the person specified by the tribunal further particulars of the grounds on which he or it relies and of any facts and contentions relevant thereto;

    (ii) grant to the person making the application such discovery or inspection (including the taking of copies) of documents as might be granted by a county court; and

    (iii) require the attendance of any person (including a party to the proceedings) as a witness, wherever such person may be within Great Britain, and may, if it does so require the attendance of a person, require him to produce any document relating to the matter to be determined;

and may appoint the time at or within which or the place at which any act required in pursuance of this Rule is to be done.

(1A) Subject to paragraph (1B), a tribunal may, on the application of an expert who has been required by the tribunal to prepare a report,

(*a*) require any person who the tribunal is satisfied may have information which may be relevant to the question or matter on which the expert is required to report to furnish, in writing, such information as the tribunal may require;

(*b*) require any person to produce any documents which are in the possession, custody or power of that person and which the tribunal is satisfied may contain matter relevant to the question on which the expert is required to report;

and any information so required to be furnished or document so required to be produced shall be furnished or produced, at or within such time as the tribunal may appoint, to the Secretary of the Tribunals, who shall send the information or document to the expert.

(1B) A tribunal shall not make a requirement under paragraph (1A) of this Rule:

(*a*) of a conciliation officer who has acted in connection with the complaint under section 64 of the Sex Discrimination Act, or

(*b*) if it is satisfied that the person so required would have good grounds for refusing to comply with the requirement if it were a requirement made in connection with a hearing before the tribunal.

(2) A party on whom a requirement has been made under paragraph (1)(i) or (1)(ii) of this Rule on an *ex parte* application, or (in relation to a requirement under paragraph (1)(i)) on the tribunal's own motion, and a person on whom a requirement has been made under paragraph (1)(iii) may apply to the tribunal by notice to the Secretary of the Tribunals before the appointed time at or within which the requirement is to be complied with to vary or set aside the requirement. Notice of

an application under this paragraph to vary or set aside a requirement shall be given to the parties (other than the party making the application) and, where appropriate, in proceedings which may involve payments out of the Redundancy Fund or Maternity Pay Fund, the Secretary of State if not a party.

(2A) A person, whether or not a party to the proceedings, upon whom a requirement has been made under paragraph (1A) of this Rule, may apply to the tribunal by notice to the Secretary of the Tribunals before the appointed time at or within which the requirement is to be complied with to vary or set aside the requirement. Notice of such application shall be given to the parties and to the expert upon whose application the requirement was made.

(3) Every document containing a requirement under paragraph (1)(ii) or (1)(iii) of paragraph (1A) of this Rule shall contain a reference to the fact that, under paragraph 1(7) of Schedule 9 to the 1978 Act, any person who without reasonable excuse fails to comply with any such requirement shall be liable on summary conviction to a fine, and the document shall state the amount of the current maximum fine.

(4) If the requirement under paragraph (1)(i) or (1)(ii) of this Rule is not complied with, a tribunal, before or at the hearing, may dismiss the whole or part of the originating application, or, as the case may be, strike out the whole or part of the notice of appearance, and, where appropriate, direct that a respondent shall be debarred from defending altogether: Provided that a tribunal shall not so dismiss or strike out or give such a direction unless it has sent notice to the party who has not complied with the requirement giving him an opportunity to show cause why such should not be done.

Procedure relating to expert's report

7A. (1) In any case involving an equal value claim where a dispute arises as to whether any work is of equal value to other work in terms of the demands made on the person employed on the work (for instance under such headings as effort, skill and decision) (in this Rule hereinafter referred to as 'the question'), a tribunal shall, before considering the question, except in cases to which section 2A(1)(a) of the Equal Pay Act applies, require an expert to prepare a report with respect to the question and the requirement shall be made in accordance with paragraphs (2) and (3) of this Rule.

(2) The requirement shall be made in writing and shall set out:

(a) the name and address of each of the parties;
(b) the address of the establishment at which the applicant is (or, as the case may be, was) employed;
(c) the question; and
(d) the identity of the person with reference to whose work the question arises;

and a copy of the requirement shall be sent to each of the parties.

(3) The requirement shall stipulate that the expert shall:

(a) take account of all such information supplied and all such representations made to him as have a bearing on the question;
(b) before drawing up his report, produce and send to the parties a written

summary of the said information and representations and invite the representations of the parties upon the material contained therein;

(c) make his report to the tribunal in a document which shall reproduce the summary and contain a brief account of any representations received from the parties upon it, any conclusion he may have reached upon the question and the reasons for that conclusion or, as the case may be, for his failure to reach such a conclusion;

(d) take no account of the difference of sex and at all times act fairly.

(4) Without prejudice to the generality of Rule 12(2)(b), where a tribunal requires an expert to prepare a report, it shall adjourn the hearing.

(5) If, on the application of one or more of the parties made not less than forty-two days after a tribunal has notified an expert of the requirement to prepare a report, the tribunal forms the view that there has been or is likely to be undue delay in receiving that report, the tribunal may require the expert to provide in writing to the tribunal an explanation for the delay or information as to his progress and may, on consideration of any such explanation or information as may be provided and after seeking representations from the parties, revoke, by notice in writing to the expert, the requirement to prepare a report, and in such a case paragraph (1) of this Rule shall again apply.

(6) Where a tribunal has received the report of an expert, it shall forthwith send a copy of the report to each of the parties and shall fix a date for the hearing of the case to be resumed; provided that the date so fixed shall be at least fourteen days after the date on which the report is sent to the parties.

(7) Upon the resuming of the hearing of the case in accordance with paragraph (6) of this Rule the report shall be admitted as evidence in the case unless the tribunal has exercised its power under paragraph (8) of this Rule not to admit the report.

(8) Where the tribunal, on the application of one or more of the parties or otherwise, forms the view:

(a) that the expert has not complied with a stipulation in paragraph (3) of this Rule, or

(b) that the conclusion contained in the report is one which, taking due account of the information supplied and representations made to the expert, could not reasonably have been reached, or

(c) that for some other material reason (other than disagreement with the conclusion that the applicant's work is or is not of equal value or with the reasoning leading to that conclusion) the report is unsatisfactory,

the tribunal may, if it thinks fit, determine not to admit the report, and in such a case paragraph (1) of this Rule shall again apply.

(9) In forming its view on the matters contained in paragraph (8)(a), (b) and (c) of this Rule, the tribunal shall take account of any representations of the parties thereon and may in that connection, subject to Rule 8(2A) and (2B), permit any party to give evidence upon, to call witnesses and to question any witness upon any matter relevant thereto.

(10) The tribunal may, at any time after it has received the report of an expert, require that expert (or, if that is impracticable, another expert) to explain any

matter contained in his report or, having regard to such matters as may be set out in the requirement, to give further consideration to the question.

(11) The requirement in paragraph (10) of this Rule shall comply with paragraph (2) of this Rule and shall stipulate that the expert shall make his reply in writing to the tribunal, giving his explanation or, as the case may be, setting down any conclusion which may result from his further consideration and his reasons for that conclusion.

(12) Where the tribunal has received a reply from the expert under paragraph (11) of this Rule, it shall forthwith send a copy of the reply to each of the parties and shall allow the parties to make representations thereon, and the reply shall be treated as information furnished to the tribunal and be given such weight as the tribunal thinks fit.

(13) Where a tribunal has determined not to admit a report under paragraph (8), that report shall be treated for all purposes (other than the award of costs or expenses under Rule 11) connected with the proceedings as if it had not been received by the tribunal and no further account shall be taken of it, and the requirement on the expert to prepare a report shall lapse.

Procedure at hearing

8. (1) Subject to paragraphs (2A), (2B), (2C), (2D) and (2E) of this Rule the tribunal shall conduct the hearing in such manner as it considers most suitable to the clarification of the issues before it and generally to the just handling of the proceedings; it shall so far as appears to it appropriate seek to avoid formality in its proceedings and it shall not be bound by any enactment or rule of law relating to the admissibility of evidence in proceedings before the courts of law.

(2) Subject to paragraphs (1), (2A), (2B), (2C) and (2D) of this Rule, at the hearing of the originating application a party (unless disentitled by virtue of Rule 3(2)), the Secretary of State (if, not being a party, he elects to appear as provided in Rule 7(5)) and any other person entitled to appear shall be entitled to give evidence, to call witnesses, to question any witnesses and to address the tribunal.

(2A) The tribunal may, and shall upon the application of a party, require the attendance of an expert who has prepared a report in connection with an equal value claim in any hearing relating to that claim. Where an expert attends in compliance with such requirement any party may, subject to paragraph (1) of this Rule, cross-examine the expert on his report and on any other matter pertaining to the question on which the expert was required to report.

(2B) At any time after the tribunal has received the report of the expert, any party may, on giving reasonable notice of his intention to do so to the tribunal and to any other party to the claim, call one witness to give expert evidence on the question on which the tribunal has required the expert to prepare a report; and where such evidence is given, any other party may cross-examine the person giving that evidence upon it.

(2C) Except as provided in Rule 7A(9) or by paragraph (2D) of this Rule, no party may give evidence upon, or question any witness upon, any matter of fact upon which a conclusion in the report of the expert is based.

(2D) Subject to paragraph (2A) and (2B) of this Rule, a tribunal may, notwithstanding paragraph (2C) of this Rule, permit a party to give evidence upon, to call witness and to question any witness upon any such matters of fact as are referred to in that paragraph if either:

   (a) the matter of fact is relevant to and is raised in connection with the issue contained in subsection (3) of section 1 of the Equal Pay Act (defence of genuine material factor) upon which the determination of the tribunal is being sought; or

   (b) the report of the expert contains no conclusion on the question of whether the applicant's work and the work of the person identified in the requirement of the tribunal under Rule 7A(2) are of equal value and the tribunal is satisfied that the absence of that conclusion is wholly or mainly due to the refusal or deliberate omission of a person required by the tribunal under Rule 4(1A) to furnish information or to produce documents to comply with that requirement.

(2E) A tribunal may, on the application of a party, if in the circumstances of the case, having regard to the considerations expressed in paragraph (1) of this Rule, it considers that it is appropriate so to proceed, hear evidence upon and permit the parties to address it upon the issue contained in subsection (3) of section 1 of the Equal Pay Act (defence of genuine material factor) before it requires an expert to prepare a report under Rule 7A. Where the tribunal so proceeds, it shall be without prejudice to further consideration of that issue after the tribunal has received the report.

(3) If a party shall fail to appear or to be represented at the time and place fixed for the hearing, the tribunal may, if that party is an applicant, dismiss or, in any case, dispose of the application in the absence of that party or may adjourn the hearing to a later date: provided that before deciding to dismiss or disposing of any application in the absence of a party the tribunal shall consider any representations submitted by that party in pursuance of Rule 7(3).

(4) A tribunal may require any witness to give evidence on oath or affirmation and for that purpose there may be administered an oath or affirmation in due form.

Decision of tribunal

9. (1) A decision of a tribunal may be taken by a majority thereof and, if the tribunal shall be constituted of two members only, the chairman shall have a second or casting vote.

(2) The decision of a tribunal, which may be given orally at the end of a hearing or reserved, shall be recorded in a document signed by the chairman.

(3) A tribunal shall give reasons for its decision.

(4) The reasons for the decision of the tribunal shall be recorded in full form in a document signed by the chairman.

(4A) There shall be appended to the document referred to in paragraph (4) of this Rule a copy of the report (if any) of an expert received by the tribunal in the course of the proceedings.

[Paragraph (5) is omitted because it has no relevance in proceedings involving an equal value claim.]

(6) The clerk to the tribunal shall transmit any document referred to in para-

graphs (2), (4) and (4A) of this Rule to the Secretary of the Tribunals who shall as soon as may be enter it in the Register and shall send a copy of the entry to each of the parties and to the persons entitled to appear who did so appear and, where the origination was sent to a tribunal by a court, to that court.

(7) Any document referred to in paragraphs (4) and (4A) of this Rule shall be omitted from the Register in any case in which evidence has been heard in private and the tribunal so directs and in that event any such document shall be sent to the parties and to any superior court in any proceedings relating to such decision together with the copy of the entry.

(8) The Register shall be kept at the Office of the Tribunals and shall be open to the inspection of any person without charge at all reasonable hours.

(9) Clerical mistakes in any document referred to in paragraphs (2) and (4) of this Rule, or errors arising in such a document from an accidental slip or omission, may at any time be corrected by the chairman by certificate under his hand.

(10) The clerk to the tribunal shall send a copy of any document so corrected and the certificate of the chairman to the Secretary of the Tribunals who shall as soon as may be make such correction as may be necessary in the Register and shall send a copy of any corrected entry or of any corrected document containing reasons for the tribunal's decision, as the case may be, to each of the parties and, in the case of a corrected entry, to the persons entitled to appear who did so appear and, where the originating application was sent to the tribunal by a court, to that court.

(11) If any decision is:

(a)　corrected under paragraph (9) of this Rule,
(b)　reviewed, revoked or varied under Rule 10, or
(c)　altered in any way by order of a superior court,

the Secretary of the Tribunals shall alter the entry in the Register to conform with any such certificate or order and shall send a copy of the new entry to each of the parties and to the persons entitled to appear who did so appear and, where the originating application was sent to the tribunal by a court, to that court.

(12) Where by this Rule a document is required to be signed by the chairman but by reason of death or incapacity the chairman is unable to sign such document it shall be signed by the other members of the tribunal, who shall certify that the chairman is unable to sign.

Costs

11. (1) Subject to paragraphs (2) and (3) of this Rule, a tribunal shall not normally make an award in respect of the costs or expenses incurred by a party to the proceedings but where in its opinion a party (and if he is a respondent whether or not he has entered an appearance) has in bringing or conducting the proceedings acted frivolously, vexatiously or otherwise unreasonably the tribunal may make:

(a)　an order that that party shall pay to another party (or to the Secretary of State, if, not being a party, he has acted as provided in Rule 7(5)) either a specified sum in respect of the costs or expenses incurred by that other party (or, as the case may be, by the Secretary of State) or the whole or part of those costs or expenses as taxed (if not otherwise agreed);

(b) an order that that party shall pay to the Secretary of State the whole, or any part, of any allowances (other than allowances paid to members of tribunals, experts or assessors) paid by the Secretary of State under paragraph 10 of Schedule 9 to the 1978 Act to any person for the purposes of, or in connection with, his attendance at the tribunal.

(1A) For the purposes of paragraph (1)(a) of this Rule, the costs or expenses in respect of which a tribunal may make an order include costs or expenses incurred by the party in whose favour the order is to be made in or in connection with the investigations carried out by the expert in preparing his report.

(2) Where the tribunal has on the application of a party to the proceedings postponed the day or time fixed for or adjourned the hearing, the tribunal may make orders against or, as the case may require, in favour of that party as at paragraph (1)(a) and (b) of this Rule as respects any costs or expenses incurred or any allowances paid as a result of the postponement or adjournment.

(3) Where, on a complaint of unfair dismissal in respect of which:

(i) the applicant has expressed a wish to be reinstated or re-engaged which has been communicated tot he respondent at least seven days before the hearing of the complaint, or

(ii) the proceedings arise out of the respondent's failure to permit the applicant to return to work after an absence due to pregnancy or confinement,

any postponement or adjournment of the hearing has been caused by the respondent's failure, without a special reason, to adduce reasonable evidence as to the availability of the job fron which the applicant was dismissed, or, as the case may be, which she held before her absence, or of comparable or suitable employment, the tribunal shall make orders against that respondent as at paragraph (1)(a) and (b) of this Rule as respects any costs or expenses incurred or any allowances paid as a result of the postponement or adjournment.

[Paragraph (4) is omitted because it has nor elevance in proceedings involving an equal value claim.]

(5) Any costs required by an order under this Rule to be taxed may be taxed in the county court according to such of the scales prescribed by the county court rules for proceedings in the county court as shall be directed by the order.

Miscellaneous powers of tribunal

12. (1) Subject to the provisions of these Rules, a tribunal may regulate its own procedure.

(2) A tribunal may, if it thinks fit:

(a) extend the time appointed by or under these Rules for doing any act notwithstanding that the time appointed may have expired;

(b) postpone the day or time fixed for, or adjourn, any hearing (particularly as respects cases under the provisions of any enactment providing for conciliation for the purpose of giving an opportunity for the complaint to be settled by way of conciliation and withdrawn);

(*c*) if the applicant shall at any time give notice of the withdrawal of his originating application, dismiss the proceedings;

(*d*) except in proceedings under the 1966 Act, if both or all the parties (and the Secretary of State, if, not being a party, he has acted as provided in Rule 7(5)) agree in writing upon the terms of a decision to be made by the tribunal, decide accordingly;

(*e*) subject to the Proviso below, at any stage of the proceedings order to be struck out or amended any originating application or notice of appearance or anything in such application or notice of appearance on the grounds that is scandalous, frivolous or vexatious;

(*f*) subject to the Proviso below, on the application of the respondent, or of its own motion, order to be struck out any originating application for want of prosecution;

Provided that before making any order under (e) or (f) above the tribunal shall send notice to the party against whom it is proposed that any such order should be made giving him an opportunity to show cause why such an order should not be made.

(2A) Without prejudice to the generality of paragraph (2)(b) of this Rule, the tribunal shall, before proceeding to hear the parties on an equal value claim, invite them to apply for an adjournment for the purpose of seeking to reach a settlement of the claim and shall, if both or all of the parties agree to such a course, grant an adjournment for that purpose.

(2B) If, after the tribunal has adjourned the hearing under rule 7A(4) but before the tribunal has received the report of the expert, the applicant gives notice under paragraph (2)(c) of this Rule, the tribunal shall forthwith notify the expert that the requirement to prepare a report has ceased. The notice shall be without prejudice to the operation of Rule 11(1A).

(3) Subject to Rule 4(2) and (2A), a tribunal may, if it thinks fit, before granting an application under Rule 4 or Rule 13 require the party (or, as the case may be, the Secretary of State or, in the case of an application under Rule 4(1A), the expert) making the applicaiton to give notice of it to the other party or parties (or, in the case of an application by an expert, the parties and any other person in respect of whom the tribunal is asked, in the application, to impose a requirement). The notice shall give particulars of the application and indicate the address to which and the time within which any objection to the application shall be made, being an address and time specified for the purposes of the application by the tribunal.

(4) Any act other than the holding of a pre-hearing assessment under Rule 6, the hearing of an originating application or the making of an order under Rule 10(1), required or authorised by these Rules to be done by a tribunal may be done by, or on the direction of, the President or the chairman of the tribunal or any chairman being a member of the panel of chairmen.

(5) Rule 11 shall apply to an order dismissing proceedings under paragraph (2)(c) of this Rule.

(6) Any functions of the Secretary of the Tribunals other than that mentioned in Rule 1(2) may be performed by an Assistant Secretary of the Tribunals.

Notices, etc.

17. (1) Any notice given under these rules shall be in writing.

(2) All notices and documents required by these Rules to be presented to the Secretary of the Tribunals may be presented at the Office of the Tribunals or such other office as may be notified by the Secretary of the Tribunals to the parties.

(3) All notices and documents required or authorised by these Rules to be sent or given to any person hereinafter mentioned may be sent by post (subject to paragraph (5) of this Rule) or delivered to or at:

(*a*) in the case of a notice or document directed to the Secretary of State in proceedings to which he is not a party, the offices of the Department of Employment at Caxton Hall, Tothill Street, London SW1H 9NF, or such other office as may be notified by the Secretary of State.

[Sub-paragraph (b) is omitted because it has no relevance in proceedings involving an equal value claim.]

(*c*) in the case of a notice or document directed to a court, the office of the clerk of the court;

(*d*) in the case of a notice or document directed to a party:

    (i) his address for service specified in the originating application or in a notice of appearance or in a notice under paragraph (4) of this Rule; or

    (ii) if no address for service has been so specified, his last known address or place of business in the United Kingdom or, if the party is a corporation, the corporation's registered or principal office in the United Kingdom, or, in any case, such address or place outside the United Kingdom as the President or a Regional Chairman may allow;

(*e*) in the case of a notice or document directed to any person (other than a person specified in the foregoing provisions of this paragraph), his address or place of business in the United Kingdom, or if such a person is a corporation, the corporation's registered or principal office in the United Kingdom;

and if sent or given to the authorised representative of a party shall be deemed to have been sent or given to that party.

(4) A party may at any time by notice to the Secretary of the Tribunals and to the other party or parties (and, where appropriate, to the appropriate conciliation officer) change his address for service under these Rules.

(5) The recorded delivery service shall be used instead of the ordinary post:

(*a*) when a second set of documents or notices is to be sent to a respondent who has not entered an appearance under Rule 3(1);

(*b*) for service of an order made under Rule 4(1)(iii) or (1A).

(6) Where for any sufficient reason service of any document or notice cannot be effected in the manner prescribed under this Rule, the President or a Regional Chairman may make an order for substituted service in such manner as he may deem fit and such service shall have the same effect as service in the manner prescribed under this Rule.

(7) In proceedings brought under the provisions of any enactment providing for conciliation the Secretary of the Tribunals shall send copies of all documents and notices to a conciliation officer who in the opinion of the Secretary is an appropriate officer to receive them.

(8) In proceedings which may involve payments out of the Redundancy Fund or Maternity Pay Fund, the Secretary of the Tribunals shall, where appropriate, send copies of all documents and notices to the Secretary of State notwithstanding the fact that he may not be a party to such proceedings.

(9) In proceedings under the Equal Pay Act, the Sex Discrimination Act or the Race Relations Act the Secretary of the Tribunals shall send to the Equal Opportunities Commission or, as the case may be, the Commission for Racial Equality copies of all documents sent to the parties under Rule 9(6), (10) and (11) and Rule 10(5).

List of statutes and regulations

Index